SUBVERSIVE INSTITUTIONS

The Design and the Destruction of Socialism and the State

From 1989 to 1992, all of the socialist dictatorships in Europe (including the Soviet Union) collapsed, as did the Soviet bloc. Yugoslavia, the Soviet Union, and Czechoslovakia dismembered, and the cold war international order came to an abrupt end. Based on a series of controlled comparisons among regimes and states, Valerie Bunce argues in this book that two factors account for these remarkable developments: the institutional design of socialism as a regime, a state, and a bloc, and the rapid expansion during the 1980s of opportunities for domestic and international change. When combined, institutions and opportunities explain not just when, how, and why these regimes and states disintegrated, but also some of the most puzzling features of these developments – why, for example, the collapse of socialism was largely peaceful and why Yugoslavia, but not the Soviet Union or Czechoslovakia, disintegrated through war.

Valerie Bunce is Professor in the Department of Government at Cornell University. She currently serves as Chair of the ACLS/SSRC Committee on Eastern Europe and has previously been the Director of the Russian and Eastern European Studies Program at Cornell. She is the author of *Do New Leaders Make a Difference?,* and she has published widely, in English, Russian, Hungarian, and Croatian, on politics and government. Her research has been supported by numerous bodies, including the U.S. Institute for Peace, the German Marshall Fund, the National Endowment for the Humanities, the Carnegie Endowment, and the Russell Sage Foundation.

CAMBRIDGE STUDIES IN COMPARATIVE POLITICS

General Editor
PETER LANGE   Duke University

Associate Editors
ROBERT H. BATES   Harvard University
ELLEN COMISSO   University of California, San Diego
PETER HALL   Harvard University
JOEL MIGDAL   University of Washington
HELEN MILNER   Columbia University
RONALD ROGOWSKI   University of California, Los Angeles
SIDNEY TARROW   Cornell University

OTHER BOOKS IN THE SERIES

The series list continues after the Index.

SUBVERSIVE INSTITUTIONS

The Design and the Destruction of Socialism and the State

VALERIE BUNCE

CAMBRIDGE
UNIVERSITY PRESS

PUBLISHED BY THE PRESS SYNDICATE OF THE UNIVERSITY OF CAMBRIDGE
The Pitt Building, Trumpington Street, Cambridge, United Kingdom

CAMBRIDGE UNIVERSITY PRESS
The Edinburgh Building, Cambridge CB2 2RU, UK   http://www.cup.cam.ac.uk
40 West 20th Street, New York, NY 10011-4211, USA http://www.cup.org
10 Stamford Road, Oakleigh, Melbourne 3166, Australia

First published 1999

Printed in the United States of America

Typeface Garamond 11/13 pt, *System* DeskTopPro$_{/UX}$® [*BV*]

*A catalog record for this book is available from
the British Library*

Library of Congress Cataloging-in-Publication Data

Bunce, Valerie, 1949–
Subversive institutions : the design and the destruction of
socialism and the state / Valerie Bunce.
p. cm. – (Cambridge studies in comparative politics)
ISBN 0-521-58449-3 (hc.). – ISBN 0-521-58592-9 (pbk.)
1. Socialism – Europe, Eastern – History. 2. Socialism – Soviet
Union – History. 3. Europe, Eastern – Politics and government – 1989–
4. Soviet Union – Politics and government – 1985–1991. I. Title.
II. Series.
HX240.7.A6B86 1999
320.53'15'0947 – dc21   98-38293
                                                CIP

ISBN 0 521 58449 3 hardback
ISBN 0 521 58592 9 paperback

To Ron and Nick

CONTENTS

PREFACE

This book seeks to explain two recent, remarkable, and related events: the collapse of socialism in the Soviet Union and Eastern Europe from 1989 to 1990 and the dismemberment soon thereafter of the Soviet, Yugoslav, and Czechoslovak states. The forces that seem to have driven these processes were the interaction between the institutional design of socialist regimes and states, on the one hand, and the considerable expansion of opportunities for change in the 1980s. The end of socialism and of the state, therefore, were both abrupt and long in the making. And both sets of events spoke to the power of socialist institutions even as these institutions were collapsing.

Embedded in the issues of regime and state collapse, however, is a series of other important questions that this study addresses as well. In particular, there are the variations in how and when these regimes and states ended. Why, for example, were some regime transitions peaceful and others violent? Why did Yugoslavia end in war, and the Soviet and Czechoslovak states through a peaceful process? Why did socialism collapse, first, in Poland and Hungary, and only later in the Soviet Union – despite the immediacy of the Gorbachev reforms in the latter? This leads to a final puzzle that speaks to commonalities rather than variance. Why did *all* the Communist parties of the region, despite their differences in socialism and circumstances, lose their hegemonic position? The answers to these questions are also largely historical-institutional in nature.

In the course of addressing these issues, this book also pursues two other objectives. One is to use the socialist experience in order to address questions of broader theoretical and geographical significance. It is not just that the recent collapse of regime and state in the eastern half of Europe speaks nearly by definition to a broad range of the literature in comparative politics – including, for example, the work on nations, nationalism, and secession; on revolution; on the role of institutions in politics; and on transitions from dictatorship to democracy and from one international regime to another. It is also that the socialist context provides us with a large number of cases and, through its mixture of similarities and differences, facilitates controlled comparisons and robust conclusions.

The other objective of this book is to challenge the recent assumption that the knowledge accumulated about European socialism over the course of the cold war period was deficient, because specialists failed to anticipate the events of 1989 and after, and largely irrelevant, because a new era has begun and socialism has become yesterday's news. This book begs to differ on both counts. First, as the long bibliography testifies, those who specialized in the region do have a great deal to say – and said it, moreover, without the advantages of hindsight. Second, much of what they had to say focused on institutions and their consequences, a topic that, while long of interest to specialists in the Soviet Union and Eastern Europe during the socialist era, has only recently occupied center stage in the disciplines of political science and sociology. Finally, without these arguments and without knowledge of the institutional and historical evolution of socialism, we could not have explained why, when, and how socialist regimes and states ended – and the variations therein. This book, then, explains what happened by relying not just on recent studies but also on older investigations carried out by scholars years before the end of the socialist story was in sight.

This book testifies, therefore, to the power of the past – that is, the socialist past and past work by specialists in the field. In this sense, it has been, like the revolutions that toppled socialism and the state, long in the making. Indeed, this book was begun twenty years ago when I, like others, began to puzzle over several trends in the Communist world: economic decline and a seeming reversal of power distributions, wherein the strong (or the party-states) were acting as though they were weak and the weak (or the societies they dominated) as though they were strong. Moreover, both trends were in clear evidence, whether the focus of the analysis was on Soviet-style socialism or the Yugoslav variant of self-management, on the domestic political economy of European socialism or its international equivalent, the Soviet bloc.

Since that time, I have benefited greatly from the work of a large number of scholars in Communist area studies and in comparative politics. Many of those scholars are thanked by virtue of their inclusion in the bibliography. As for the particular arguments presented here, I would like to thank those who in various ways helped me to refine my arguments at the 1995 National Endowment for the Humanities summer seminar at Cornell University and at seminars I presented at Harvard University, the University of Montreal, the University of Maryland, the University of Michigan, the Woodrow Wilson Center for Scholars, and Central European University (Budapest). I am also indebted to a number of colleagues, who made helpful comments at various stages of this project: Mark Beissinger, Ellen Comisso, Grzegorz Ekiert, Matt Evangelista, Chip Gagnon, Bela Greskovits, Abbey Innes, Mark Kramer, Jan Kubik, Hector Schamis, Lilia Shevtsova, Jack Snyder, Katherine Verdery, Veljko Vujačić, Sharon Wolchik, and Igor Zevelev, and, especially for their detailed comments, Maria Csanádi, Voja Stanovčić, and Sidney Tarrow.

A final thanks goes to the Carnegie Endowment for Peace, the American Council of Learned Societies, the National Endowment for the Humanities, the U.S. Institute of Peace, and the German Marshall Fund. All five provided support in various ways to bring this project to completion.

1

THE COLLAPSE OF
SOCIALISM AND
SOCIALIST STATES

Political systems are not in the habit of committing suicide.
Milovan Djilas (1988)

From 1989 to 1990 socialism collapsed throughout the territories that, during the cold war era, had comprised the Soviet Union and Eastern Europe.[1] What followed was the formation of new regimes committed, albeit in quite varying degrees, to the construction of liberal economic and political orders (Dawisha, 1997; Roeder, 1994). Although the success of these regime experiments has yet to be determined, particularly in those cases where the ex-Communists won the first competitive elections (see especially Fish, 1998; Bunce, 1995a), the future of European socialism – in its dictatorial form – is no longer in question. It has vanished from the entire region, after having defined for forty-five years not just the political economy of the eastern half of Europe, but also the very structure, if not the stability, of the postwar international order.

What quickly followed these developments was another set of equally abrupt and perhaps even more surprising changes: the termination of four states in the region. The first to go was the German Democratic Republic, which in September 1990 joined its neighbor, the German Federal Republic, to form a single state. While the speed of German unification was unexpected and had a great deal to do with the convergence between Chancellor Helmut Kohl's "chutzpah" and President Gorbachev's reform needs, the fact of it was not (see, e.g., McAdams, 1997; Levesque, 1997). The border separating the two Germanies had been an artificial construct

1

of the cold war. Once that war ended, so did the geographical and ideological boundary dividing the German nation.

The disappearance of the German Democratic Republic was then followed by the collapse of three more states in the post-Communist region: Yugoslavia, beginning in June 1991, the Soviet Union following the unsuccessful coup d'etat in August of the same year, and Czechoslovakia after the summer 1992 parliamentary elections. In these cases, state multiplication, not reduction, was the result (on the importance of this and other distinctions about state dismemberment, see Buchanan, 1991). As a consequence, no less than twenty-two new states emerged from those territories that had once featured a mere three.

Indeed, this number could change in the future. In 1997, the leadership of Belarus began to take steps to reintegrate with Russia – a process that has generated enormous conflict within Belarus while pleasing, to be sure, all those deputies within the Russian Duma who, under the leadership of Gennadi Zyuganov, had supported a proclamation in March 1996 to reestablish the political boundaries of the former Soviet Union (see Vinogradov, 1996: 1). At the same time, the war in Chechnia provided ample testimony to the continuing struggle between a weak center and a powerful and at times secessionist periphery within the Russian Federation – a struggle that also seems to be taking place in Bosnia following implementation of the Dayton Accords and their creation, more in theory than in practice, of a single, confederal Bosnian state (see, e.g., Lynch and Lukić 1996; Stern, 1994; Solnick, 1996, 1998b; Treisman, 1996, 1997; Hughes, 1994; Kirow, 1995; Hayden, 1995b). Just as regimes are still in the making in the post-Communist world, then, so are states.

The purpose of this book is to explain these recent and dramatic changes in Europe by analyzing the role of socialist-era institutions in constructing and then destroying the regime and the state. The irony of the collapse of socialism, then, was that the very institutions that had defined these systems and that were, presumably, to defend them as well, ended up functioning over time to subvert both the regime and the state. European socialism, in short, was hoist by its own petard.

Four interrelated issues are addressed in this study. The first, examined in Chapters 2 and 3, investigates the institutional design of European socialism, and the long-term consequences of that design for economic performance and for the distribution of power between the center and the periphery. Here, I concentrate on three socialist playing fields: the regime, the state, and the Soviet bloc. The second concern, which is the focus of Chapter 4, is why all the European socialist regimes collapsed – and collapsed when and how they did. In Chapter 5, I turn our attention to state dismemberment and examine why, following regime collapse, the Soviet, Yugoslav, and Czechoslovak states divided, whereas other states in the region remained intact. This leads to the final questions to be examined in this study (in Chapter 6): why did Yugoslavia end violently, and why was the dissolution of both the Soviet and Czechoslovak states peaceful?

THE PUZZLES OF REGIME COLLAPSE

There is no shortage of explanations – produced primarily after the fact (but see Bunce, 1985; Csanádi, 1997; Rigby, 1990 and, earlier, 1977) – of why state socialism collapsed.[2] These various explanations have provided a rich inventory of key factors and include economic decline and the growing gap between the promises and the performance of socialism; rising corruption within the party; the Communist Party's loss of whatever political legitimacy it once enjoyed; the formation of civil society within the nooks and crannies of state socialism and its growing capacity to function as a regime alternative; and the capacity of the Helsinki process to redistribute moral and political resources between once hegemonic Communist parties and once postrate societies. Finally, there are the proximate and powerful effects of the Gorbachev reforms in a context already characterized by economic and political decay.

All of these lines of argument are, no doubt, relevant to the story of socialist collapse, and all of these factors figured prominently, it must be noted, in studies that predated the actual collapse of the system. They lack, nonetheless, a certain explanatory bite, in large measure because the cases examined tend to be limited in number,[3] and because the variable matrix developed tends to be either too cluttered to produce a parsimonious explanation or too simple to account for the hows and when – and the variations therein – of the departure of socialist dictatorships from the European stage.

All of this leaves us with some thorny questions that have yet to be answered. For example, why did *all* of the socialist regimes in the region fall – and within such a short span of time? An easy answer could be constructed that emphasized some combination of the following: the nature of socialism itself and its inherent flaws, the overarching importance of the Gorbachev reforms, and demonstration effects. However, to argue along these lines is difficult. First, if socialism was in fact fatally flawed, then why did it manage to live for so long? A robust account of the collapse of socialism, then, must worry not just about 1989, but also about the many decades of socialism that predated its spectacular collapse – decades that included, for instance, the survival of these regimes in the face of the crises of 1953–1956, 1968, and, for Poland, a variety of other years as well (see, e.g., Ekiert, 1996; Kubik, 1994; Ost, 1990). Second, the binary cold war terminology to the contrary, the socialist experience is better understood as socialist experiences. There were in fact significant differences among the European socialist dictatorships, and these differences were along virtually all the dimensions that would seem to be highly relevant to not just the practice but also the decline of socialism.

Let us take the three countries that eventually dismembered as one example. Here, one can observe the signficantly greater national diversity of Yugoslavia and the Soviet Union than Czechoslovakia; the revolutionary origins of socialist Yugoslavia and the Soviet Union versus the rise of communism in postwar Czechoslovakia as a response more to the onset of the cold war than domestic support for such an outcome (though domestic support was, nonetheless, present and to a more significant degree than in, say, Romania or Poland); the contrast between Soviet-style socialism, which was exported to Czechoslovakia after the war in "ready-to-wear" fashion (Brus, 1977), versus the distinctive Yugoslav model of workers' self-management; the enclosure of the Soviet Union and Czechoslovakia within a tightly integrated regional system dominated by the Soviet Union and explicitly counterposed to the West versus the contrasting Yugoslav alternative of nonalignment in the international system; and the longer and more consistent history in Yugoslavia of political and especially economic liberalization versus the absence of either, except for brief moments, in socialist Czechoslovakia and the Union of Soviet Socialist Republics. To all these contrasts can be added yet another: economic performance. Whereas Yugoslavia was in severe economic straits from the late 1970s to the end of the following decade when the regime and the state unraveled, Czechoslovakia registered during that same time frame steady if unspectacular economic growth, while the Soviet Union fell in between these two extremes of economic performance (Rutland, 1992).

With such evident differences among the European socialist dictatorships, therefore, it becomes hard to account for the regionwide collapse of socialism by speaking of socialist commonalities – whether with respect to the shared and purportedly fatal flaws of the system or to equality in regime "receptivity" to either the Gorbachev reforms or regional demonstration effects. These variations in socialism – across country and over time – also make it hard to bridge the methodological gap between explanations that focus on causes and those that focus on events (see, e.g., Abbott, 1992).

If all the socialist regimes shared the fact of collapse, moreover, they varied nonetheless in when and how this happened. Why did the process begin in Eastern Europe in general and Poland and Hungary in particular? While most empires fray, first, at their edges (witness, for instance, the rebellious Polish tradition within the Russian Empire), it was, after all, in the Soviet Union and not in Eastern Europe where Gorbachev had placed the very future of socialism at the top of the political agenda (see Bunce, 1989; Levesque, 1997; Tökes, 1996). Similarly, why did the end of these regimes occur in such varying ways – for instance, pacting in Poland and Hungary, mass mobilization in Czechoslovakia and East Germany, and a mixture of reform from above and below in the Soviet Union (see especially Levesque, 1997, for an overview; and on the Soviet case, Urban, 1990; Fish, 1996)?

The most puzzling aspect of the end of socialism, however, was its largely peaceful character. Although in a few cases, such as Romania and Yugoslavia, Communist leaders behaved in predictable ways by deploying the military to defend themselves and the regimes they led, if not "owned," in most cases, these parties simply gave up the ghost – sometimes immediately, as in Hungary, when the Communists agreed to a round table with the opposition in the summer of 1989, and sometimes after pursuing for a brief while some alternatives to outright capitulation, as in Czechoslovakia, East Germany, and Bulgaria. This apparent acquiescence in the face of challenges to their power was in violation not just of what one would have expected, given the long-established economic and political preeminence of these Communist parties and their willingness in the past to use violence to get what they wanted, but also of one of the most widely accepted maxims of politics. As Marx once put it: ruling classes do not give up power willingly.

Finally, there is the question of the relationship between regime and state collapse. It is obvious that the two are connected, given the sequencing in the Soviet, Yugoslav, and Czechoslovak cases of regime and then state collapse. This is a pattern, moreover, that testifies to the simultaneous spatial and political multiplication of sovereignty (to borrow from Tilly, 1993) that is typical of most revolutionary situations, including those that had earlier given rise to socialism in Yugoslavia, the Soviet Union, and China (see especially Walton, 1984; Motyl, 1987; Pipes, 1968). However, why and how changes in the organization of political power joined in the Soviet, Yugoslav, and Czechoslovak cases with changes in the spatial boundaries of that power are questions that remain unanswered. This is largely because the regime "story" has tended to be the focus of one body of work and the state "story" quite another.

THE PUZZLES OF STATE DISMEMBERMENT

This leads to a second set of puzzles – in this case, surrounding the disintegration of the Yugoslav, Soviet, and Czechoslovak states.[4] At the most general level, we must remember that states tend to be sticky – despite all the talk for many years of their impending decline, if not growing irrelevance in a globalized world featuring competing identities, competing sovereignties, and the expanding influence of transstate actors (Kautsky, 1962; Strange, 1995; Tilly, 1992b; Cable, 1995; Hann, 1995; Held, 1996; Evangelista, 1998). States have tended to endure, primarily because they are jealous of their authority and their boundaries, and because they have considerable resources at their disposal to crush or co-opt those groups that challenge them. Indeed, these generalizations even seem to apply to states, such as Sri Lanka, India, Nigeria, Canada, Belgium, and Spain, that have faced – and are continuing to face – powerful pressures for decentralization along national and/or territorial lines, or, in some instances, an actual reconfiguration of state boundaries (see, e.g., Brown, 1989; Brown, 1993; Martiniello, 1995, 1998; Martin, 1995; Linz and Stepan, 1996: 100–107; Bossuyt, 1995; Conversi, 1994b; Harun-or-Rashid, 1990). Secession, therefore, tends to be the exception and not the rule, a generalization often overlooked in recent years in the rush to account for interethnic conflict and state weakening (for a similar set of observations, see Fearon and Laitin, 1996; Brown, 1989). Moreover, demands for secession do not, by any means, arise automatically in response to either regime transition or the development of nationalist movements (see, e.g., Brass, 1985; Hroch, 1996; Horowitz, 1985, 1994; Bossuyt, 1995). Rather, they seem to be the product of contingent and uncommon circumstances.

At the same time, one can argue that the Soviet, Yugoslav, and Czechoslovak states were sufficiently strong that they should have been able to survive the threats of political fragmentation. Although specialists in the politics of the region recognized, long before the events of 1989, that Communist regimes were weak in many respects, they also tended to assume that Communist *states* were strong (Evangelista, 1995). Indeed, one of the purported successes of Communist revolutions, whether home-grown or imported, was the construction through Stalinization of states that had the administrative, economic, and coercive capacity to control their spatial environment. This was particularly the case for the Soviet Union – a superpower, a regional hegemon, and the leader, as well as the founder, of the world socialist movement.

Yet another asset was that Yugoslavia, the Soviet Union, and Czechoslovakia were all in Europe – the home, it must be remembered, of the modern state. It would be shortsighted to argue, of course, that European boundaries were and are written in stone. One has only to remember the long and nasty history of state building in Europe, the many complications to and delays in nation- and state-formation in the eastern half of the continent in particular, and, more recently, the threats to European state sovereignty represented by regionalist movements within many of these states and, looking externally, by the process of European integration[5] (see, e.g., Anderson, 1974; Daalder, 1973; Tilly, 1975; Szucs, 1983; Bunce, 1998a; Gourevitch, 1979; Safran, 1994; Finer, 1983; Linz, 1973; Martiniello, 1995).

The fact remains, however, that state boundaries in Europe did remain unchanged throughout the cold war era, a period of forty-six years, thereby setting a European record. Nor was this "accidental" – to revive for a moment the familiar jargon of the Communist period. During the cold war there developed a widespread assumption among Euratlantic policy makers that stable state boundaries in Europe – and even in the Third World (see Jackson and Rosenberg, 1982) – were the foundation, along with bipolarity and nuclear weapons, of the extraordinary postwar "long peace" (Gaddis, 1986; but see Bunce, 1993). As a result, influential international actors, whether leaders of states or multilateral institutions, agreed that stable borders in Europe were to be maintained at virtually all costs. Indeed, this was one reason why from 1989 to virtually the end of 1991 Western powers responded to the growing crisis within Yugoslavia with calls for the continuation of the state (see, e.g., Crawford, 1996; Woodward, 1995a; Burg, 1995). The relevance of this consensus for our concerns here has been brought home by Donald Horowitz (1981: 167):

> Whether a secessionist movement will emerge at all is determined by domestic politics, by the relations of groups and regions within the state. Whether a secessionist movement will achieve its aims, however, is determined largely by international politics, by the balance of interests and forces that extend beyond the state.

This brings us to another question that is hard to answer. Why did the boundaries of the new states that came into being assume the form that they did, and so quickly? While it is clear that all three states broke up in the face of powerful secessionist claims put forward by cultural communities,[6] it is also clear that these cultural communities (and their political leadership) varied substantially from each other – within and across these states – in their levels of cohesion and in their commitment to secession. Compare, for example, the differences between the behavior of Macedonians versus Slovenians in Yugoslavia or Kazakhs versus Lithuanians in the former Soviet Union. Moreover, the correlation between cultural group boundaries and the boundaries of the new states that formed was not that high, except in Czechoslovakia. In addition, as the history of state formation suggests, quick determination of boundaries tends to be the exception, not the rule.[7]

The final puzzle focuses on differences, rather than similarities among the Yugoslav, Soviet, and Czechoslovak experiences of state dismemberment. Yugoslavia ended through bloody wars of secession. This was in sharp contrast to the peaceful partition of both the Soviet Union at the end of December 1991 and Czechoslovakia a year later. However, a quick inventory of possible explanations for this contrast – or one that manages to highlight plausible causes that produce the needed pairing of Czechoslovakia and the Soviet Union against Yugoslavia – leads to a number of dead ends.

On the one hand, these states had some important characteristics in common – for instance, their diversity and their socialist past. However, these could hardly account for the variation of interest here. On the other hand, where they differed produces the wrong set of contrasts. Thus, for example, the Soviet Union and Yugoslavia were exceptional in their diversity along national, religious, and socioeconomic lines and along the dimensions as well of regional elite support of state dismemberment and political and economic liberalization. Moreover, again in contrast with Czechoslovakia, both of these states featured a relatively low correlation between national boundaries and the boundaries of the nation-states that formed in the aftermath of state dismemberment. This included, moreover, a large community of Russians outside of Russia and Serbs outside of Serbia. Finally, in terms of the structure of the games of dismemberment, Czechoslovakia and Yugoslavia were similar in that both featured – unlike Russia – a process that was dominated by interrepublican, rather than center-republican bargaining.

At the same time, while there were reasons to assume that the end of Yugoslavia would be violent, there were also compelling reasons to expect the same for the Soviet Union. It was not just that nationalist mobilization in the Soviet Union, as in Yugoslavia, had grown increasingly violent over time (see Beissinger, 1995a). It was also that the Soviet Union was a superpower in practice and, even more importantly, in the minds of virtually all Russian elites. Thus, the Soviet state and Russia were widely seen as interchangeable and, thereby, indivisible entities (see Zimmerman, 1994). As a consequence, Russia and expansionism and certainly not Russia and "contractionism," would seem to have necessarily gone together – in 1991, as over the long expanse of Soviet and Russian imperial history. Why, then, did the Russian elite accede to the breakup of the state?

A COMPARATIVE PERSPECTIVE

Both the end of the Soviet, Yugoslav, and Czechoslovak states and the collapse of socialist regimes throughout the eastern half of Europe force us to confront a number of difficult questions. While these questions flow naturally from the recent and dramatic changes in the eastern half of Europe and include, necessarily, the larger puzzle of why and how the postwar international order collapsed, they also speak to issues of broader geographical, theoretical, and temporal significance. Central to the story of regime and state collapse in the eastern half of Europe is what has become a familiar set of developments the world over. Here, I refer to such staples of the current political scene as nationalism, secession, interethnic conflict, state weakening, and the transition from dictatorship to democracy. Indeed, what is significant about the cases analyzed in this book is that they represent a remarkably efficient summary, if you will, of global trends.

Not surprisingly, these trends have come to dominate contemporary debates in comparative and international politics. Many of the puzzles laid out earlier are, simply, the application to the eastern European realm of such widely debated issues as the following. Why do some regimes collapse and others survive in the face of extraordinary pressures? Why and how do states and empires end, and why is regime collapse accompanied at times – but only at times – by state dismemberment? Why do nations arise when and where they do, and why do they sometimes mobilize in pursuit of the political project of greater autonomy within the existing state or the more radical project of independent statehood (also see Medrano, 1995, on this issue)? Finally, why do some (but only some) seemingly entrenched authoritarian regimes give way to democratic orders?

The significant overlap between the issues addressed in this book and the literature on nationalism, revolution, and democratization lead us to the following observations. First, because our cases feature a helpful mix of similarities and differences with respect to *all* of these issues, they constitute an ideal laboratory for their study. This is true, moreover, whether our interest is solely in the European socialist experience (which, we must remember, covered more than 20 percent of the world's land mass and, as a territory, now includes twenty-seven political entities) or in a larger world, which has been registering a roughly similar story of nationalism, regime transition, and state decline.

Just as useful for comparative study, moreover, is the "atypicality" of some of the recent developments in the socialist world. Here, I refer, for example, to the primarily bloodless revolutions that brought an end to European socialist dictatorships and the surprisingly bloodless collapse of the Soviet "empire-state" (on this terminology, see Beissinger, 1995a,

1996; Suny, 1995). It is through deviations, rather than the norm, then, that we can often gain our greatest insights into the workings of politics.

The comparisons drawn in this book will also help us cut across some of the artificial boundaries that too often separate scholarly debates. For example, as it now stands, theorists of revolution have little to say about either secession or nationalism (but see Walton, 1984). This is despite the role of both in most revolutionary dynamics. Moreover, discussions of great reforms, revolution, and regime transition tend to be parallel, rather than intersecting, despite their often common origins in political and economic crises. At the same time, analysts of the state all too rarely interact with analysts of empires, and neither speak very much in turn to those who work on international regimes. Finally, students of nationalism often seem to forget that nationalist movements are one category within the larger construct of social movements (see McAdams, Tarrow, and Tilly, 1997).

This book, therefore, is guided by two concerns. The first is to explain recent developments in the eastern half of Europe – by engaging in a series of comparisons that are informed by what happened in this region and by comparative theory. The other is to use this analysis to say some things of broader relevance about nationalism, revolution, and regime transition. To these two objectives can be added a third. The collapse of communism in Europe has prompted a spirited debate about the value of area studies versus comparative analysis (see, e.g., Schmitter and Karl, 1994; Bunce, 1995b; Shea, 1997; Collier, 1998; Hall and Tarrow, 1998).

Part of what has driven this debate is a widespread presumption that Communist area studies failed to predict the momentous changes in eastern Europe from 1989 to 1992. This book begs to differ. As the references throughout this study testify, there were many in this field of study whose work delineated, in detail and from the vantage point of theory, the many problems confronting European socialist dictatorships during their last decades. These observations, moreover, were grounded in a theoretical framework that only later became the rage in political science in general – that is, institutional analysis. Thus, while many political scientists working on Western democracies were absorbed with, say, public opinion, political parties, and voting behavior, specialists in socialist dictatorships were struggling with quite a different set of issues, such as defining the institutional structure of European socialism and tracing its particular strengths and weaknesses, costs and benefits (see, e.g., Vajda, 1981; Rigby, 1977; Nove, 1979, 1980; Höhmann, 1979; Csanádi, 1997; Hirszowicz, 1986; Harding, 1984; Burg, 1983; Pravda, 1981; Wolchik, 1991; Bunce, 1983a, 1983b, 1985). This was, of course, one of the advantages in working on systems where both civil and political society were weak; where the state directed both the polity and the economy through an elaborate array of institutions; and where there was a considerable gulf separating high from low politics. Institutions, in short, were hard to ignore (and see Solnick, 1998a).

Having laid out these larger issues, let me now turn to some of the organizational details of this study. I begin that discussion by defining some terms.

DEFINITIONAL QUESTIONS

This analysis focuses on four interrelated processes: regime collapse, state collapse, nationalism, and secession. By *regime collapse*, I refer to the disorganization of political power (to reverse the common definition of regime), or, put another way, the multiplication of sovereignty (see Tilly, 1993, on revolutionary situations). In the specific context of European socialist dictatorships, this refers to the Communist Party's loss of political hegemony, with such hegemony understood as *the* defining feature of European socialism and, as a result, *the* necessary condition for its very existence. In practice, this occurred in several ways – for example, through a pacted transition where the Communist Party and the opposition made a series of agreements about regime transition (as most notably in Hungary and Poland, but also elsewhere – see especially Elster, 1996); through mass mobilization against the regime (as in Czechoslovakia and the German Democratic Republic); through Communist Party–initiated reforms that deregulated politics and economics (as in the Soviet Union); and through various combinations of these processes (as in Bulgaria and Yugoslavia, the latter evidencing significant variations by republic).[8]

Thus, what was crucial was not just a decline in the capacity of the regime to extract compliance (which is the familiar story of revolutionary situations the world over), but also a process wherein the Communists were forced to share the stage with other political actors (including various new Communist and socialist parties) and thereby compete with them for political power. *Deregulation* of politics, therefore, was central to regime collapse in the socialist context. At the least, this produced a political oligopoly, as in much of the southern tier of eastern Europe after 1989 (see especially Pusić, 1997; Fish, 1998). At most, this produced in relatively quick fashion a competitive political order and, thus, a full-scale transition to democracy. What is implied here is that regime collapse in the world of socialist dictatorships, as elsewhere, was a product of both short-term crises and long-term developments, with the latter including economic decline, divisions within the party, and the growth of civil and political society.

State collapse is usually defined as the loss of the state's coercive monopoly (see, e.g., Skocpol, 1979; Foran and Goodwin, 1993).[9] Such a definition, however, tends to confuse issues of regime and state and, at the same time, overlooks the boundary functions of the state while treating state collapse as a dichotomous rather than a continuous variable. Thus, for example, while the French, Russian, and Chinese revolutions all involved the end of the regime and the end of the state's coercive monopoly, they varied in the extent to which existing geographical boundaries were challenged – and challenged successfully (but see Walton, 1984, on the importance of looking at rebellion within revolution). Moreover, in all three cases, we see not just a crisis that decisively weakened the state, but also long-term leakage in the capacity of the state to monopolize coercion and extract compliance. In this study, state collapse is understood to involve the reduction and then the collapse of the state's coercive and spatial monopoly.[10]

This leads us to two more key terms: the nation and nationalism (see especially Hobsbawm, 1992; Gellner, 1983; Greenfeld, 1992; Armstrong, 1992; Eley, 1996; Wolfe, 1982; Young, 1976; Smith, 1986, 1989, 1992; and the helpful theoretical summaries provided by Young, 1993, and Danforth, 1995: chap. 1). Here, I can be succinct. *Nation* is defined in this study as a shared sense among a group of people that they have a common cultural identity that distinguishes them from other groups. That identity comes about through shared historical experiences that have produced common cultural symbols and common institutions. It may or may not include, however, a common religion and/or language – though this is the norm or has been, at least, since the final quarter of the nineteenth century (Hobsbawm, 1992).

In the continuing debate among primordialists, constructivists, and instrumentalists (see especially Young, 1993; Esman, 1994), my position is that the nation, while often having some primordialist origin, is, nonetheless, primarily constructed through density of shared experiences. Thus, the nation is neither a given, nor is it a stable construct. Instead, it is "forever assembled, dismantled and reassembled" (Wolfe, 1982: 391, quoted in Danforth, 1995: 26) in response to the interaction among three factors: geographical proximity, the density of intragroup interaction, and the continuing struggle among people over political power, money, and cultural symbols.

Lest there by any doubt about these observations, consider, for example, the development of the Serbian and Croatian nations. This was a process that spoke to the power of contrasting imperial experiences and contrasting opportunities for state building in creating two nations out of what could have been, under other circumstances, one (see Čirković, 1996; Roksandić, 1991; and, more generally, Anderson, 1991).

Nationalism enters the scene when the nation, or at least political leaders claiming to speak for the nation, focus on a political project. That project can involve, at the least, demands for greater national autonomy within the state or empire, and, at most, mobilization in pursuit of independence from the state and, where successful, the construction of a new state.

Finally, in this book *secession* is understood to be the departure of a region, or regions, from the state. This situation typically arises through a three-stage process, wherein political leaders of a spatially concentrated nation, eyeing a mixture of threats and expanded opportunities in the political environment, begin to demand major changes in the political and economic relationship of the region to the center. What then commences is bargaining between the state and leaders of the region, with bargaining understood loosely to include demands, promises, and threats. In the final stage, bargaining leads to a shrinkage in state boundaries through the territorial subtraction of the region from the state.

What is implied here is that boundaries matter a great deal – to the center and to the region. As Ian Lustick (1990) reminds us, state boundaries are very important. They not only align politics (and economics) with geography but

> specify who and what are potential participants or objects of the political game and who and what are not. Their differential demographic implications and the different political myths associated with different borders also help determine which interests are legitimate, which resources are mobilizable, which questions are open for debate, which ideological formulas will be relevant, which cleavages could become significant, and which political allies might be available. (Lustick, 1990: 56; also see Lustick, 1987)

Thus, it is hardly surprising that the leaders of most states are jealous of their authority and their territory. The departure of a region subtracts resources, reconfigures the distribution of power and money, and redefines preferences. In the process, moreover, secessionist pressures also often invite an increase in external threats to the state, if not outright foreign interventions (see, e.g., Brown, 1993; Brubaker, 1995; Van Evera, 1994; Esman and Telhami, 1995). At the same time, the precedent of one region leaving could tempt other regions to do the same to the point where the state vanishes, along with the power of state elites.

This does not mean, however, that secession can be reduced to a simple game, wherein a "keeper" (the state) bargains with a "leaver" (the secessionist region) (see, e.g., Hechter, 1992; Hechter and Appelbaum, 1982; Hechter and Levi, 1979; Furtado and Hechter, 1992). One problem is that "keepers" may not be "keepers" at all costs.[11] For example, central leaders did very little in fact to resist the division of Norway and Sweden in the early twentieth century. A state's defense of its territory, therefore, is not as predictable as death and taxes. It is best understood as a variable and not a constant.

Second, there can be a sharp disjuncture between what nations and their leaders actually want, as has been particularly well documented for Czechoslovakia prior to its division in 1993 (see Wolchik, 1994; Innes, 1997). Thus, just as regions can stay within a state, despite popular support for independence from the state, so regions can secede without having popular support (or, indeed, even elite support) for such actions.

Third, the preferences of nations and their leaders are in practice extraordinarily fluid over the course of bargaining about center-periphery relations. They are vitally affected, for example, by the politics and economics of the moment, calculations of costs and options, and the particular institutional arenas framing the bargaining process (see especially Innes, 1997; Gagnon, 1995). For example, might the Yugoslav state have survived if all-Yugoslav competitive elections had been held prior to republic-level elections (see Linz and Stepan, 1996)? Might the Czechoslovak state have survived, if the process of dismemberment had taken place within the confines of a new constitution, not that of the socialist era (Wolchik, 1995)? Finally, to step outside of the region, might Quebec have become an independent state had the various referenda on independence been held at different times – or held under the assumption that the economic costs of leaving Canada would be short-term and not long-term in nature (Martin, 1995)?

Finally, and perhaps most importantly, a secessionist outcome may be less the culmination of struggles over autonomy and independence that pit a secessionist region against the center than a *by-product* of a host of other struggles over money, power, and policy that are going on within the center and within the region, as well as between the regions and between the center and the regions (see Hroch, 1996). In this sense, secession can often be an offshoot of other ongoing political struggles, rather than a direct outcome of bargaining over the future contours of the state.

What all this suggests is that secessionist outcomes *emerge* from a long and complex process. This insight is particularly instructive for the cases I examine in this book. Thus, for example, the end of the Yugoslav, Soviet, and Czechoslovak states all began with struggles over power and reform and not over existing state boundaries. Moreover, while some regional leaders, such as Vladimír Mečiar of Slovakia, threatened secession for strategic reasons, but did not really want that outcome, others, such as Slobodan Milosević of Serbia, pursued precisely the opposite course (see especially Kadijević, 1993; Jović, 1995a, 1995b; Hadžić, 1994a; Miller, 1997). Finally, some regions within the socialist federations left the state because of public and elite support of that action (as with the Baltic states, Slovenia, and Croatia). However, some left because of elite and not public support (as with the Czech and Slovak cases), and, indeed, some left despite the absence of *either* public or elite support for secession (as with, for instance, Kazakhstan, Belarus, Bosnia, Macedonia, and, arguably, Russia). What is striking about the recent dismemberment of the three European socialist states, therefore, is the sheer diversity of conditions under which republics left these states and these states, in turn, vanished from the European stage.

ANALYZING THE COLLAPSE

With these definitional considerations in mind, let us now turn to the final issue to be addressed in this chapter: my approach to analyzing the collapse of socialism and the state.

COMPARISON

The analysis presented in this book is based on two core assumptions. The first is that the comparative method – or controlled comparisons among a limited number of cases – can be a powerful tool for uncovering causal relationships (see, e.g., Przeworski and Teune, 1970; Lijphart, 1971; King, Keohane, and Verba, 1994; Ragin, 1987). This is particularly so when four conditions are met. One is that the question(s) to be addressed must be well specified. Another is that case selection must be driven entirely by the puzzle to be explained – and not by, say, the "sunk case capital" of the analyst. Still another is that the number of cases selected must be small enough to ensure full knowledge of causal dynamics, careful operationalization of variables, and confidence that apparent similarities and differences are in fact real (see Locke and Thelen, 1998), yet large enough to hold the number of plausible causes (identified by theory) to a minimum.

The final condition, which is more controversial, is to combine, where possible, two approaches: sampling on the independent variable, where cases are chosen on the basis of seemingly similar contexts producing divergent outcomes; and sampling on the dependent variable, where case selection follows the opposite logic, with the same outcome observed in seemingly diverse contexts (see Lijphart, 1971; Przeworski and Teune, 1970; Collier and Mahoney, 1996). The first approach is widely preferred by many comparative methodologists (see especially King, Keohane, and Verba, 1994). By allowing for variance in the dependent variable while limiting the number of potentially causal factors, this method approximates the standards of statistical approaches. This, in turn, enhances the claim to generalizable findings (see Varshney, 1997, for one good example of its benefits).

However, while sampling on the dependent variable has been criticized for introducing biases into the analysis, this second approach nonetheless has merit – particularly when combined with the first method (see Ragin, 1998; Dion, 1998; Collier, 1998). By examining similar outcomes across apparently diverse contexts, this approach can go far in eliminating a range of plausible causes (which is precisely the overarching goal of the scientific method) and in defining what constitutes necessary (but not sufficient) conditions. The redundancy of the outcome but the constrained number of redundant causes, in short, can be quite illuminating. As such, this approach to case selection can augment one that samples on the independent variable – especially since the latter, constrained by the need to both limit cases yet vary outcomes, can produce conclusions that rest precariously on single instances of each observed outcome.

In this study, I use the comparative method and do so in a manner that meets these four conditions. Thus, I address three specific issues: why state socialism collapsed and collapsed when and how it did; why the Soviet, Yugoslav, and Czechoslovak states ended (whereas other states, so similarly situated, did not); and why the end of the Soviet Union and Czechoslovakia was peaceful and the dismemberment of Yugoslavia violent. Consequently, this book is engaged in several sets of comparisons, each of which is tailor-made to answer the particular question at hand.

Thus, when the concern is with the similar outcome of regime collapse, I compare these in many ways diverse regimes with each other and search for regionwide commonalities. In order to avoid the problems of sampling on the dependent variable, however, this comparison is supplemented in two ways. One is to introduce a diachronic perspective by looking at socialist regimes over the course of their lives. This allows us to vary the dependent variable (by tapping into the contrast between durable versus dissolving regimes), while using continuity of context to hold many causes constant. The other is to compare the socialist dictatorships with other kinds of dictatorships, such as those that have been characterized as bureaucratic authoritarian (O'Donnell, 1979).

When our interest is in variations in regime collapse, I will again compare the socialist dictatorships with each other. In this instance, however, the focus is on key sources of differentiation that, within an overall context of similarities, we must remember, could logically account for divergent patterns in the mode and timing of regime termination. As with all the other comparative exercises in this book, so in this one plausible lines of explanation will be defined by theory.

Finally, when the focus shifts to state disintegration, I will compare the Soviet Union, Yugoslavia, and Czechoslovakia with other states in the region and with each other. While the first contrast will help explain why these postsocialist states and not others ended, the second will help identify why they ended in different ways. As an additional source of information on this question, I will bring in other cases from outside the region that feature some of the same characteristics that distinguish the Soviet Union, Yugoslavia, and Czechoslovakia – for example, the presence of large national minorities, secessionist pressures, and regime transition – but that feature variable outcomes with respect to state survival. The Spanish case in particular proves to be unusually helpful in this regard, since it resembles the socialist states that dissolved in so many ways, but minus the outcome of state dissolution.

INSTITUTIONS AND OPPORTUNITIES

The second assumption underlying this study is drawn from recent work on institutions, revolution, social movements, nationalism, and secession.[12] Although the focus of much of this work is, not surprisingly, quite different, and although the particular language used to connote key processes is quite variable as well, there is within this body of research, nonetheless, a striking convergence in the line of argumentation – a convergence that serves as the theoretical foundation for this book. In particular, demands for political change – whether radical or incremental, whether by publics, the nation, or "nations," and whether targeted on elites, the regime, or the state – tend to arise when two factors converge. The first is more long-term and focuses on the formation of solidaristic and resourceful political groups – that is, groups that have shared economic, political, social, and cultural experiences; that have developed a common identity, a common set of goals, and a common definition of the enemy; and that are empowered not just by their solidarity but also by ideology, organization, and leadership. Whether such groups form depends heavily on the institutional design of the system and its specification of the political playing field; the rules of the game; and, by virtue of the institutional format, the distribution of roles, interests, incentives, and resources. Thus, the formation, the

identities, the power, and the proclivities of groups reflect in large measure
how the system within which they operate is structured (and see Solnick,
1998a).

Though a product of long-term developments, political contention is
usually prefaced by short-term and dramatic shifts in political context.
This leads to the second factor, what social movement theorists have
termed an expansion of the political opportunity structure (see especially
Tarrow, 1994; also see Keeler, 1993). This refers to a growing elasticity in
the political environment, wherein existing political alignments are dis-
turbed, political access widens, the policy agenda is reordered, and the
costs of mobilization decline alongside the benefits of standing passive on
the sidelines. In practice, this typically refers to major shifts in policies,
institutions, or leaders, with the most dramatic cases being those that affect
all three – for example, great reforms, regime transition, war, and revolution. As Mark Beissinger (1995a: 4; 1993) has argued with respect to
nationalist mobilization in the Soviet Union during the Gorbachev era:

> The easing of repression, disarray within ruling circles, moments of state
> weakness, the example of successful challenge by other groups in analo-
> gous situations, or even a sudden loss of accustomed group status all
> encourage challenges to the ways in which the existing political order
> defines its physical and human boundaries. These conditions make chal-
> lenge appear possible, not only by providing counterelites with the po-
> litical space necessary to mobilize populations. They also do so by provid-
> ing weakened targets: on the one hand, the state, whose existing
> definition of the boundaries of the community – itself a central part of
> the political order – is never fully accepted by society; on the other hand,
> other groups whose status and position depend upon the authority of the
> state and its rule-enforcement capacity.

The result of these developments and others implied in the notion of
an expanded opportunity structure is to redefine – or at least threaten to
redefine – the resources available to publics, elites, and elites-in-waiting,
along with the array of risks and incentives attached to the various demands publics and elites might make and the actions they might subsequently take. In the process, the parameters on what is politically possible
and desirable are expanded considerably; new forms and degrees of "group-
ness" can materialize as well (see Fish, 1995); and such seeming "con-
stants" as the regime, the state, and the nation can become subject to
contentious politics. Indeed, this is precisely the story in a nutshell of the
fall of socialism and the state.

The approach taken in this book, then, is to explain regime and state
collapse by engaging in a series of comparisons that allow us to trace the

interaction between two factors. One is the institutional design of socialism and its long-term consequences for the regime, the bloc, and the state. The other is the shorter-term effects of major political and economic changes throughout the 1980s. Why socialism and the state collapsed in the eastern half of Europe from 1989 to 1992 was in effect because both of these factors pushed in the same direction. In all cases, they deregulated the party's economic, political, and social monopoly, and, in some cases, they also deregulated the spatial monopoly of the state. In the first instance regimes dissolved, and in the second states dissolved as well.

CONCLUSIONS

Among the most enduring issues of politics and political science – and among the most relevant issues for the contemporary world – are the following. Why do dictatorships fall? Why do publics rebel? Why do states end? How do new states form? How and why do nations and nationalist movements come into being? Why do some nationalist movements succeed in leaving the state? Finally, why are all these various instances of major shifts in politics sometime violent and sometimes peaceful?

The recent and dramatic collapse of socialist dictatorships in Europe and of the Soviet, Yugoslav, and Czechoslovak states provides us with a rare opportunity to investigate *all* of these questions – and in a setting that is at once variable and yet well controlled. As we will discover, many of the answers to these questions can be traced to the same source: the interaction between institutions and opportunities. These answers in turn afford us yet another luxury: to build bridges between, while assessing, the recent scholarly work on revolution, nationalism, and regime transition.

2

DOMESTIC SOCIALISM: MONOPOLY AND DEREGULATION

Here, you can't just say "workers," because the whole working society has a common denominator of losses and limitations. For the worker it means he earns little and is cheated; the writer, that he is not allowed to write or told to write as he doesn't wish to; for the teacher, that he must say things that are untrue . . . thus, all are in some way oppressed by the system.

Lech Walesa (quoted in Singer, 1985: 764)

In this chapter, I lay out the institutional design of European socialism and assess its long-term consequences for the party, the society, and the economy. As we will discover, in the early years the institutions that defined socialism produced strong regimes, weak societies, and robust economic growth. Socialist institutions, therefore, served the interests of the party in general and its leadership in particular. However, as these regimes matured, a quite opposing set of outcomes began to materialize. These regimes depended for their very survival on maximizing growth and safeguarding the economic and political monopoly of the party, yet their institutional structure began gradually but surely to undermine growth and to deregulate the party's monopoly. European socialism, therefore, began to devolve and to decline long before it officially ended.

SIMILARITIES AMONG PARTY-STATE DICTATORSHIPS

All dictatorships feature by definition a political monopoly or, put differently, certain political results (see especially Przeworski, 1986; Bunce, 1991a, 1991b). However, aside from this core organizing principle, dictatorships tend to exhibit substantial variation – for example, along such dimensions as the ideological basis of the regime, the composition of its ruling stratum, the organizational design of the dictatorship, and the relationship of the state to the economy and to the international system.

What distinguished "actually existing socialism" as a type of dictatorship – whether the model constructed first in the Soviet Union and, after World War II, in China and virtually all of Eastern Europe, or the variation on state socialism of self-managing pluralism that evolved in socialist Yugoslavia – were four key factors. The first was the ideological mission of the ruling elite. Unlike most dictatorships, which tend to be concerned with stability, if not a version of cultural and class nostalgia, and which operate within a capitalist economic framework, socialist regimes were future-oriented, avowedly anticapitalist and premised on a commitment to rapid transformation of the economy, the society, and, following that, in theory at least, the polity as well.

These ideological concerns had several distinct consequences. One was to carry to the extreme both the late developer model and the model of import substitution by, for example, creating fully autarkic economies, starving the agricultural and the consumer sectors, speeding the rate of urbanization, generating unusually high rates of savings, and targeting investment toward both education and heavy industry. Another consequence was to make a fetish of growth by concentrating on the production of the markers of modernization. These markers were largely defined, it must be noted, not by international markets, level of socioeconomic development, factor endowments, or, more generally, changing definitions over time of modernity and high technology, but rather by the historical roots of socialism in the late nineteenth century and, thus, by nineteenth-century standards of modernity. This, plus the constraints on development in the periphery of capitalism, bequeathed to the entire region one striking legacy of the socialist experience, a legacy that has made the current transition to capitalism all the more painful (Balcerowicz, 1995). As one Czech economist put it, thanks to socialist development policies, eastern Europe had become one large "museum" of the industrial revolution.

A second defining feature of socialist dictatorships was the construction in all cases of a conjoined economic and political monopoly that rested in the hands of the Communist Party. This monopoly originated, on the one hand, in the absence (or, for Yugoslavia, the limited role) of private ownership,[1] markets,[2] a bourgeoisie, and competition in politics and economics, and, on the other, in their replacement with a Leninist party dictatorship, a transformative ideology, central planning, and state ownership of the means of production. Thus, instead of pluralism, there was a "mono-organizational" order (see especially Rigby, 1990, and, earlier, 1977; and see Höhmann, 1979; Nove, 1979; Vajda, 1981; and on socialism as the "opposite" of capitalist liberal democracy, Horvat, 1982). As a result, Communist parties had enormous economic and political resources at their disposal, they lacked competitors, and they were bent on rapid development. In this way, the political monopoly begat the economic monopoly – and vice versa (see especially Nove, 1979; Daniels, 1979).

The hegemonic role of the party in politics and economics had two crucial implications, aside from the obvious one of creating what was, even by the standards of dictatorship, an extraordinarily powerful elite stratum. One was that the investment hunger built into socialist economies (Kornai, 1979) had its equivalent in the "power hunger" built into socialist polities. Characteristic of these systems, then, was a widespread sense, even among the top elite, of resource deficits and a compelling drive to expand (Csanádi, 1997; Gaidar and Yaroshenko, 1988; Gorlin, 1983). At the same time, the party's dual monopoly meant that politics and economics were extraordinarily interdependent. This was even the case in Yugoslavia, where market socialism (introduced largely after 1965) had, purportedly, divided the two, but where in practice the costs of socialist economics, or the inefficiencies derived from the politicization of economic decision making (Rutland, 1992), were combined with all the costs of markets, namely the high levels of unemployment and the boom and bust cycles that are characteristic of the integration of peripheral and poor economies into the global capitalist system (see, e.g., Comisso, 1979; Milenkovitch, 1971; Woodward, 1995b; Županov, 1983; Tašić, 1993).

Indeed, the term "interdependence" puts the case too weakly. In all of the socialist systems, we see in fact a *fusion* between politics and economics. Just as politics provided the answers to the questions of economics (i.e., what is to be produced, how is it to be produced, and how is the product to be distributed; see Lindblom, 1977), so economics provided the answers to the questions of politics – or, in Lenin's immortal and concise phrasing, "kto-kogo."

This leads us to a third feature shared by all socialist systems: the fusion of not just the polity and the economy, but also the party and the state. Although the state had separate institutions that existed side by side with party institutions, this did not mean (as some analysts tended to assume when analyzing party-state relations during the Communist period) that the state functioned as an autonomous source of political and economic power and, thus, as a powerful constraint on the party. Rather, to understand what fusion meant in this case we need to recognize at the outset that the party-state was the sum total of a complex array of dyadic linkages between appointed positions that extended from the very bottom of the system (for instance, within enterprises, schools, hospitals, local governments, and neighborhood associations) to its apex. These appointed positions were located within the party or within the state bureaucracies, and the linkages – which were *the* mechanisms for distributing political power and economic resources – tied party positions to each other or to positions within the state. The end result was that the party-state produced in effect a single, extraordinarily detailed tapestry that covered the entire system (see especially Csanádi, 1997).

If one were to make a distinction between the party and the state, it would be that the party represented the more dominant threads within this tapestry. The state, in particular, relied on the party for personnel (because the party appointed members of the state, and because members of the state apparatus were also party members and often held simultaneously positions in the party); for the very design of its institutions; for all of its resources; and for the specification of its considerable, if always deliberately ambiguous, economic, social, and administrative tasks (which the party then took upon itself to define and refine). Moreover, the state apparatus was never free in an institutional sense to make decisions. This was because party positions intervened at every strategic point in the structure, and because the pinnacle of the system, with respect to decisional authority, was occupied by the party – specifically, the Politburo and the Central Committee. Thus, the party and the state were neither separate nor equal. The state was heavily dependent upon the party and, thus, the junior partner in the alliance.

What also distinguished European socialist systems and what constitutes the final key characteristic of state and self-managing socialism is what has been implied in the discussion thus far – that is, the extraordinary institutional penetration of the party-state. As Michael Mann (1987) has argued, all regimes can be arrayed along two dimensions: penetration and despotism. While other kinds of dictatorship have, unfortunately, come close at times to being the equal of socialism in the latter, none has approximated the institutional capacity of socialist systems to orchestrate developments within their environs. This capacity reflected not just the economic and political monopoly enjoyed by the party and the sheer size, density, and sectoral as well as geographical coverage of the party-state, but also the party's ideological commitment to reinventing its environment. What this meant for the system was, for example, a tendency toward what Stephen Cohen (1985) has termed excess.

While this is easy to forget from the vantage point of, say, the Brezhnev era, socialism in Europe was in practice addicted to change – in policies, leaders, and institutions. It was a system that lacked the kinds of constraints that, in more pluralist political settings, moderate and correct the course of public policy – for instance, the ever present possibility of enterprise and electoral failures, and the considerable pressures on elites within capitalist economies, whether situated within a democratic or a dictatorial political context, to juggle their own political needs with the demands of capital and labor. Thus, just as excess meant in practice that decision makers within these systems became fixated with the idea that "big is better," whether big enterprises, big collective farms, big dams, or big states (Graham, 1993; Gaidar and Yaroshenko, 1988), so the "Magnitigorsk mentality" pushed these systems to produce, especially in their early years, extraordinarily high rates of investment, urbanization, and, it must be added, literacy. Excess also led, especially when combined with fusion and the commitment to rapid transformation, to regularized cycles, wherein "bunched" crises, at once economic and political, alternated with major reforms, with the end result that the system was rarely at rest. This in turn produced, among other things, human tragedies on a grand scale – for example, the death of twenty to thirty million peasants in response to the Great Leap Forward in China and the death of millions during the drive for collectivization in the Soviet Union.

For the mass public, the penetration of the party-state, along with its other characteristics, translated into the surrender of autonomy. Put another way, as it developed throughout the eastern half of Europe, socialism managed to destroy and/or prevent the development of political *and* civil society (Vinogradov, 1996). It did so by rejecting bourgeois law and individual rights; by erasing the boundary separating the private from the public and the economy from the polity, while erecting virtually impenetrable boundaries between the domestic and the international environment; and by preventing the existence of any associational life, political organizations, or social movements that existed separate from the party-state's institutional web. As a consequence, mass publics were rendered dependent on the party-state for jobs, income, consumer goods, education, housing, health care, and social and geographical mobility. Thus the party-state, and no other set of institutions, held sole responsibility for the allocation of power, money, and status.

If absolute control over the mass public was one objective of Communist Party leaders, then so was the exercise of control over all those individuals who were in positions to distribute resources within the command political economy – for example, party bosses, ministerial officials, and enterprise directors. This was a far more difficult proposition. The sheer size of the party-state made monitoring difficult, while the fusion of economic and political resources and the absence of competition made rent-seeking behavior quite tempting. The problem, in short, was one of principals controlling a vast array of potentially independent and resource-rich agents (Solnick, 1998a). The solution to this dilemma was to make use of a series of mechanisms to enhance bureaucratic compliance: terror, job insecurity, and nonstandarized operating procedures, coupled with the party's appointment monopoly, taut planning, ideological incentives, and rapid economic growth. What was to keep lower-level officials in line, then, was a mixture of fear, uncertainty, ambition, and élan.

What was also used to assure compliance was the very structure of the party-state itself – in particular, its atomization. As Maria Csanádi (1997) has argued on the basis of an extraordinarily rich empirical base, party-states are best understood as "fractal" structures. By this she means that each unit within the system reproduced the overall structure of the system. This, plus the already noted dyadic linkages that tied single positions to each other throughout this large and dense structure, meant that individuals located within the structure were just that: individuals. They were isolated from each other and operated under a veil of considerable uncertainty – about their jobs, about the flow of resources, and about the interests and the behavior of others located elsewhere within the party-state system. Thus, like the prerevolutionary Leninist party upon which its organizational structure was based, the socialist party-state was a peculiar blend of external domination and internal atomization.[3] While the former secured the party's economic and political monopoly, the latter guaranteed – at least in theory – a monopoly within the monopoly.

PLURALIZING THE PARTY

What differentiated European socialism from other dictatorships, then, was the party's commitment to rapid transformation, its interwoven relationship with but dominance over the state, and its enormous organizational capacity to orchestrate politics, economics, and social relationships within its geographical boundaries. All of this would seem to point to an obvious conclusion. Socialism in Europe was ideally structured to reproduce itself –

by maximizing the control of the party over itself and over the state, the economy, and the society and by maximizing in the process the growth rate of the economy. However, the institutions of socialism came to have quite different consequences. Over time and certainly by accident, the institutional framework of socialism functioned to deregulate the party's monopoly and to undermine economic growth. This set the stage for crisis and reform – and, ultimately, for the collapse of all of these regimes.

Key to this process of the involuntary subversion of socialism was the role of socialist institutions in generating high levels of intraelite conflict along horizontal and vertical lines. This occurred in large measure because these systems combined the following characteristics: a stress on planned and rapid transformation; high rates of turnover in elite positions (especially in the early years of socialism, when the old system was destroyed and the new system imposed); overlapping and poorly specified administrative responsibilities attached to elite positions; pooled economic, political, and social resources and, thus, interdependent and highly fluctuating outcomes; close interdependence between the upper and lower reaches of the party, because the former needed the latter to procure resources and meet planned objectives, while the latter depended upon the former for allocation of resources and for security of job and life; and the role of the party not just as the sole distributor of power and privilege but also as the sole market for any and all claims to power and privilege. The final point is crucial. Monopoly in this context produced monopsony. With but one arena for the mediation of all conflicts, the commitment to rapid transformation, the extraordinarily high stakes attached to winning and losing, and, finally, an extraordinarily fluid economic, political, and social environment, the stage was optimally configured for political struggles among politicians who were at once very insecure and very ambitious (on intraelite divisions and limits to central control, see, e.g., Arbatov, 1991: 248–250; Zaslavskaya, 1984; "Korrenoi vopros," 1988).

What also encouraged intraelite conflict was the succession problem at the very top of socialist systems. It was not just that there was no institutionalized mechanism for succession (since this would create resourceful rivals), that the stakes attached to winning or losing were very high, that there was no fixed term of office for the first or general secretary, or that those engaged in the struggle at the apex of the system were experienced and highly professional politicians and policy makers who were, as a result, in an unusually strong position to lobby, criticize, broker new coalitions, and, indeed, mount campaigns to become the next first or general secretary – a combination of characteristics that gave real meaning to the usually hyperbolic phrase "power struggle." It was also that these struggles necessarily affected virtually every other member of the apparatus. This was because succession struggles – whether unleashed by the death of the leader, by policy reversals and/or public protests that quickly unraveled the leader's governing coalition – involved necessarily major shifts in the composition of the Politburo, its coalitional structure, and, thus, its policy priorities (Daniels, 1979).

In addition, given the institutional "echoes" of such systems, all these changes translated in turn into changes in all those positions throughout the party-state apparatus that fanned out from the Politburo and that were appointed by the subset of the Politburo that made up the Secretariat. Moreover, even if members of the apparat retained their posts during a succession crisis, they still had to respond to changes at the top. They did so by shifting their political allegiances and their policy commitments, while sizing up their opportunities for upward political mobility.

In all political systems, of course, whether dictatorships or democracies, an ambitious and disputatious elite stratum has important effects on public policy and regime-society relations. This is because elites make policies, and a divided elite invites the formation of new coalitions and, thus, the representation of new interests; the consideration of new directions in public policy; and expanded room for maneuver for mass publics in general and the opposition and social movements in particular. However, the institutional design of socialism made these systems unusually "elite sensitive." Thus, instability at the top in the socialist context invariably caused a chain reaction that destabilized the entire system by affecting all of its social, political, and economic nooks and crannies. This was one of the costs of fusion and interdependence in a setting that was both institutionally elaborate and despotic.

HOMOGENIZING SOCIETY

If the party elite was weakened by conflict at the top that, particularly during succession periods, divided and fragmented the rest of the apparatus, then those outside the apparatus were, at the same time, far from playing the role of disinterested bystanders. Ellen Comisso (1991) has succinctly summarized one continuing theme in the history of socialist dictatorships: "When the party divides, society enters." It is not surprising, therefore, that the socialist experience evidenced a robust correlation between instances of intraparty conflict and outbursts of public protests – as, for example, in Czechoslovakia and East Germany in 1953, in Hungary in 1956, in Czechoslovakia in 1967–1968, and in Poland in 1956, 1968, 1970–1971, 1980–1981, and many of the years thereafter.

It is tempting to focus on these dramatic episodes and their implication of a zero-sum relationship between the power of the party and the society under socialism (and see, more generally, Migdal, 1988). It is equally important, however, to recognize the existence of other sources of power available to publics that allowed them to engage in a variety of more "everyday" forms of resistance (drawing upon Scott, 1985). Although these were also a product of the structure of the system and contributed to the weakening of the party, they were more incremental in their development and somewhat independent of shifts in high politics. Here, I refer, first, to the power that came from the party's commitment to full employment – a commitment that, along with the labor hunger of enterprises (see Kornai, 1979), produced the infamous deal wherein workers pretended to work and enterprise directors pretended to pay them. The absence of unemployment was particularly important in the socialist context, because of the fusion between politics and economics. Thus, in giving workers job security, their political power was necessarily augmented. Moreover, the regime was deprived of one mechanism that capitalist systems have long used to police their publics – elastic labor markets.[4]

Publics in socialist systems also benefited from what can be termed the homogenization of their positions and, thus, their interests. The party's economic, political, and social monopoly, its commitment to rapid socioeconomic development, limited wage inequalities, and stable prices for consumer items, its preference for large enterprises and large collective farms, and its creation of consumer-deficit societies all worked together to give publics in the European socialist systems a remarkably uniform set of experiences (Bunce, 1993). Whether citizens engaged in political, economic, social, or cultural activities, they were controlled in what they could do by the party. Thus, the party did not just orchestrate elite recruitment, voting, attendance at rallies, and the content of the mass media. It also functioned in the economy as the only employer, the only defender of workers' rights (through party-controlled unions), the only setter of production norms, and the only allocator of vacation time (while being the only builder and maintainer of vacation retreats). At the same time, the party allocated all goods and set all prices. Finally, it was the party (sometimes through enterprises) that was the sole distributor of housing, education, health care, transportation, and opportunities for leisure-time activities.

Thus, in a Marxist sense (which should, after all, have some application to supposedly Marxist systems), publics under socialism occupied a virtually identical structural location. This was the case, whether we focus on the redundancy of life experiences as we move from one individual to the next, or from one role, such as that of a producer, to another role, such as that of a consumer. To borrow from T. H. Rigby's succinct and insightful formulation, these were "mono-experiential" systems.

What also contributed to this homogenization was another characteristic of socialist systems: their bias toward systemic uniformity. For example, when prices were changed, they were changed everywhere by the same amount at the same time. When shortages appeared in one place, they tended to appear in most others. And when social mobility expanded, it expanded everywhere, and when it slowed, virtually everyone was affected. As noted earlier, moreover, this pattern extended as well to politics. Thus, when politicians at the top turned over, politicians virtually everywhere else tended to follow suit and a wide range of economic and social policies also shifted accordingly – and in the same direction at roughly the same time. In the "good times," uniformity was an advantage, since it meant that virtually everyone reaped some and similar benefits. Thus, in the early years, social mobility was widespread, economic performance was robust, and many supported the system by virtue of its successes and opportunities (see Brus, 1977). In the "bad times," however, such as when mobility slowed and the economy declined, virtually everyone outside the top reaches of the party-state paid a price – and, what is more, roughly the same price. As Vojin Dmitrijević (1995: 39) has observed, "Common interests are best realized when they are perceived to be in jeopardy" (and see Sadikov, 1986).

All of this fed, of course, into large-scale popular discontent, as Edward Gierek, the Polish party leader, discovered, when his attempts throughout the 1970s to raise prices in order to reduce state subsidies and thereby finance Poland's growing external debt were repeatedly met with public protests. This brings to mind an old political adage that was put to good use by Barrington Moore (1978) in his masterful study of injustice and protest (and see Luebke, 1997). Nothing gets people into the streets faster than shared isolation, agreement on a common enemy, and shocks that are sudden and similar.[5]

The homogenization of socialist societies had several consequences, aside from the obvious one of building subtle but durable bonds among people who were, ostensibly, isolated from each other. In particular, shared and similar experiences produced strikingly uniform interests. Homogenization also generated a common definition of the enemy. For mass publics, this included a pronounced tendency, aided by the complete absence of transparency in economic and political decision making (see Brada, 1994), to assume that bad and seemingly unfair outcomes were produced in quite deliberate fashion by the party – or what was commonly referred to as "the power." This interpretation even dominated when, as in Poland and Yugoslavia in the 1970s and 1980s, the party had lost its capacity to control the economy and was quickly losing popular support as a result of widespread shortages – in other words, even when "the power" was behaving for all to see in an obviously counterrational way (see, e.g., Ermakoff, 1997, on counterrational elites).

Homogenization also encouraged individuals within socialist systems to divide their personalities into a public and conformist self, on the one hand, and a private and more rebellious self, on the other – what was referred to in the East German setting as a *Nischengesellschaft*, or niche society (which was the subject of many sociological studies in Poland in particular, beginning in the 1960s – see, e.g., Szczepanski, 1970). This lack of "transparency," if you will, in public opinion in socialist systems had three important consequences (see, e.g., Lohmann, 1994; Kuran, 1992; Bunce and Chong, 1990). One was to depress protest in the short-term, since it was hard for unhappy individuals to be confident in assuming that, if they took to the streets, a number of others would quickly join them. Another was to create the potential for rapidly expanding protests, once some core group of people revealed its true preferences – usually in response to major changes in politics that both divided elites and threatened publics. Finally, because the preferences of publics were falsified and public acquiescence was the norm, political authorities found it easy to overestimate their support and to underestimate the support of the opposition forces (as with, for instance, Edward Gierek's miscalculations about rebellious Poles in 1980 and the Polish Communists misforecasting of Solidarity's support in the June 1989 Polish elections).

All three consequences, of course, were crucial in shaping the events of 1989, the subject of Chapter 4. But all three speak as well to our concern in this chapter: the hidden, surprising, and growing power of socialist publics as a consequence of the design of the system in which they lived and worked. Thus, while these dictatorships had enormous resources to control their publics, they also transferred – quite by accident – significant resources to those publics. The problem was not simply the creation of homogenized publics with similar experiences, similar interests, a similar definition of the enemy, and similarly misleading public stances. It was also that the very structure of the system had deprived its leaders of those mechanisms that allow leaders in more pluralist settings to keep publics divided and to diffuse protest – for example, substantial socioeconomic inequalities that are understood to be the result of some combination of the overall functioning of the economy, employer decisions, the "market," personal merit, and personal luck; direct ties between money and purchasing power and between levels of income and patterns of consumption, both of which focus responsibility on the individual; and hierarchy in the economy coupled with democracy in the polity (with the latter producing such arguments as citizens merely getting the leaders they deserve). Thus, what the institutions of European socialist dictatorships lacked in part was the capacity to obfuscate regime responsibility for unpopular outcomes.

This is not to argue, however, that socialist publics were in a position to do whatever they wanted. Indeed, there were substantial variations across country and time in the levels and frequency of public unrest in the European socialist regimes. For example, in the more repressive systems, such as Albania, Bulgaria, Romania, East Germany, and the Soviet Union and in systems that had featured protests in the past that were then put down by Soviet armed intervention, such as Hungary and Czechoslovakia, the costs of protest were high and publics tended, as a result, to be more quiescent (see, e.g., Ekiert, 1996; Bozoki and Sukosd, 1993), while engaging, nonetheless, in some subtle forms of protest, such as work slowdowns.

In Yugoslavia and Poland, however, overt protests were far more common, in large measure because these two countries featured some distinctive characteristics that proved optimal for the generation of political protests. In Poland, for example, where Stalinization was less extreme, where the church had carved out some autonomy, and where protests in 1956 had produced neither a crackdown nor a Soviet invasion, but, rather, a remarkable accession to popular demands (including decollectivization of agriculture, along with Gomulka's return to power), political protests were unusually frequent, as were strikes – the latter consistently over the last twenty years of the regime until its formal farewell in 1989 (see, e.g., Staniszkis, 1984, 1991; Ekiert, 1996; Kubik, 1994; and see Bilandžić, 1979; Bokovoy, 1997, on Yugoslavia).

What also facilitated political mobilization in Poland were two other factors rarely combined in Eastern Europe. One was widespread antagonism toward Soviet power and, before that, the Russian imperial presence, and the other was the ethnic and religious homogeneity (for tragic historical reasons) of Polish society. Thus, while there is much to be said for protest as a well-established Polish tradition dating back to the partitioned Poland of the nineteenth century, there is also something to be said for the ways in which specific Polish experiences during socialism and the composition of Polish society interacted with the more general institutional characteristics of socialism to produce an ideal formula for political protest. What

the Polish context managed to combine, in short, was resentment, resources, and opportunities.

It was no accident, then, that Polish publics played three important
roles in both anticipating and laying the groundwork for the subsequent
collapse of socialism. In 1956, 1980–1981, and 1988–1989, they demonstrated what societies within a socialist dictatorship could accomplish, if
sufficiently organized and angry. They also repeatedly exposed the limits
of Communist Party rule at home. Finally, they exposed as well the limits
to Soviet intervention in Eastern Europe. In this sense, just as the 1905
revolution in Russia was the "great dress rehearsal" for 1917 (as Trotsky
put it), so the rise of Solidarity in Poland in 1980–1981 was the great
dress rehearsal for 1989.

DIVIDED ELITES AND COHESIVE PUBLICS

We can now combine the public "story" of socialism with our earlier
"story" of elites and their divisions. A straightforward conclusion presents
itself. Contrary to its purpose, the institutions of socialism deregulated the
system – by pluralizing and thus weakening the party and by homogenizing and thus empowering the society. As these systems aged, these redistributive tendencies became more pronounced. This reflected, first, the
growing complexity of a modern, industrial economy and the society that
necessarily went with it. With complexity, the interests of the party began
to differentiate; the party found it harder to plan efficiently and implement
the plan; and economic performance became more dependent upon the
participation and the cooperation of both experts and labor. Moreover, as
society became more complex, it also began to outgrow its Stalinist
"britches" (see especially Lewin, 1988).

Islands of autonomy, in short, began to develop, particularly where a
more liberalized political environment was joined with comparatively high
levels of socioeconomic development and public resentment of communism
– as in Poland and Hungary, the two "leaders" of 1989. This generalization, moreover, can be applied to regions within socialist states that featured similar characteristics and that were, within their larger contexts, the
leaders as well of regime destruction: Slovenia within Yugoslavia and the
Baltic republics within the Soviet Union.

At the same time, for a variety of reasons, including remorse, self-
interest, and worries about economic and administrative efficiency, the
party elite decided to end the terror and to give elites in virtually all of
these systems by the mid-1950s security of life (on de-Stalinization, see,

e.g., Azrael, 1970; Dallin and Breslauer, 1970). During the Brezhnev era, this was extended to job security as well – not just in the Soviet Union, but also throughout Eastern Europe, including Yugoslavia (see, e.g., Breslauer, 1982; Colton, 1986; Bunce, 1983b). Stability in cadres had several important consequences. One was to reduce the capacity of the upper reaches of the party to control what happened elsewhere within the apparatus. This was in part because these changes were joined with the pressures already noted, including the impact of complexity; in part because the costs of deviance declined, while ambition remained high; and in part because the slowdown in political mobility created both an insulated if not self-satisfied and corrupt elite at the center and an elite in the periphery that was increasingly entrenched and highly resentful of declining opportunities to move onward and upward (see, e.g., on the Soviet case, Bahry, 1987; Lane and Ross, 1995).

Another consequence of the end of the terror was to empower society, because citizens were increasingly incarcerated in a "velvet prison" (Haraszti, 1987) that limited deviance, but that allowed room within those limits for some political, economic, and social maneuver. Just as with the elites within the party-state apparatus, so within the society the costs of deviance began to decline just as the resources available for autonomous actions began to slowly but surely accumulate. The evidence of the growing power of mass publics – and a major cost for the regime of forfeiting the terror and job insecurity and using these changes, as well as a rejection of major reform, to maintain elite consensus at the center – was what scholars have termed, variously, the "social compact" or the "social contract" (see especially Pravda, 1981; Bunce, 1981; Hauslohner, 1987; and, earlier, Gitelman, 1970). This was an implicit deal struck in the 1960s between the regime and the society, wherein publics agreed to comply with the regime and tolerate declining opportunities for social mobility in exchange for a well-developed social security net, price stability, steady if unspectacular improvements in the standard of living, increased access to consumer goods, and a relatively depoliticized environment.

Put more baldly, by the early 1970s most of the Communist parties in the eastern half of Europe settled for less by paying more. They asked for political acquiescence rather than demanding enthusiastic support, and they used money, goods, and minimalist work norms, rather than terror and ideological campaigns, to purchase short-term political stability. The hope in all this was that there would be an additional dividend. "Happy" workers would be more productive than "angry" ones (see, especially, Bunce, 1983b, on the corporatist deal). Thus, the remarkable absence throughout much of the region of public protests during the 1970s and

1980s (with the invariable exceptions of Poland and Yugoslavia) did not signal by any means the existence of either repressive regimes or postrate publics. Instead, it spoke to the existence of a low-level equilibrium, wherein weak dictatorships forced to buy public support (in part because of their fears of public unrest) ruled over a citizenry that could not change politics but that could, at the margins at least, dictate economic and social policy.

ECONOMIC DECLINE

This leads us to the final trend associated with the aging of socialist regimes: the decline in economic performance. The economic slowdown made its first appearance in the early 1960s in the most developed socialist state: Czechoslovakia. By the end of that decade, however, this trend began to be registered throughout the socialist region and became by the end of the 1970s a well-entrenched and vexing problem (see especially Vanous, 1982). The economic slowdown reflected the perverse incentives generated by state ownership, monopoly, fusion, and autarky. In particular, the form of economic rationality generated by these systems was growth-deflating, rather than growth-enhancing, given the cumulative burdens on the economy generated by hidden inventories, captive consumers, low rates of technological innovation, the labor and capital hunger of enterprises, and the reliance on queues, connections, and corruption, rather than prices and income, to indicate and allocate supply and demand. As time passed, these costs increased, as principal-agent problems mounted, as distributive coalitions hardened (see Olson, 1982), and as corruption spread in the presence of shortages and in the absence of penalties. This in turn made it difficult for these economies to make the needed shift from extensive to intensive growth – from the creation of new sources of labor and capital (as during Stalinization) to the efficient utilization of existing labor and capital stock (and see Arbatov and Oltmans, 1984).

What also contributed to the economic slowdown was, of course, the factors already mentioned: the growing complexity of the economy and the society and, hence, its limited "planability" (Nove, 1980); the slowdown in elite circulation and the rise of corruption and provincial satrapies; and the growing burdens on the economy of levels of public consumption that increasingly outstripped the expansion of the surplus (see especially Bunce, 1985). Thus, beginning in the 1970s, virtually all of the socialist regimes in Europe were in a difficult bind. An expanding surplus was vital to the survival of the regime, because it was a major component of both regime legitimacy and political stability – the former because of regime ideology and the latter because of the need to keep intraelite conflict within bounds while pacifying a restive and expectant public. However, precisely because the party had pluralized and the public had homogenized, the demands on the surplus had increased and economic growth was thereby undermined.

To get the growth needed, a major overhaul of the system was necessary – in particular, economic reforms that would involve a movement from planning to markets, from public to private ownership, from shadow to real prices, and from isolation from to participation in the global economy. Thus, the economy could be saved, but at the risk of ending the regime by threatening all those interests that depended on the party-state monopoly – that is, not just the "usual suspects," such as party elites, planners, and enterprise directors, but also those, such as workers and consumers, who had been forced to make their deals with the devil. Just as virtually everyone was implicated, so everyone would be threatened by reform – even when they claimed to champion it.[6] What would save the system, then, could very well destroy it. But to avoid destroying the system in the short term would surely dig its grave in the longer term.

A major strength of capitalist liberal democracy is the resonance between short-term and long-term rationality and between what is rational for individuals and for the system as a whole. Indeed, it is precisely this resonance that explains why such systems are so good at reproducing themselves. By contrast, the defining feature of the socialist dictatorships in Europe was the clear tension between these various pairings of rationality. What then follows from this observation is obvious: socialist systems lacked the capacity to be viable and durable over time.

THE STRUGGLE OVER REFORM

Not surprisingly, when confronted with these dilemmas, all the socialist regimes in Europe began to wrestle seriously with the question of reform by the early 1970s (and even earlier in the Soviet Union, Yugoslavia, Poland, and Hungary).[7] The reforms they eventually adopted, however, fell far short of overhauling the entire system – not just because of the power of vested interests but also because of the fear of following the dangerous precedent set by the Czechoslovak reform movement of 1967–1968 (Kramer, 1998). The reforms adopted were also quite variable. The Soviet Union and Czechoslovakia – and, to a greater extreme, Romania, Bulgaria, East Germany, and Albania – maintained their Stalinist economic and political systems, but added some innovations: expanded trade outside the bloc (Romania, the Soviet Union, and Bulgaria), a more independent and nationalist foreign policy (Romania and Albania), and significant expansion of public consumption (the Soviet Union, East Germany, and Czechoslovakia). Poland, Yugoslavia, and Hungary, the remaining socialist regimes in the region, liberalized their domestic politics and expanded public consumption, while increasing considerably their trade with the West – in combination, in the Yugoslav and Hungarian cases in particular, with the introduction of significant market-oriented economic reforms.

None of these responses, however, resolved the institutional dilemmas of socialism (see Bunce, 1985). The rates of economic growth, while decent in Czechoslovakia and East Germany over the course of the 1970s and 1980s (albeit hardly on par with the past and at a rate that expanded, rather than reduced the East-West income gap), declined substantially during the same period in the Soviet Union. Growth fell even further in the heavily debt-ridden economies of Poland, Hungary, Yugoslavia, Romania, and Bulgaria, though the latter two, given political repression, found it easier than their neighbors to cut back on external borrowing. This created in Poland, Hungary, and Yugoslavia in particular a more exaggerated version of the tensions among growth, stability, and monopoly that had first materialized throughout the socialist region by the beginning of the decade.

By the 1980s, socialism was in dire economic and political straits. The only solution was to liberalize politics and economics – the former to unblock resistance to reform and the latter to render the economy more efficient. This was the solution that Gorbachev proposed in the second half of the 1980s, a solution that ended socialism by trying to save it. But that is the story of Chapter 4.

CONCLUSIONS

This chapter has focused on the institutional commonalities of socialism in Europe and their consequences for the regime, the economy, and the state. Three arguments have been presented. First, what defined all the socialist dictatorships of the Soviet Union and Eastern Europe was an ideology committed to rapid socioeconomic transformation; an institutional structure that fused politics and economics, the public and the private, the party and the state; and, finally, a political party that managed through fusion, centralization, and organizational penetration to monopolize political, economic, and social life. The institutional design of European socialism rendered socialist elites unusually powerful, even by the standards of dictatorships in general (O'Donnell, 1979).

Second, this combination of traits had the perverse effect over time of undermining the very foundations of all the socialist systems in Europe. In particular, elites were increasingly divided and disputatious; publics became more resourceful and more autonomous from the party-state; and the economy began to stagnate. Thus, the party's economic and political monopoly – the linchpin of the system – began to unravel as resources became scarce and were redistributed from the top to the lower levels of the party and from the party to the society.

Finally, attempts to save socialism in the 1970s tended in most cases to make a bad situation worse. The disappointing growth rates of the 1960s were followed in the next decade by even slower growth rates, if not actual economic decline, as in Poland and Yugoslavia. At the same time, publics empowered by the social compact and a liberalization of politics (the latter in Poland, Hungary, and Yugoslavia in particular); elites empowered by stability in cadres, corruption, and ossified distributional networks; and, more generally, the impact on both elite and mass developments by the contradiction between growth and stability all led to a simple conclusion. Major reform was as necessary as it was politically impossible.

The choice narrowed down to two unpalatable alternatives. One was introducing needed reforms and thereby destroying the system, either through the reforms themselves and their deregulation of the party's economic and political monopoly or through massive protests that would be unleashed once the "privileged" position of both publics and elites was threatened and the cap removed from public participation and intraparty conflict. The other option was to put off needed reforms and keep party elites, ministerial officials, and enterprise directors mollified while placating the public with economic but not political benefits. This possibility, however, could only buy short-term stability, since economic growth could not keep up indefinitely with the costs of purchasing compliance.

These arguments provide, of course, some important clues to the puzzle of why these regimes – and, indeed, all of them – eventually collapsed. What is missing from our story, however, are three considerations: why the collapse took place at the end of the 1980s and not earlier, why the collapse began in Hungary and Poland and then moved elsewhere, and why regime collapse was followed in the Soviet, Czechoslovak, and Yugoslav cases by state collapse. These issues will be addressed in Chapters 4 through 6. In the next chapter, I continue the institutional discussion by focusing on two remaining socialist playing fields: federal states and the Soviet bloc.

FEDERALISM AND THE SOVIET BLOC: MONOPOLY AND DEREGULATION

Federalism is the process by which unity and diversity are politically organized. . . . It unites without destroying the selves that are uniting.
                                            Carl Friedrich (1966: 286–287)

It is the state that makes the nation and not the nation the state.
    Colonel Jozef Piłsudski (quoted in Hobsbawm, 1992: 44–45)

In the preceding chapter, we focused on institutional similarities among all the European socialist systems. As we discovered, the structure of socialism created – in theory – strong regimes, weak societies, and rapid economic growth. What happened as socialism evolved, however, was a redistribution of power from the party to the society and expanding limits on economic growth. Thus, the eventual and seemingly sudden collapse of socialism was in fact long in the making. It was the product, ironically, of the very institutions that were to preserve and protect the hegemony of the Communist Party.

While institutional commonalities provide the raw material for explaining the regionwide collapse of socialism, they are less helpful in explaining the variations in regime collapse and in the capacity of socialist states to survive the end of the regime. To address these issues, we need to shift our focus from similarities among socialist systems to differences.

In this chapter, we focus on two such differences by analyzing the institutional design of the Soviet bloc and socialist federations. As we will see, the bloc and the federations were surprisingly similar in their design and their internal dynamics. Both involved adding a horizontal layer to "generic" socialism – at the international level in the case of the bloc and at the domestic level in the case of socialist federations. This layer was defined, moreover, in the same way – that is, as a unit that was at once spatial, cultural, political, economic, and administrative. Finally, the political economy of the bloc and the federation followed a pattern typical of center-periphery dynamics. Thus, the key players in the bloc – and the focus, therefore, of bargaining and redistribution – were the Soviet Union as the core versus the Eastern European elites (and the societies they led) as the periphery. At the same time, the key players within socialist federations were the central party-state apparatus versus the republican apparatus (and the societies they led) that fanned out from the center.

These similarities had three important consequences. One was to provide units that were in a position to capture and to hoard those resources that the center leaked over time. Thus, the redistributive dynamics of socialism shifted resources from the Soviet Union to Eastern Europe and from the center to the republics. The second was to tie the fate of the state and the bloc to the fate of the regime. Finally, the very structure of the bloc and the federation put into place the necessary conditions for the rise of nations and nationalist movements in the peripheral units. With the collapse of the regime, this translated into the formation of newly sovereign states, as Eastern Europe was liberated from Soviet domination and as the republics within the federations were "liberated" from the state. In this way, political change in the Soviet bloc and in the socialist federations was at once ideological, national, and territorial.

THE SOVIET BLOC

All of the European socialist regimes, with the exception of Albania and Yugoslavia,[1] were members of the Soviet bloc, a hierarchical regional system that was dominated by the Soviet Union and tightly integrated along economic and political-military lines. What was striking about the bloc was that its structure, as realized through the Warsaw Treaty Organization and the Council for Mutual Economic Assistance, repeated at the international level the essential characteristics of domestic socialism (see especially Bunce, 1985, 1991b). More specifically, the power of the Soviet Union over its client states in Eastern Europe was secured through bilateral ties controlled by the Soviet Union; through Soviet regional dominance in ideology, political authority, national security, markets, and primary products; and through the Soviet role as a regional hegemon defining and defending the boundaries of the bloc and monopolizing interactions between the bloc and the international system. The Soviet bloc, therefore, was highly centralized and radial in its structure – much as was the case with domestic socialism and, for that matter, empires.

Soviet largesse in money, power, and primary products, moreover, was matched by Eastern European deficits in all three areas – a contrast that paralleled in the domestic realm the considerable gap in formal terms between the resources of the party-state and those of society. Thus, like the Communist Party at home, the Soviet Union functioned within the bloc as a political and economic monopoly, controlling all resources and eliminating all competitors. Indeed, the domestic and the regional monopolies did not just duplicate each other; they were also interwoven. Eastern European publics depended upon their ruling parties for money, power, and status, and ruling parties in Eastern Europe depended in turn on the Soviet Union for the same.

For the Soviet Union and virtually all of the Eastern European states, socialism was a two-tiered structure. In this way, the fate of virtually all of the Eastern European parties and, thus, societies was tied through a complex chain of dependencies to the fate of the Soviet Union in general and its Communist Party in particular. It is, therefore, hardly surprising that there were striking similarities among all the bloc political economies, that the Eastern European client states tended to adhere closely to the economic and political dictates of the Soviet Union, and that deviations from Soviet expectations invited at the least harsh words, economic pressures, and personnel changes instigated by the Soviets and, at most, Soviet military intervention – as in Hungary in 1956, Czechoslovakia in 1968, and, indirectly, Poland in December 1981.

However, it is also not surprising, given such a structure and given our discussion in the preceding chapter regarding the long-term costs of domestic socialism, that other, less obviously "bloc-affirming" and "socialist-affirming" developments tended to occur as well. In particular, the Eastern European regimes encased in the bloc, already vulnerable because they owed their very founding and survival in most cases to the Red Army, were rendered even more vulnerable as a consequence of their long-term dependence on the Soviet Union for political power and economic growth. These regimes were often caught, as a result, in a crossfire. While their international patron demanded stability, growth, and ideological conformity, their publics and reformers within these parties – resentful of Soviet domination and empowered by regime weakness and the divisions that came from continuous Soviet meddling in intraparty affairs – demanded quite different things: economic and political liberalization, higher levels of public consumption, an independent foreign policy, and a national road to socialism (if not to another destination entirely).

THE BURDENS OF EMPIRE

For the Soviet Union, this produced growing contradictions among the interests that were to be realized through empire. In the ideal world, Eastern Europe would follow Soviet dictates, and this would enhance Soviet power in the international system and Soviet national security, while contributing in the domestic realm to Soviet growth and stability. However, the real world was another story. On the one hand, the Soviets could use either pressure or bribery to induce the Eastern European regimes to conform to Soviet dictates. However, pressure could destabilize the bloc and thereby undercut Soviet security and stability, whereas bribery would necessarily undermine Soviet growth in the short term and domestic stability and security in the longer term. And the longer-term scenario seemed quite likely, since bribery could easily slip into standard operating procedure. On the other hand, the Soviets could opt for loosening the bloc by transforming it, for example, into an alliance. However, this would also have negative consequences, aside from the obvious one of limiting Soviet control over Eastern Europe and thereby limiting the contributions of "semiempire" to growth, stability, and security. In particular, publics throughout the region and reformers within the Eastern European parties could use a liberalized international environment in order to protest and to demand significant changes in the system, and the weak regimes throughout the region could, as a result, collapse.

The contradictions generated by fusion and monopoly that were built into the domestic logic of European socialism, then, were also characteristic of intrabloc dynamics. At the regional level, however, it was the Soviets – as the dominant Communist Party that functioned at the same time as the regional hegemon – that bore most of the costs.

The tightly integrated structure of the bloc also meant that changes in the Soviet Union, whether in policy or personnel, tended to spread rapidly to Eastern Europe – whether the Soviets wanted that to happen or not and, quite often, in a form and level of intensity that the Soviets neither expected nor welcomed. The bloc structure, therefore, tended to *magnify* Soviet developments as they traveled westward. Thus, Brezhnev's stability in cadres and his corporatist deal (see Bunce, 1983b) were duplicated in the extreme in Eastern Europe, particularly in the northern tier, and the

Eastern European regimes, taking up a variety of reformist and antire-
formist cues from Soviet high politics, tended to shift quickly to either the
left or the right of the Soviet Union. Thus, while Romania under Ceausescu
was an example of unreconstructed Stalinism, if not socialist patrimonialism (Linden, 1986), so Hungary by the late 1960s featured what was by
Soviet standards an unusually liberalized economic and political environment. In a similar vein, while de-Stalinization in the Soviet Union led to
considerable intraparty conflict, in Hungary it did the same and more by
leading in 1956 to the collapse of Communist Party rule. Finally, while
the Khrushchev succession led to a quick victory for Brezhnev and some
divisions within the Communist Party of the Soviet Union, in Czechoslovakia ambiguous signals emanating from Moscow during the struggle for
power produced a showdown within the party between reformers and hard-
liners, the fall of Novotný as the general secretary, and a Communist Party
that first encouraged and then lost control of a popular movement that was
at once reformist and nationalist (see especially Mlynar, 1980). In this
sense, "Soviet sensitivity" was the bloc equivalent of the "elite sensitivity"
characteristic of domestic socialism.

Another cost of the bloc's structure was that the transmission belt that
tied Eastern European publics to their parties and their parties in turn to
the Soviet Union was quite capable of operating in the opposite direction
as well. Divisions within the Eastern European parties and the public
protests that often accompanied and then exaggerated these developments,
therefore, carried the distinct possibility of destabilizing Soviet high politics. Thus, one factor influencing the Soviet decision to invade Czechoslovakia in 1968 was not just the obvious one of preventing the regional
diffusion of "socialism with a human face," but also the less apparent but
nonetheless compelling worry that rising Slovak nationalism might very
well invade the Ukraine – a republic within the Soviet Union abutting
Slovakia that had several representatives on the Soviet Politburo at the
time and that featured a historical record rich in instability and dissent,
both nationalist and ideological (see especially Hodnett and Potichnyj,
1970; Kramer, 1998; Dawisha, 1980; Remington, 1969; Golan, 1973; and
Beissinger, 1996, on the impact of the revolutions of 1989 on Ukraine).

Indeed, such fears do not seem to have been misplaced, though assuming the worst and being wrong was, no doubt, a rational strategy for the
Soviet leadership at the time of the Czechoslovak crisis. During the last
decade of Communist Party rule, for example, there was evidence that the
rise of Solidarity in Poland, a movement that was both nationalist and
anti-Communist, influenced the subsequent development of similar protest
movements in the Baltic states (Vardys, 1983). These movements in turn

were ready to go with the introduction of the Gorbachev reforms, and their sheer size and cohesion put them in an optimal position to influence the rise of nationalist movements elsewhere in a Soviet Union that was rapidly disintegrating along geographical as well as ideological lines (see Muiznieks, 1995).

To these many costs of the bloc can be added one more that also echoed developments within domestic socialism: the tendency for economic and political problems to "bunch." Thus, crises in one arena or in one state tended, given bloc integration, the fusion of politics and economics, geographical proximity, and socioeconomic redundancy, to spread easily to the others. The end result was that crises within the bloc tended to run rampant in both a geographical and a sectoral sense. The bloc, therefore, proved to be the perfect host for communicating the diseases of European socialism. As one Soviet general put it during the Czechoslovak crisis of 1968: "All it will take to bring the entire house [bloc] down is just one spark" (quoted in Mlynar, 1980: 143). The structure of the Soviet bloc, then, did not just fuse politics and economics; it also fused regime fates.

The redistributive tendencies of domestic socialism, elaborated in the previous chapter, therefore, also shaped intrabloc dynamics, with the Soviet Union substituting in this context for "the party" and Eastern Europe for "the society." Thus, once again we find divided parties – in this instance, divisions within the Eastern European parties and between the Soviet party and the dependent parties in the periphery. We also find a tendency toward homogenization, with Eastern European societies gaining strength not just from the "monoexperiential" character of domestic socialism but also from sharing two common enemies: their domestic Communist parties and the Soviet Union. Indeed, to anticipate the discussion in Chapter 4, this is one reason why publics were so quick to mobilize in Eastern Europe in 1989 and why these protests are best understood as *both* nationalist and anti-Communist.

The consequences of these parallels between domestic and regional socialism, moreover, were remarkably similar. Once again, monopoly generated monopsony, with the Soviet Union consigned to a position within the bloc of being *the* target for any and all demands issued by Eastern European parties and publics. This meant that Eastern European regimes and, especially, societies gained leverage from their very weakness – a weakness that meant that societies in the periphery could in stairstep fashion blackmail a Soviet Union unusually vulnerable to such behavior. Just as the Soviets had the most to lose from Eastern European regimes collapsing in economic and political disarray, so the Soviets monopolized all the resources necessary to solve the problems of the region. Moreover, the

Eastern European regimes could easily gang up on the Soviet Union, given the radial structure of the bloc, the redundancy and the geographical proximity of the bloc's political economies, and the less-than-subtle hint that problems in one country could very well spread right to the doorstep of the Soviet Union. The obvious message was that payoffs for bloc membership should spread as well.

The domestic story of socialism, then, was duplicated at the regional level. Thus, within the bloc there was a decline over time in the willingness of these parties to use repression and violence, a trend that described not just domestic developments but also Soviet behavior in response to deviance in Eastern Europe. One sharp contrast brings this point home. Prior to 1989, the three greatest threats to socialist regimes in Eastern Europe were the Hungarian Revolution of 1956, the Czechoslovak reform movement of 1967–1968, and the rise of Solidarity in Poland in 1980–1981. In the first case, the Soviets used considerable violence to restore Communist Party hegemony; in the second, the invasion was largely peaceful, if not oddly apologetic; and in the third case, the Soviets opted to work through the proxy of a domestic and fully peaceful imposition of martial law.

What was also repeated was the social compact, with its implication of weak regimes buying public acquiescence in the short term. Here, it was not just that the public consumption burdens on the Eastern European regimes were unusually large, especially beginning in the late 1970s, when lower growth and, in Poland and Hungary, mounting external debts made it harder and harder for these regimes to finance such consumption (see Bunce, 1981, 1985). It was also that the bloc equivalent of these burdens – or the costs of empire for the Soviet Union – were also large and, what is more, larger each year, beginning in the early 1970s. This was evident, for example, in patterns over time in the distribution of the regional defense burden and in the extension of explicit and implicit subsidies from Moscow to the client states, as well as in less easily measured indicators, such as the successful resistance of Eastern Europe to Soviet pressures for greater bloc integration during the Brezhnev era and, by the late 1960s onward, the increasingly diverse character of socialism within the bloc's periphery (Vanous and Marrese, 1983; Bunce, 1985).

Squeaky wheels, therefore, got the grease in the bloc, a practice that had one other implication. When Soviet publics traveled in Eastern Europe, as they tended to do in considerable numbers by the 1970s, they were confronted with what they saw as a consumer paradise. The colonies appeared richer than the imperial center, a contrast that was embittering and that subsequently had the benefit of easing public and elite acceptance in the Soviet Union of the formal dismantling of the empire in 1990.

Let us now close with one final parallel between domestic and regional socialism. If we join the discussion here with the analysis presented in Chapter 2, we find, at the most general level, a growing gap at home and within the empire between the formal and informal distribution of power. In brief, the sharp contrast between the strong and the weak in formal terms was muddied in reality by the weak gaining strength and the strong accumulating constraints. This gap testifies to the long-term decline of socialism as a domestic and a regional system and to the culpability of socialist institutions in producing that decline. It provides, in short, the foundations for an explanation of why socialist regimes and the Soviet bloc collapsed.

This gap also contains a hint of an answer to one of the most puzzling features of regime and bloc disintegration – that is, the seeming ease with which Communist parties surrendered their political hegemony in the domestic sphere and the Soviet Union the same within the region. While this will be developed further in the next chapter, we can observe here that the size of this gap and the growing costs of exercising "shallow" power had one consequence: it made exit a relatively attractive option to many Communist elites. Moreover, just as Gorbachev diversified his assets by reaching out to the West while reforming socialism and the bloc and did so prior to the collapse of the system, so did domestic Communists, especially in the more liberalized systems of Poland, Hungary, and Yugoslavia. At least some of the Communists in these countries recalculated the costs and benefits of porous hegemony and shifted their assets. In this way, they made the transition before the transition by reinventing their identities and their sources of power. No longer apparatchiks, some became "entrepreneurchiks" (see especially Tarkowski; 1990; also see Urban, 1991; Gaidar and Yaroshenko, 1988; Gaidar, 1995; Staniszkis, 1991; Wasilewski and Wnuk-Lipinski, 1995; Lane, 1997) – though others, of course, stayed in politics and became social democrats (see Bunce, 1998d; and Rose, 1996).

We can now turn to a second variation on socialism: socialist federations. While this was a domestic and not an international configuration, it bore a striking resemblance in structure and consequences, nonetheless, to the Soviet bloc.

FEDERAL VERSUS UNITARY STATES

While most of the socialist states in Europe were unitary, three were federal: the Soviet Union, Yugoslavia, and, following the Soviet invasion in 1968, Czechoslovakia. As with all federal systems, whether socialist or otherwise, this meant that there was a layer – at once political, administrative, and geographical – that was sandwiched between the center and the localities, that featured its own political leadership and representational bodies, and that shared power with the center in decision making and implementation, while functioning at the same time as a key level within the state's administrative chain of command (on federalism, see, e.g., Riker, 1964; Elazar, 1982, 1993). However, what differentiated these cases of federalism from others outside the Communist area was the combination of three additional features.

The first – and most obvious – was that socialist federalism operated within the context of a dictatorship. This is unusual in and of itself, but particularly so, given the fusion and centralization of economic and political resources characteristic of these dictatorships in particular. At issue for all three federalized socialist systems, then, was linking regionally defined monopolies to the larger economic and political monopoly of the Communist Party. This was no small task, and it opened up the very real possibility of monopolies that were competitive, rather than embedded (see, e.g., Stanovčić, 1989). It also meant that all powers were in practice shared between the center and the regions, rather than the situation more typical of federations, wherein some powers are shared and other powers are earmarked for either the center or the regions (see Riker, 1964).

A second characteristic was that the regions in these cases featured their own economic and political institutions – including, significantly, their own Communist parties. These were joined, moreover, by an elaborate array of regionally based and regionally controlled social and cultural institutions. Among the most important of these for subsequent developments, including the rise of nations and nationalism, were schools, academies of sciences, and the mass media.

Finally, as in Canada, India, and Belgium, federalism was national, as well as spatial.[2] Thus, the fifteen republics that made up the Soviet Union, the six republics that made up Yugoslavia, and the two republics that composed federal Czechoslovakia were all based on distinctive national profiles. To these units were added in the Soviet Union and Yugoslavia a number of other smaller and less politically and culturally empowered administrative units, such as autonomous provinces, autonomous districts, and the like. During the socialist period, for example, the Soviet Union comprised fifteen republics and an additional thirty-eight administrative units incorporated within the republics of Russia, Georgia, Azerbaijan, Uzbekistan, and Tadzikistan. All of these units were defined in national and territorial terms. In similar vein, Yugoslavia comprised six republics and, within Serbia, the two autonomous provinces of Vojvodina and Kosovo. As a result, in all three of the federal socialist systems 90 percent or more of the population had national homelands (see, e.g., Roeder, 1991, on the Soviet case).

The idea and the practice of national federalism, not surprisingly, emerged initially in the first and most nationally diverse socialist state: the Soviet Union. There is little consensus as to why the Bolsheviks decided to reconstruct the Russian Empire and to deal with its tremendous size and diversity by creating a system, unprecedented at the time, wherein the party-state would be federalized and the political-administrative units of the federation would be defined in national-territorial terms.[3] Whether this decision reflected a belief that nationality was important or umimportant for the development of the state and socialism and whether the goal was to celebrate national diversity or extinguish it are important questions, but ones, nonetheless, that are unlikely ever to be answered in any definitive way. However, what is not debatable is that there was an inescapable political logic behind national federalism. As Philip Roeder (1991: 1999) has astutely observed:

> Appreciating the strategic value of organizational weapons, political entrepreneurship, and mobilization resources, the architects of the Soviet regime came to understand that federal units could expand their control over the politicization of ethnicity. Within each homeland the regime created a cadre of party and state officials drawn from the indigenous ethnic group but dependent upon Moscow for its members' positions.

The very same logic was applied several decades later, we must insert briefly, when the Soviet Union introduced another institutional innovation – that is, the Soviet bloc. As with domestic federalism, so the bloc was based on recognizing the existence of national diversity, reinforcing that diversity through an elaborate institutional structure and ensuring, in the process, that the national units in question – or states within the bloc, like regions within the socialist federations – would be led by Communist parties that dominated their particular national environs, but that were dependent on the center for political power and economic resources. The assumption in both settings, therefore, was the same. By constructing a nest of dependencies, the Communist Party could assure systemwide compliance by – and not just while – institutionalizing diversity.

This assumption, however, proved to be untenable. In practice, Soviet federalism (which was later copied in Yugoslavia after the revolution[4] and Czechoslavakia after the Soviet invasion in 1968) had remarkably similar consequences to those that were detailed already for the Soviet bloc and, echoing the discussion in Chapter 2, to domestic socialism in general. To put the matter succinctly, federal institutions – their mandates to the contrary – *redistributed* political power and economic resources from the center to the regions (Derlugian, 1995; Lapidus and Walker, 1995).

Federalism had these effects, first, because it institutionalized national distinctions and thereby rendered membership in a nation a key marker of individual and group identity. For example, national identity was a key category in the census;[5] these three states extended official recognition of multiple national languages; republics were defined and named by reference to the titular nation; and each of these three states devoted considerable resources to the development of national cultures. They also, of course, played national groups off against each other – a practice that was evident as well in the nonfederal socialist states that featured significant minority populations (see Verdery, 1993a, 1993b). Moreover, the subtext of regime policy on the national question in these federal systems, while often exhibiting the tensions between diversity now versus the blending of nations in the future (see especially "Natsional'naia politika," 1989, and *Jedanaesti kongres*, 1978: 92–93) and while exhibiting biases in favor of the dominant national group (particularly in the Soviet Union and Czechoslovakia), nonetheless made the point repeatedly that membership in a nation was a critical component of identity (see especially Hodnett, 1967).[6]

If the institutions and the policies of federal socialist states were important in developing individual national identity or, at the very least, reinforcing a national identity already well established by the time socialism made its entrance (as with, for example, Slovaks, Estonians, Latvians, Lithuanians, Armenians, Croats, and Serbs – see, e.g., Leff, 1988; Pusić, 1996; Henderson, 1994; Taagepera, 1993), they were also important in developing to a greater extent than in the past the collective identity we associate with "the nation." As Ronald Suny (1992: 24–25) has observed:

> One of the central ironies of Soviet history is that a regime dedicated to effacing nationality and to creating a supra-ethnic community and a party that posited that class rather than nationality was the key determinant of the social structure have presided over a process in which modern nations have been formed within the union they governed.

In this sense, the federalized socialist systems were, indeed, multinational in their composition. The social contract, as discussed in the previous chapter, had its equivalent in a "national contract" (Nahaylo and Swoboda, 1989: 352). Rather than creating an overarching sense of unity, these regimes recognized and constructed national diversity. This was a process that was only exaggerated by the destruction of other divisions within the population, such as class (see Verdery, 1993a) and by the homogenizing effects of creating a common enemy – which, in the federal context, was invariably the center.[7]

This complicated considerably the smooth functioning of two-tiered socialism, because it produced not one party and one society, but many – and managed, given the tendencies of socialism in general and the institutional elaboration of diversity at the republican level, to homogenize these national parties and these national societies. Moreover, with the policy of promoting "national in form and socialist in content," and with the existence of many nations but only one state, the very concept of citizenship became dual. One part of citizenship was based on membership in the ideological-political community – that is, citizenship attached to the socialist regime-state – and the other on membership in a national community. As a consequence, the concept of nation-state in these cases straddled rather uncomfortably three quite different and potentially competing dimensions of life within socialist federations: ideology, nationality, and territory (see especially Brubaker, 1996).

The dissonance among these in the formation of individual and collective identities meant, for example, that if the first was devalued, then the second and third could take precedence. This was a particular issue in the Russian case, given the domination, numerically and politically, of both Russians and the Russian Federal Republic. It was hard to distinguish, for example, between Russian and Soviet identity and between the notion of a state and the notion of an empire, with the latter distinction blurred throughout Russian history (Vujačić, 1996). This helps explain, in turn, the slow development of Russian nationalism in comparison with, for example, its Lithuanian counterpart (see, e.g., Dunlop, 1993a, 1993b; Arutiunian and Drobizheva, 1987; Lieven, 1993; Senn, 1990; Karklins, 1993; Kirkh, Iarve, and Khaav, 1988).

If the socialist federations were multinational, moreover, they were also, at least potentially, "multistate" as well. The design of these systems put into place virtually all of the building blocks that are necessary for the rise of nationalist movements and for the formation of states – all within, it must be emphasized, an ostensibly single state. This they did, for example, by recognizing or, in some cases, creating a common language; by expanding education; by building a nationally defined intelligentsia; by developing at the republican level a stable core of economic, representational, coercive, social, and cultural institutions, each of which was led by powerful, durable, and "nativized" elite cadres; by providing considerable economic and political resources to these republican elites; and by enclosing all of these developments within well-defined geographical and administrative perimeters (see, e.g., Rybovski and Tarasova, 1990; Goldman, Lapidus, and Zaslavsky, 1992; Zaslavsky, 1992; 1993).

Thus, if we define states as those political entities that combine a coercive monopoly, legally based claims to sovereignty,[8] and stable boundaries that enclose relatively well-defined nations and relatively well-defined economic, political, and social institutions, then the republics within the socialist federations came very close indeed to being states (and see Thomson, 1995, on "stateness"). One could even argue, especially given the institutional density of the republics within the socialist federations, that republican claims of stateness were stronger than similar claims made by, for example, states in Africa following decolonization (see Jackson and Rosenberg, 1982; Curtin, 1996). All that these republics seemed to lack during the socialist period was full autonomy from the center, a window of opportunity to leave the state, and formal recognition of statehood by the international community.

The strong claims to being both a nation and a state allowed for and contributed to the growth of interrepublican diversity. This followed logically from constructing republics as major and relatively homogenized bundles of politics, culture, society, and economics; from structuring the system in a radial fashion, such that republics were in an institutional sense separated from each other and directly connected, instead, to the center; and from giving republics, as a result, their own identities, their own interests, and, thus, their own positions within the games that allocated money, power, and status in socialist systems (see, e.g., Bahry, 1987, 1991; Berkowitz and Mitchneck, 1992; and, on the post-1991 Russian state, Treisman, 1996, 1997; Solnick, 1996, 1998b; Derlugian, 1995). Relative homogenization from within (though this varied on the national dimension across republic and time) and diversity from without meant in turn that the consensus around what defined socialism and even the state began to fray along national and geographical lines. Competitive conceptions of politics, in short, emerged, and these conceptions were organized by space and nation. As Rudolf Rizman (1995: 6) has observed for developments in Slovenia versus Serbia a good decade before the formal collapse of the Yugoslav state:

> Thus, behind the "Yugoslav idea" stood intractable problems: some understood unification to mean equality, voluntary union and recognition of specific national individuality, while for others it stood for a unitarian, hegemonistic or simply enlarged "Great State" political project.

Diversity also meant that conflict within the federalized socialist states was not just between the party and the society or between higher- and lower-level party units. It also took the form of conflicts between the center and the republics, since these had become a defining and dominant dimension of political and economic interactions. Sovereignty, as a result, tended to assume a zero-sum quality. Thus, whenever power at the center contracted, as was typically the case during periods of succession, crisis, and reform, vertical conflicts erupted between the center and the republics. This occurred, for instance, during the struggle for power after Lenin's death (Harris, 1998); during the "Bratislava spring" within (or perhaps alongside) the "Prague Spring" of 1967–1968; and during the Croatian crisis in Yugoslavia in 1971–1972, followed by a series of crises in Kosovo lasting up to the present day (and, for a long-term view of these developments, see Leff, 1988; Hodnett, 1967; Nahaylo and Swoboda, 1989).

While crises invariably empowered republics within the socialist federations, so did crisis management strategies (see Županov, 1983). As argued in Chapter 2, Leonid Brezhnev (and Tito in Yugoslavia and Gustav Husak in Czechoslovakia) consolidated his power by in effect giving it away – to everyone through depoliticization and reduced control of the center over the economy, to publics through the social compact, and to elites through security of tenure. For the republican party elites, this meant a decline in mobility opportunities and in access to economic resources (Bahry, 1987). This also provided republican elites with the time and the incentives to build and then feather their republic-based institutional nests. This process was only facilitated, moreover, by the density of institutions at the republican level and by the fusion of politics and economics within localities and within republics (Hough, 1969; and, on the role of provincial elites in general in the development of nationalist movements, Mann, 1995). As John Slocum (1995: 12) has elaborated for the Soviet Union:

> The Soviet federal system created a structure of incentives and opportunities that, in the context of the command-administrative economic system, encouraged the growth of regional "mafias," local networks of corruption and influence that greased the interlinked workings of government, party and industry, typically extending outward from the desk of regional party secretaries.

Thus, while principal-agent problems were considerable in all of the socialist states, especially with the policy of stability in cadres (for the Soviet case, see, e.g., Arbatov, 1991; Lane and Ross, 1995; Zaslavskaya, 1984, 1986), they took a particular form in the federalized systems. This was because these systems – like the Soviet bloc with respect to its member states – provided a geographical and national locus for the development and the expression of autonomy. The end result was the creation of an optimal environment for the republicanization of sovereignty and for the rise within the republics of "ethnopolitical machines" (Suny, 1992, 1993).

If the institutions of socialism functioned over time to undermine the domestic regime of socialism, as argued in the previous chapter, and the international regime of socialism, or the Soviet bloc, as argued earlier in this chapter, then the institutional design of socialist federations seemed to do precisely the same with respect to the state. All three socialist playing fields, as a result, built what was termed during the Bolshevik Revolution *dvoevlastie* (dual power) – or what theorists of revolution have characterized as the multiplication of sovereignty (see especially Tilly, 1993). The only difference among these three settings was whether the process of deregulation was simply ideological or both ideological and spatial. In the cases of federalism and the bloc, it was the latter.

Before we draw this chapter to a close, however, we need to focus for a moment on one national federation in particular – Yugoslavia. This is in recognition of the greater decentralization of the Yugoslav federation, the distinctive Yugoslav road to socialism, and, in comparison with the Soviet Union and Czechoslovakia, the far more contested and violent end of that state.

YUGOSLAV EXCEPTIONALISM

What made Yugoslavia different from the rest of Eastern Europe was, first, the legitimacy of Communist Party rule as a consequence of the victory of the Partizans in two wars that took place simultaneously on Yugoslav soil from 1939 to 1945 – that is, World War II, which produced Italian and German occupation, and a civil war, which decided the political form postwar Yugoslavia would take (see, e.g., Bokovoy, 1997; Irvine, 1991; and, more generally, Bilandžić, 1979). These victories led in turn to Tito's move after the war to dominate the Balkans and, in light of the developing struggle over zones of influence after World War II, to a break with Stalin in 1948 and eventually with the Soviet model of socialism.

Domestic legitimacy, a strategic location, and loss of the Soviet Union as a socialist patron produced by the 1950s a series of distinctive economic innovations in Yugoslav socialism, including workers' self-management, or *samoupravljanje* (which was eventually extended to the polity and the social system as well); market socialism (which combined markets with public ownership of the means of production); a mixed public and private agricultural sector (though Poland was to follow suit in this regard after 1956); and, especially after 1965, free movement of labor and integration of Yugoslavia with the global economy (see Irvine, 1997a).

On the political side, Yugoslavia was distinguished from the 1960s onward by a relatively liberalized political environment[9] – though, as else-

where, the pattern was jagged over time, reflecting periodic bouts of repression in response to intraparty conflict and popular protest. In addition,
there was a substantial decentralization of the party and the state to the six
republics making up the Yugoslav federation. This was particularly notice-
able following adoption in 1974 of yet another new constitution. Finally,
socialism in Yugoslavia was premised on nonalignment, or *nesvrštanje*, in
the international system. In practice, this meant in effect highly strategic
flirtations with both sides in the bipolar postwar international order.

In many respects, then, the innovative features of the Yugoslav model
distinguished the domestic and international politics and economics of this
socialist regime from its Soviet-style neighbors. The result was that socialist Yugoslavia was, by regional socialist standards (especially from the late
1960s onward) unusually decentralized, unusually liberalized, and unusually situated with respect to East-West economic and political-military
rivalries. However, the advantages of hindsight suggest that these many
distinctions – which were played up by Yugoslavs, their leaders, and those
who analyzed the system during the socialist era – are perhaps more accu-
rately interpreted as differences in degree and timing rather than differences in kind.

For example, Yugoslavia was not the only but rather merely the first
socialist state in the region to carry out market-oriented economic reforms
and to participate in the global economy. Moreover, the long-term and
ultimately destructive oscillation between planning and markets that was
treated as a defining feature of Yugoslav landscape was characteristic, albeit
in less exaggerated form, of many of the other socialist states, including
the Soviet Union (beginning with the abortive Lieberman reforms in
1953), Hungary (with the introduction of the New Economic Mechanism
in 1968), and Poland (which from 1956 onward exhibited repeated attempts at reforms, which were then sabotaged). Thus, while the Yugoslav
economy was distinctive in its capacity to advertise its economic problems
through such "unsocialist" indicators as rising rates of inflation and unemployment (see especially Woodward, 1995b), those problems and the
solutions they generated were hardly unique to the Yugoslav model.

Similar arguments, moreover, can be made with respect to politics. For
example, Yugoslavia was the first but hardly the only socialist state to
liberalize its politics. Moreover, the substantial variations over time and
across republics in political liberalization in Yugoslavia could be said to
provide a summary in effect of the range of political developments that
took place throughout the European socialist region as a whole from the
introduction of the de-Stalinization reforms in the mid-1950s through
1989. Indeed, even the strikes and demonstrations that became common-

place in Yugoslavia in the 1980s, most notably in Serbia and Slovenia, were also characteristic of Poland during the same period. To this can be added one more parallel. Republicanization of Yugoslav politics after 1974 became a key factor in the Soviet Union slightly more than a decade later and, we must remember, in Czechoslovakia from 1966 to 1968, as well as during and after the revolution of 1989.

All this is to argue, then, that Yugoslavia was both similar and different. Its similarities exposed this regime, like its socialist neighbors, to a series of problems that were long in evidence and that eventually led to its downfall (see, e.g., the telling analyses of Županov, 1983; Golubović, 1988; Goati, 1989). Its differences meant in effect that the Yugoslav regime was not so much distinctive as unusually quick to register the costs of socialism. It developed – or, rather, degenerated – faster than its neighbors, and this is one reason why the regime and the state both collapsed and did so violently. The other reasons for violent collapse, which focus on the details of Yugoslav federalism, will be addressed in Chapter 6, when we compare similarities and differences in the dismemberment of the Soviet, Czechoslovak, and Yugoslav states.

CONCLUSIONS

A number of scholars have argued that socialist federations constructed, quite by accident, nations, nationalist movements, and eventually nation-states at the republican level (see especially Brubaker, 1996; Suny, 1992, 1993; Ramet, 1984; Burg, 1983; and, much earlier, Hodnett, 1967). However, far less commonly noted have been two other arguments advanced in this chapter. The first is the existence of a number of similarities between Yugoslav self-managing socialism and what is commonly referred to as state or Soviet-style socialism. This reinforces a point made in the previous chapter – that is, the inherent weakness of *all* of the European socialist dictatorships, including, and perhaps especially, Yugoslavia.

The other argument focused on the striking institutional similarities between national federalism and the Soviet bloc. These similarities meant that both were prone at the least to redistributive pressures – that is, shifts in the distribution of political power and economic resources from the center to the republics and from the Soviet Union to Eastern Europe – and at most to decomposition along republican or sovereign state lines. At the same time, the fate of both the bloc and the federal states was closely tied to the fate of the regime. In this sense, there were four, not three federations in the European socialist world: Yugoslavia, the Soviet Union, Czechoslovakia, and the Soviet bloc.

Both of these observations help us understand why the collapse of Communist Party rule led to both the collapse of the Soviet bloc and the dismemberment of the Soviet, Yugoslav, and Czechoslovak states. They hint, moreover, at a less obvious implication. If the breakup of the Soviet, Yugoslav, and Czechoslovak states is assumed to be a product of nationalism, then why not view the revolutions in Eastern Europe in the same way? Indeed, one cost of the design of both socialist federations and the Soviet bloc was not merely to fuse the regime and the state (or bloc). It was also to splice the nation and socialism and, thereby, create the potential for pitting one against the other. Thus, it was the combination of reform and nationalism that seemed to have ended both the state, as has been commonly observed, and, less commonly noted, the regime and the bloc.

LEAVING SOCIALISM

Never was any event so inevitable, yet so completely unforseen.
Alexis de Tocqueville (on the French Revolution)

All of the socialist regimes in Europe depended for their survival on maximizing economic growth and maintaining the party's economic and political monopoly. Indeed, these two preconditions for rule were inextricably linked. If the economy faltered, especially over an extended period of time, then the regime would necessarily weaken in the face of deregulatory pressures. Thus, already contentious elites would become more so; the capacity of the upper levels of the party to control its lower levels would atrophy; and the party would be forced to renege on its promise to publics and elites alike to expand resources. As a consequence, the upper levels of the party and its lower levels, the regime and the society, would each go its separate way.

What also made growth imperative was the absence of political capital. Because they had become evermore flaccid dictatorships, these regimes had fewer and fewer mechanisms, aside from socioeconomic transfers, for either forcing or encouraging the compliance of ministries, enterprises, local party secretaries, and even publics. Thus, in addition to the irony that the party's monopolistic structure was itself a mechanism for deregulation was yet another one. Regimes that had long castigated capitalism for its short-term horizons and that prided themselves on the long-term vistas enabled by planning, state ownership of the economy, and Communist Party rule were increasingly placed in the position of making decisions in response to a

single question: what have you done for me lately? Thus, machine politics
– with its defining characteristics of a political monopoly, elaborate dependency chains, a disinterest in ideology, and a stress on delivery now –
was not terribly different in Moscow from what it was in Chicago under
the first Mayor Daley. This is a point made long ago by the most insightful
analyst of the Chicago machine, Milton Rakove (1975).

But a regime under stress is one thing and regime collapse another.
This is an important distinction that alerts us to the frequency of the
former and the infrequency of the latter, and that serves as the Achilles
heel of most theories of revolution with their predisposition for over-
predicting the incidence of revolution. As argued in Chapter 1, however,
social movement theorists have given us a way out by emphasizing the
interaction between resources and expanded opportunities for change (see
especially Tarrow, 1994). It is the latter – that is, the growing elasticity
in socialist politics over the course of the 1980s and the reduced constraints, as a result, on what elites and publics imagined, wanted, demanded, and did – that will be the subject of this chapter. When joined
with the redistributive dynamics of socialist institutions, the dramatic expansion of opportunities for change throughout the socialist world in the
1980s provide us with an explanation for the collapse of socialism by the
end of the decade.[1]

THE POLITICAL OPPORTUNITY STRUCTURE

There are three developments that predictably open up regimes to new
directions, including the possibility of exit: leadership succession, great
reforms (to use the common characterization of the major reforms introduced in Russia by Alexander II), and significant shifts in the international
system that reorder domestic politics. What is striking – and, indeed,
distinctive in a historical sense – about the European socialist experience
during the 1980s is that all three factors were present. There was a major
succession in the Soviet Union in 1985, which unleashed similar struggles
in all of the Eastern European states that were members of the Soviet bloc.
Moreover, there were major successions as well during this decade in the
two remaining Eastern European states that fell outside the Soviet orbit:
Yugoslavia and Albania in 1980 and 1985, respectively. Thus, because of
the structure of the bloc and because of the deaths of Brezhnev, Tito, and
Hozha in particular, *all* of the socialist regimes in Europe had to contend
with a more fluid and, thus, more uncertain elite environment over the

course of the 1980s. One reason why the collapse of socialism was region-wide, aside from the commonalities of socialist systems outlined in Chapter 2, was that the succession struggles of the 1980s had regional reach.

LEADERSHIP SUCCESSION AND REFORM

Leadership succession is important for regime change, not just because of the obvious – that is, the infusion of new political blood – but also because of the uncertainties and shifting incentives generated by struggles for political power. Here, I refer, for example, to the sudden expansion of the political market for critiques of the status quo, for new ideas about domestic and foreign policy, and for the representation of new interests and new groups. Thus, successions produce a more fluid policy environment, as well as elite stratum, and they function, as a result, as mechanisms for both personnel and policy change. This is the case, moreover, for both dictatorships and democracies (Bunce, 1981).

In the socialist cases, leadership succession functioned as a particularly powerful mechanism of change. This was in part because of the reform mania that was built into socialist systems and was intrinsic to their elite political cultures (see Csanádi, 1997)[2] and also because of the particular characteristics of socialist succession processes. Thus, in that particular context, what was distinctive was that leadership turnover lacked routinization. Mandates, as a result, were always provisional. Moreover, the process combined a legacy of accumulated political and economic problems bequeathed by a previous administration that had become, through sheer length of tenure and the monopoly enjoyed by the party, exceedingly ingrown and insulated. In addition, the struggle for power was decided not by a mass electorate and the vague appeals, unrealistic promises, and sound bites that are intrinsic to, say, democratic elections, but, rather, by highly experienced, ambitious, and discriminating "selectorates" (to borrow from Hodnett, 1975) composed of "first secretaries-in-waiting," if not "in-the-making." Finally, the resolution of the struggle involved the transfer of considerable appointment and policy-making powers to the victorious coalition. What all these features meant was that socialist successions managed to combine considerable incentives with considerable capacity for changes in both leadership and policy. They opened wide "the window for reform" (Keeler, 1993).

If this was usually the case, then it was even more so in the context of the 1980s. At that time, several factors were present that guaranteed a succession process that would involve major struggles over power and policy and that would, as a consequence, hold the potential for reinventing the apparatus, public policy, and the regime itself. One factor was the dismal performance of socialism; that is, the long-term trends, evident throughout the region, of poor economic performance, rising corruption, and declining control of the party over the economy, the society, and, indeed, itself. While all of these disturbing developments were a direct product of the very design of socialism, as argued in Chapter 2, they also testified to a more subtle and long-term by-product of the very workings of the system: the costs of having a political leadership too long in power. For example, both Hozha and Tito had led their systems since World War II; Brezhnev was in power for eighteen years; and Todor Zhivkov of Bulgaria first came to office in 1954 and did not leave (and then under duress) for thirty-five years. Indeed, the last succession in the Soviet bloc prior to Gorbachev's rise to power in 1985 was fifteen years earlier in East Germany.

This leads us to the second factor. Long-term stability in cadres meant that the socialist successions of the 1980s involved not just some long-delayed changes in leadership, but also a rotation in political generations. This was crucial, because the nature of these systems – for instance, the tendency of elites to mount systemwide campaigns and to introduce sudden and thoroughgoing shifts in policy directions – produced, not very surprisingly, unusually distinct political generations, particularly with respect to the party apparatus.

Thus, one important aspect of Gorbachev's rise to power was that he and his allies were members of the *shestidesiatki*, or the generation of the 1960s. This was a political generation that, thanks to Stalinist excesses, had experienced significant personal mobility, while taking pride in the larger story of Soviet international mobility. This was also a group that had joined the party after World War II and had become professional politicians and policy makers during the Khrushchev era. Finally, the *shestidesiatki* were frustrated during the Brezhnev era by the contradictory developments of the rise of the Soviet Union as a global power and significant improvements in the Soviet quality of life, on the one hand, and, on the other, the considerably less welcome trends of rising corruption and public cynicism, a breakdown in central control, and a slowdown in economic growth in general and their opportunities for political mobility in particular. Members of this group, in short, shared experiences and perspectives, and they were ideally suited for introducing major reforms, once the opportunities to do so finally presented themselves. They were, perhaps, the last believers in their own power and in the system, and they combined this with anger about their personal situation and the direction socialism had taken (see, e.g., Cohen, 1985; Arbatov, 1991; Gorbachev, 1993; 3–35).

The passing of one political generation and the rise to power of a new one (which was the case throughout the region), when combined with the problems facing socialism and the more general dynamics built into social-ist succession struggles, unleashed major struggles over power and policy throughout socialist Europe over the course of the 1980s. As a result, all matter of posssibilities, within the frame of economic and political liber-alization, were on the table. This led either to long-term and tense stale-mates over reform, as most notably in Yugoslavia and Poland over much of the 1980s, or to the introduction of great reforms, as in the Soviet Union following Gorbachev's rise to power in 1985. In either case, however, power and policy were extraordinarily fluid, and the political opportunity structure expanded considerably. The time of politics and policy "as usual" had passed, and the very survival of these regimes came more and more into question.

INTERNATIONAL CHANGE

This leads us to a third and final factor that loosened the political oppor-tunity structure: significant changes in the international system that had powerful domestic repercussions. Here, we need to look back to a series of decisions in the 1970s that can be conveniently summarized as détente and that constituted in effect a silent revolution. Détente reduced – and also regulated and set parameters on – East-West conflict by, for instance, recognizing Soviet-American equality, legitimating the Soviet takeovers in Eastern Europe, and rendering more porous the cultural, economic, and political boundaries that had for so long isolated the eastern from the western halves of Europe. In reducing the uncertainty surrounding East-West relations and in poking holes in the wall dividing Europe, détente could be said to have ended the cold war, although this was formally to take place nearly twenty years after Nixon and Brezhnev began the process of what the Soviets termed *razriadka*, or a lessening of tensions (see, e.g., Lynch, 1992; Garthoff, 1985; Evangelista, 1998).

These developments had enormous consequences for the domestic and international politics and economics of the entire socialist region. For ex-ample, in the Soviet case, Brezhnev's power was bolstered by *razriadka*, and he had what he needed to construct an elaborate policy package, con-sisting of cutbacks in the military, expanding domestic public consump-tion, stability in cadres, rejection of economic and political liberalization, and termination of regional economic autarky. The assumption in all of this was that the Soviet Union had finally "arrived," and that economic growth and political stability could be well served – and served efficiently – by the social compact, loans from and trade with the West, and a domestic political environment that was decidedly illiberal, but, nonetheless predictable and secure (see, e.g., Bunce, 1983b; Volten, 1982; MccGwire, 1987).

What Brezhnev did not foresee, however, were two sets of costs. One was the very different understanding of détente in the East versus the West. It was precisely this contrast in perceptions and assumptions that drove the two superpowers apart in reaction to Portuguese decolonization in Africa followed by the revolution in Afghanistan. The other set of costs grew directly out of Brezhnev's strategy for shoring up the political and economic problems of socialism. In particular, by exposing inefficient economies to a global economy in need of recycling petrodollars, by exposing insular dictatorships to the corrupting influences of the West, and by locking in personnel and policy priorities, Brezhnev managed to undermine rather than to save socialism. He stayed in power, but only to oversee systemic decay.

Central to the decline of the Soviet Union under Brezhnev was the passage of the Helsinki Final Act in 1975. This functioned to undermine regime and state in the socialist world by legitimating international intervention in domestic affairs; by providing an international norm of human rights and the possibility of organizing oppositional activities within socialist states around that norm (which proved to be particularly important in more hard-line regimes, such as the Soviet Union and Czechoslovakia – see Thomas, 1997); and by legitimating the right of nations to self-determination, a consequence that was particularly influential in the story, addressed in the next chapter, of state dismemberment.[3] Through the Helsinki process and through other mechanisms, then, the larger dynamic of détente introduced new ideas, new allies, and new resources into the socialist region. In reducing the party's control over international boundaries, then, détente qualified the monopoly upon which Communist Party rule and the socialist system itself rested. This in turn weakened these regimes while altering in significant ways the calculus of political protest in the Soviet Union and Eastern Europe.

What we see by the 1980s, then, is a lot of "give," if not turmoil, in socialist politics, reflecting the interaction during this decade among succession struggles, struggles over major reform, and more fluid international boundaries. When combined with the redistributive dynamics already in place throughout the socialist world as a consequence of the design of these systems, the stage was set for regime collapse. In the remainder of this chapter, I will work through this process.

The story begins, appropriately enough, with the Soviet Union, the first and most entrenched socialist regime. It was also, because of its age, its federal structure, and its role as both the regional hegemon and the leader of the world socialist movement, the regime in the region that most "efficiently" summarized the crises of socialism.

THE GORBACHEV REFORMS

With the death of Konstantin Chernenko in March 1985, Mikhail Gorbachev acceded to the office of first secretary of the Communist Party of the Soviet Union. This succession, which proved to be unusually quick and smooth, provided support in the extreme for the argument that leadership change in socialist states is a mechanism for policy innovation.

There were five premises (varying in their accuracy) that underlined the Gorbachev reforms as they evolved from 1985 to 1990. First, Gorbachev assumed that he was in an unassailable position of power. Second, he assumed that Soviet socialism and the Soviet state were viable and durable entities. Third, he assumed that the problems facing the system – which reflected in his view the actions and primarily the inactions of his predecessors – were quite serious and, if left unaddressed, would transform the Soviet Union into a Third World country. Fourth, Gorbachev assumed that the key problem was stagnation in the economy, the polity, and the social system. Finally, Gorbachev assumed that the resistance to reform was so substantial and the problems of Soviet socialism so considerable that the only solution was to build a domestic-international coalition for reform that spanned the Soviet Union, Eastern Europe, and the West, and that involved a virtual revolution from above (Trimberger, 1978) – or, what Timothy Garton Ash (1989) has aptly termed a "refolution" (a hybrid of revolution and reform). Thus, socialism was to be saved by building bridges to the West and to dissidents and party reformers in the Soviet Union and Eastern Europe and by introducing, at the same time, changes of considerable magnitude in the institutions and the domestic and foreign policies of the Soviet Union.

These premises led to a reform package that had as its basic theme deregulation of the institutions that had for so long defined the Soviet experience. In particular, in the domestic sphere, Gorbachev deregulated the economy through market-oriented reforms and deregulated the polity through liberalization of the media, greater tolerance for more open political debate, high turnover of party and state officials, injection of real (but not full) competition into the political system, and creation of genuinely accountable representative institutions (see, e.g., Djilas, 1988; Breslauer, 1989; Bogomolov, 1989). In the international sphere, Gorbachev deregulated the bloc – for instance, by pressing the "lesser Brezhnevs" in Eastern Europe to follow the Soviet reform model, by siding with reformers within the Eastern European parties (while reaching out to some dissidents as well), by announcing in 1988 a reduction in the size of the Soviet military and its representation in Eastern Europe, and, finally, by making speeches in Prague, Belgrade, and Helsinki from 1987 to 1988 that recognized explicitly the independence of Eastern Europe.

With respect to Eastern Europe, therefore, Gorbachev attempted to liberalize socialism and to transform the bloc into an alliance. In doing so, he walked several dangerous lines: between reducing Soviet influence in the region and using Soviet domination to build a regional base for reform; between supporting reforms that could save socialism, but at the risk, especially in Eastern Europe, of unraveling it; and between building a stronger base for empire versus starting the process of decolonization (see Bunce, 1989; Levesque, 1997).

The reach of the Gorbachev reforms extended, moreover, significantly beyond the western boundaries of European socialism. Gorbachev also in effect deregulated East-West relations – for instance, by pulling out of Afghanistan without peace or honor, by building diplomatic bridges to Western Europe and, later, to the United States, and by undermining the very structure of the postwar international order with his talk of an interdependent, not polarized world, a Soviet bloc that was evolving into an alliance, significant arms reductions, and an end to nuclear testing (for these and other initiatives, see, especially, Gorbachev, 1993). When combined, these actions were to accomplish two objectives. One was to reduce the burdens on the Soviet economy produced by an increasingly expensive Soviet foreign policy, while building at the same time an international coalition in support of reform in general and Gorbachev in particular. The other was to inject the Soviet economy and polity with a version of competition – or, as then defined, less job security, more public engagement in politics, and, in the economy, less planning and harder budgets.

All these actions, along with glasnost' (or publicity),[4] were presumed to have the beneficial effects of weakening those who opposed reform (and Gorbachev), while empowering supporters, and, at the same time, bolstering overall economic performance by using politics and the market as prods. Thus, in direct contrast to the Chinese approach to reform under Deng from 1978 to 1997, with its emphasis on marketizing the economy while holding the dictatorial polity constant, the Soviet approach under Gorbachev – an approach that resonated with the Russian historical tradition of "Great Reforms" (Bunce, 1993) – was to change both in dramatic ways. Thus, political liberalization was used to force economic liberalization, and international change was used to spur the domestic transformation, while cushioning some of its shocks.

The reform did not work entirely as Gorbachev hoped. This was in large measure because he overestimated his own power and, at the same time, underestimated how far redistribution had already gone as a result of the very institutions of Soviet socialism. Thus, he was too optimistic – about his political future and the future of reform, the regime and the state. In zigzagging left and right on reform (especially beginning in 1990) in order to balance among conflicting elites and to offset the varying costs and benefits of reform at any given moment, Gorbachev ended up being caught in the middle. He was too much the deregulator for opponents of reform or too little the deregulator for those who supported reform – either too rightist or too leftist, using Communist parlance. He was, in short, increasingly isolated, particularly by 1989–1990.

His isolation was joined, moreover, by the rise of several political rivals who outflanked him on the left and the right. One was Yegor Ligachev, who supported the initial premise of the reform that the system should be maintained but improved, and who saw developments beginning in 1987 as having gone too far in the rightist direction and thereby constituting a threat to the very ideological foundations of Soviet socialism. It bears observing now, of course, that Ligachev was entirely correct. Gorbachev was dismantling the system, albeit hardly by design.

The other opponent was Boris Yel'tsin, who supported the radicalization of reform and who was demoted from the Politburo in 1987 only to make a subsequent political comeback by outflanking Gorbachev on the right on reform and building a political base, first within the new Soviet parliament and then within the Russian republic. His perspective was that the center was vulnerable, that an emerging coalition for reform needed a leader, and that political power and economic resources increasingly resided within the republics and, thus, had to be built from the republics "up." As earlier with Ligachev, so Yel'tsin's later reading of the highly fluid situation in the Soviet Union proved to be accurate. And, with the obvious ideological and territorial fragmentation of the Soviet Union by 1990 (with the latter the focus of the next two chapters), it was Yel'tsin – and not Ligachev, or, for that matter, Gorbachev – who was in the ideal situation to triumph.

The Soviet story, therefore, can be easily summarized. The long-term and informal deregulation of Soviet socialism was combined, in the Gorbachev era, with a formal deregulation of the system. In the absence of a party monopoly and in the presence of an economic and political landscape that was both more competitive and in disarray, socialism, as it had been constituted in the Soviet Union, could not survive. Deregulated socialism, in the European context at least, was, after all, a contradiction in terms. However, it was not just that the regime was collapsing, as was the party with the significant defection of reformers to the opposition (see especially Gaidar, 1995: 103–105). It was also that political power and economic resources had been parceled along both horizontal and vertical lines.

While the end of socialism in the Soviet Union occurred gradually but nonetheless dramatically over the course of the Gorbachev era, the collapse of socialism in Eastern Europe was, with the exception of the southern tier (see Pusić, 1997; Glenny, 1997), equally dramatic but far more abrupt. In that context, the process focused for the most part on sudden and direct confrontations between the party and the society. The developments in Eastern Europe also predated, for the most part, those two events that marked the formal end of the Soviet experiment – that is, the Soviet parliament's retraction in early 1990 of Article 6 in the constitution, which had articulated the CPSU's right to a political monopoly, and the attempted coup d'etat in August 1991.

Why socialism fell more "suddenly" in Eastern Europe is a question that was answered in large measure in Chapters 2 and 3. First, given the commonalities of socialist institutions, what ailed the Soviet Union also ailed all of Eastern Europe. Second, the structure of the Soviet bloc automatically transmitted political and economic changes in the Soviet Union to its client states in Eastern Europe. Third, the two-tiered structure of the bloc had created ever more dependent regimes in Eastern Europe and had exaggerated there the redistributive thrust of socialism. As a result, these economies were for the most part in unusually bad shape, and these parties were unusually open to divisions and to the demands of a very expectant, angry, and homogenized public. This was particularly the case for the northern tier (see especially Bozoki and Sukosd, 1993). Finally, for Yugoslavia, an outsider to the bloc, we can reiterate the observation made in Chapter 3 that Yugoslavia's deviant road to socialism had produced a system that featured, to an extreme, all the costs of socialist institutional design.

Thus, all of Eastern Europe was, in comparison with the Soviet Union, unusually receptive to the influences of the Gorbachev reforms and unusually ready to translate deregulated socialism into its demise. Let us now turn to the events of 1989.

REGIME COLLAPSE IN EASTERN EUROPE

For the first few years into the Gorbachev reforms, political mobilization was far more muted in Eastern Europe than in the Soviet Union, a reversal of earlier patterns. This was because party elites in Eastern Europe, facing in many cases severe economic problems and in all cases the distinct possibility of an impending succession crisis (which had in fact begun in Czechoslovakia in 1987), tried to ignore Gorbachev's calls for reform and, in some cases, such as East Germany, even censored his speeches. Moreover, these elites had capitalized on the fragmentation and pluralization of the bloc that had proceeded apace during the Brezhnev era. Thus, they had gained some capacity to ignore Soviet pressure. Finally, Eastern European elites, along with dissidents and their allies, had learned the hard way the costs of misreading Soviet succession struggles and the reform initiatives they invariably generated. After all, similar dynamics from 1953 to 1956 and from 1964 to 1968 had produced major protests throughout the bloc, which had been cut short by either a wave of domestic repression, Soviet military intervention, or both. At the same time, Yugoslavia stood as a current and frightening reminder of the dangers involved in liberalizing both politics and economics.

By 1988, however, the situation began to change. First, it was evident (and historically unprecedented) that the Soviet reform process was moving in a decidedly more radical direction, given, for example, the selective introduction of competitive elections and not just the formation of popular fronts for perestroika, but also Gorbachev's evident support of mass mobilization. Moreover, by 1988 Gorbachev had won significant support in the West, and had stated clearly no less than three times that the Eastern European states were "free to choose." In addition, despite all this, every indicator pointed to the conclusion that Gorbachev was firmly in power, especially after Ligachev seemed to be in decline by 1988 and Yel'tsin had not yet emerged as a credible political threat. However, what proved to be the decisive shift was the outbreak of protests in Poland, beginning in the spring of 1988.

Why Poland led the way is easy enough to explain. This was a country encased in the Soviet bloc that was distinctive by regional standards in the cohesion and the strength of its civil and political society, in the weakness of its regime, in the size of its external hard-currency debt (though, in per capita terms, Hungary's debt was larger), and in its long-term stalemate on economic and political liberalization.

The details of the Polish story have been elaborated elsewhere (see, e.g., Kubik, 1994; Taras, 1993a; Bernhard, 1993; Ekiert, 1996). What is important for our purposes is the following. It was abundantly clear to party leaders in Poland by 1987–1988 that the design of the regime had to be changed in fundamental ways, if reforms necessary for the survival of the system, however amended, were to be introduced and implemented. The gap between the formal power of the party and the informal power of the society could only be bridged, therefore, through a radical political-economic reform – and one, given Poland's international position, that the Soviet Union could and would support.

At the same time, there was in Poland by the late 1980s a two-tiered struggle – that is, not just the apparent battle between the party and the society, but also within the party between soft-liners and, essentially, democratic socialists (the hard-liners were few and far between), and, within the Solidarity movement, between radicals and those who, like Walesa, supported more incremental goals and less confrontational tactics. Moreover, by the spring through the fall of 1988, the divisions within Solidarity had produced mounting protests that the leadership of Solidarity could no longer control. Walesa, in short, was under pressure to move quickly; the protests also pushed the Polish party in the same direction; and the overlap between reformers within the party and moderates within Solidarity was significant and growing.

Finally, a key player in Polish developments was the Soviet Union. It was not just that the Gorbachev reforms seemed to be a model for breaking the political impasse in Poland or that growing tensions in Poland had failed to invoke Soviet intervention – as had been the case, indirectly, in 1981. It was also that the Soviets, for example, began to sponsor in late 1988 a series of favorable articles about Lech Walesa in the Soviet media; supported the Polish round table in early 1989 between Solidarity and the Polish United Workers' Party (to be sure, one of the region's best misnomers); and accepted its resulting decision to begin a four-year transition to liberal democracy. Moreover, the Soviets took in stride the semicompetitive elections that were held in Poland in June 1989, the surprisingly strong showing of Solidarity in those elections, and the formation in August of a Solidarity-led government (contrary to the plans of Solidarity, General Jaruzelski, or the PUWP).

In this sense, Gorbachev's influence was direct and indirect, ideational and policy-oriented. He did not just loosen the boundaries of socialism and the bloc; he supported the end of both in Poland. And in the process he signaled to the rest of Eastern Europe that he was firmly in power and just as firmly committed to reforms in general and to "come what might" from the reform process in Eastern Europe in particular.

Hungary quickly followed suit, a development that can be explained by the redundancy of the bloc in general and its openness to diffusion effects, the resonance and power of Gorbachev's message, and, to focus on Hungary in particular, the combination there as in Poland, unique for the bloc, of liberalized politics and heavy hard-currency debts. Thus, Hungary and Poland were optimally situated for regime collapse. They combined very divided parties with publics that were both resourceful and resentful. What Hungary also featured was, on the one hand, a far less organized political society than Poland, and, on the other, a succession struggle in process, where the longtime leader, Janos Kadar, was replaced by Karoly Grosz, who was, by Hungarian standards, relatively conservative (see Bruszt and Stark, 1992, on the Hungarian roundtable; Tokes, 1996; O'Neil, 1996). While Hungary also went the route of a pacted transition (reflecting, as in Poland, the confluence of a liberalized political context, severe economic problems, and a divided party facing a divided but nonetheless sizable opposition), its roundtable (and subsequent constitutional actions by the Communist-era parliament) went much further in defining the new system. Moreover, elections that were to be fully competitive were put off until March 1990, in order to work out the details of the new system and to allow for the formation of viable political parties.

These decisions, along with the parliamentary model Hungary embraced, have provided an unusual stability to post-Communist Hungarian politics. However, this may reflect as well the long shadow cast by 1956. Publics in Hungary learned at that time a bitter lesson – and one that was reinforced by the earlier experience of 1848, when the Russians, serving as the gendarme of the Concert of Europe, put down the Hungarian nationalist protests.[5]

The exit from socialism was not so surprising in either Poland or Hungary, especially given the political complexion of their ruling Communist parties, their long-liberalized politics, their economic crises, and, finally, Gorbachev's reform package and his support of these "refolutions" at strategic points. What was surprising – though it should not have been, given the structure of the bloc and the continuing struggle over power and policy in the bloc's epicenter – was that East Germany, then Czechoslovakia, then Bulgaria, and then Romania followed suit in the fall and early winter of 1989. In all of these cases, where the regimes under siege were hard-line, mass mobilization (and, indeed, massive mobilization in East Germany and Czechoslovakia) against the regime rather than pacting (though pacting often followed – see Elster, 1996) was the process by which Communist Party hegemony came to a close.

Again, the details are available elsewhere (see especially Stokes, 1993; Brown, 1991; Bunce and Chong, 1990; Levesque, 1997). But what is important to note is, first, that precedent mattered. The events in Hungary and Poland, coupled with the Soviet response to them and Gorbachev's continuation in power and his continued movement toward a more radical reform stance over the course of 1989, changed considerably the calculus of protest and compliance in the remaining regimes in the region. As Mark Beissinger (1995a: 2) has observed:

> Nationalist mobilization in one context usually provokes similar mobilizations . . . in other analogous and connected contexts, as actors attempt to utilize the opening afforded by the example of others and the weakening of interconnected regimes to assert their own claims vis-à-vis the state. It is this interconnection of particular classes of polities . . . that imparts a tide-like (and not merely wave-like) quality to nationalist behavior.

Put briefly, then, the risks of protest declined significantly across the region, while the risks for party members of supporting their regimes rose just as sharply.[6] This, plus the role of the bloc as a transmission belt, a homogenizing force, and a mechanism ensuring the dependency of the Eastern European regimes on the Soviet Union, meant that the collapse of communism in Poland and Hungary was easily and quickly followed by similar developments, though at the direct instigation of mass protests, in the historically more hard-line contexts of Czechoslovakia, East Germany, Bulgaria, and Romania.

Second, Gorbachev's decision to ignore Honnecker's demands and fears, to chide him into embracing reform, and to support the East German protesters by standing mute while Hungary maintained open borders and thereby allowed the East German tourists to flee to the West played a key role in the unraveling of the German Democratic Republic. This was important for mass mobilization elsewhere in the region, because the East German regime was widely recognized as one that was unusually immune to calls for economic and political liberalization; that was relatively successful in economic terms (at least by the low standards of the Soviet bloc); and that occupied a frontline position in the cold war and, thus, center stage in Soviet foreign policy. All of these factors made the East German crisis particularly instructive for elites and publics in the remaining socialist regimes in Eastern Europe – and, indeed, in the Soviet Union as well (see Beissinger, 1996). Put simply: if there, why not everywhere?

Thus, Gorbachev's decisions, the evolution of the bloc, demonstration effects, and diffusion processes all worked in the same direction. They assured that the collapse of socialism in one country would become – and rapidly – the collapse of socialism throughout the region. However, if I were to establish priorities among these lines of explanation, I would have to emphasize, in particular, the central role of the bloc. Just as the costs of its institutional design served as one key factor pushing Gorbachev toward radical reforms, so that design had made the Eastern European regimes identical, weak, highly vulnerable to Gorbachev's messages, and prone, as a result, to rapid-fire collapse.

PEACEFUL TRANSITIONS

Finally, one more consequence of the bloc's structure must be noted. One of the most peculiar aspects of the revolutions of 1989 in Eastern Europe, as well as the collapse of socialism in the Soviet Union soon thereafter, was their largely peaceful character. While it is far from unknown for transitions from dictatorship to democracy to be peaceful, especially given the recent experiences of many countries in Latin America and southern Europe, the collapse of socialism in Eastern Europe and the Soviet Union involved a far more radical break with the past. The exit from socialism, then, is best understood as a revolutionary process (on this point, see Bunce, 1995a, 1995b; Fishman, 1990). However, it was for the most part a peaceful process of revolutionary change, a seeming contradiction in terms. What makes this all the more puzzling, moreover, is that the three countries in the region that did experience violence – Romania, Yugoslavia, and Albania[7] – have featured far less of a break with the socialist past than was the case for the peaceful revolutions that took place in Poland, Czechoslovakia, Hungary, East Germany, Bulgaria, and the Soviet Union. How, then, can we explain not just the historically unprecedented norm of peaceful revolutions, but also the existence of some deviations from that norm – and, what is more, deviations that produced less, not more change?

The bloc provides the answer. All of the regimes that collapsed peacefully were fully integrated into the Soviet bloc, and all the countries that experienced violence during the collapse of Communist Party hegemony were either completely outside the bloc (Albania), associated with it but not a full member (Yugoslavia), or a member in "poor standing" (Romania – which, for example, refused to participate in many Warsaw Pact exercises and was the only member of the bloc not to have Soviet troops stationed within its borders). This distinction proved to be crucial for two reasons. First, after 1968, the Soviet Union centralized command and control within the Warsaw Pact (Jones, 1981). As a result, every decision to deploy troops in Eastern Europe was Moscow's – and Moscow's only. Second, Gorbachev was committed to reform; his reforms depended on the construction of an international coalition in support of reform that included both the West and reformers within Eastern Europe; and key to his reform package was the transformation of Eastern Europe from a bloc to an alliance and from moribund to revitalized socialist regimes. Thus, the revolutions in Eastern Europe and the Soviet Union were peaceful, because domestic Communist parties lacked the capacity to deploy military force in order to defend their hegemony, *and* because Gorbachev refused to help them do so. However, where Communist elites had domestic control over the military and where Gorbachev's actions with respect to military deployment were largely irrelevant, as in Romania, Yugoslavia, and Albania, Communist elites acted in a manner typical of elites in most places. They used force to defend their power and privilege.[8]

Once again, then, we see the key role of three factors in the events of 1989. One was the inherent weakness of the Eastern European socialist regimes in particular. Another was the importance of the bloc's structure for when and how socialism ended. Finally, within this institutional context, the ideas and the actions of Gorbachev were crucial. Just as he began the process of regime collapse in the Soviet Union and Eastern Europe, so he ensured – at least where the bloc was in place – that socialism would depart peacefully from the region.

THE END OF SOCIALISM IN YUGOSLAVIA

This leaves us with one final case of regime collapse: Yugoslavia. The grim story of the fall of socialism in Yugoslavia has been examined in detail by others – though the focus of most of these efforts, understandably enough, is on the end of the state, not the regime, and though a consensus on what happened and why remains elusive – both because the story is so complex, and because it is so politicized (see, e.g., Gow, 1992; Magaš, 1993; Lampe, 1996; Woodward, 1995a; Cohen, 1993; Silber and Little, 1996; Tašić, 1994; Glenny, 1992; Irvine, 1997a). What we will do here is to make some observations that will give us insights into the larger question of the regionwide collapse of socialism. In the next two chapters, when we compare the dismemberment of the Yugoslav, Soviet, and Czechoslovak states, we will address the Yugoslav case in greater detail.

One helpful observation about the Yugoslav case is that it most resembled the dynamics of regime collapse in Poland. As there, the entire decade of the 1980s in Yugoslavia presented a profile of political and economic disintegration, given the actual contraction of the economy over this period (with economic growth from 1981 to 1985 one-tenth of what it had been from 1976 to 1980 – see Cohen, 1993: 73n), the protracted and highly conflictual stalemate over reform, the considerable decline in public support for the League of Communists (see Goati, 1990: 90–101), and, finally, rising public protests in Serbia, Kosovo, and Slovenia. Thus, to amend a familiar observation made about 1989: while Czechoslovakia took ten days, Poland *and* Yugoslavia took ten years.

However, there were three ways in which Yugoslavia diverged from Poland, aside from the obvious ones of being outside rather than inside the Soviet bloc and being a heterogeneous rather than a homogeneous society. In particular, Yugoslavia was an extraordinarily decentralized federation rather than a unitary state; public protest there (and the development of civil and political society) was intrarepublican rather than statewide in form and, thus, highly variable across the republics; and Yugoslavia began the decade not with mass mobilization against the regime but, rather, with Tito's death and an ensuing struggle over power that took place within a brand new, post-Tito institutional landscape.

What all these differences meant was that the end of socialism in Yugoslavia represented, by virtue of the very different trajectories followed by the republics, the full diversity of this process in the socialist region as a whole. For instance, while the Slovene story involved a strong and mobilized civil society and a Communist Party that quickly came to embrace the opposition's support of confederalization of the Yugoslav state and a rapid transition to capitalism and democracy, the Serbian story featured a politically divided but highly mobilized society (see especially *Nove stranke*, 1990), and a recentralization of the state. This, in turn, led to contrasting outcomes. In Slovenia, there was a sharp break with the regime and the state, whereas in Serbia the party maintained its economic monopoly while moving, begrudgingly, to an oligopolistic political order.

These distinctions also imply that the crisis in Yugoslavia was, if anything, more serious than the crisis in Poland. Put simply, a sharply divided society was confronting a sharply divided opposition. This in turn jells with the earlier observation in Chapter 3 that the Yugoslav road to socialism exaggerated both the tendency for socialist economies to sputter and for socialist parties to leak power and money.

Finally, these differences suggest that the end of the Yugoslav regime was, from the beginning, inextricably tied to the end of the state. Indeed, this was even more the case than in the Soviet Union because the republicanization of politics and economics was fully in place *prior* to the debates about the form and future of socialism and the state. In the Soviet Union, by contrast, the republicanization of politics was in effect a by-product of Gorbachev's reforms – though, as argued in Chapter 3, the center had in fact surrendered some of its power to the periphery during the Brezhnev era.

This leads to another set of observations. In contrast to Hungary, Poland, Czechoslovakia, and the like, the collapse of socialism in Yugoslavia was not sudden. Indeed, it is not all that easy to date when precisely this happened. On the one hand, one could point to 1989–1990, when, for instance, each of the republics held more or less competitive elections, when some of the republican constitutions were revised to deny the Communists their political monopoly, and when the central-level League of Communists disbanded (once the Slovenes and then the Croats left in January 1990). However, there are other indicators that suggest that Yugoslavia was by far the first, rather than the last socialist regime to go in Eastern Europe. For example, by the end of the 1970s the League of Communists' political and economic monopoly had been divided in effect into a number of monopolies that were, in practice far less than in theory, nested together in Matrioshka-doll fashion (to borrow from Taras, 1993b) to form a larger systemwide monopoly. This decentralized approach to socialism led Sabrina Ramet (1984) to make a convincing argument that, by the end of the 1970s, Yugoslavia had ceased to be either a regime or a state. Instead, it had become an international system composed of six, relatively autonomous dictatorial entities of varying political and economic, not to mention national, persuasions.

Indeed, the number, six, may be too small, if we include the two autonomous provinces attached to Serbia and the growing political independence of Kosovo in particular, beginning at the end of the 1970s; the Yugoslav National Army as an increasingly autonomous political actor; and the growing isolation of the Yugoslav central government. Like the natural wonder of Plitvice in Croatia, then, the country within which it was located featured multiple pools of power – which even lacked many of the waterfalls that in Plitvice at least produced a single and relatively integrated water system.

To this we can add several other developments that came early and suggest at the least regime weakening and at the most regime collapse. I refer, for example, to the sharp decline, especially in the north, of dinar usage with the explosion of inflation in Yugoslavia during the 1980s; the opening up of Yugoslav borders, even in the 1960s, and the consequent loss of the party's monopolistic control over labor and capital (Zimmerman, 1987); rising levels of unemployment (especially in the south), which violated both the premises and promises of socialism (Woodward, 1995b); and Tito's introduction in the late 1960s of republican-based militaries that existed side by side – and were not integrated with – the Yugoslav National Army (Gow, 1992). Thus, whether we adopt the standards of the essential preconditions for socialism or of what theorists of revolution define as the key indicators of regime collapse, socialism in Yugoslavia may very well have died with Tito in 1980. What happened thereafter, then, was largely a matter of working through the nasty details.

This leads to a final set of observations. The Yugoslav case helps us assess the role of demonstration effects in the collapse of socialism in Eastern Europe. On the one hand, Yugoslavia's ideological and political distance from the Soviet Union would suggest that the impact of socialist developments outside of Yugoslavia was unimportant. This interpretation, moreover, is reinforced by the points made earlier that the Yugoslav crisis was serious, even in 1980, and that the regime in some respects began to exit from the scene a good ten years before this happened in the Soviet bloc. In this sense, the many problems Yugoslavia faced functioned in effect as a substitute for the "nudge over the cliff" provided to Poland, Hungary, East Germany, and the like by the structure of the bloc, the Gorbachev reforms, and Gorbachev's actions.

However, developments elsewhere in the socialist region after 1985 were, nonetheless, important for the disintegration of Yugoslav socialism. The Soviet Union was, after all, the first and presumably the most entrenched socialist state. As a result, the introduction of radical reforms and the collapse of socialism there – and throughout the bloc – were necessarily instructive events for the Yugoslav party leadership and diverse oppositional groups. This was particularly the case, since the crisis in Yugoslavia was well advanced by the time Gorbachev and his reforms made their entrance. Moreover, there were the obvious parallels between Yugoslavia and the Soviet Union. For example, both were federations; both were highly diverse in national terms; and both socialist regimes had strong claims to historical legitimacy. Finally, and perhaps most importantly, the Soviet Union had long functioned as the Yugoslav "other." It was in reaction to, if not fear of, the Soviet Union that the Yugoslav model came into being. Market socialism, after all, was, among other things, a scathing critique of the Soviet model, as was nonalignment in the international system. Moreover, each time there was a crisis in the Soviet Union and each time the Soviets intervened in Eastern Europe, the Yugoslav political elite responded in dramatic ways – as when, for example, it altered the plan for the defense of Yugoslavia in reaction to the Soviet invasion of Czechoslovakia (see, e.g., Gow, 1992).

Thus, while it would be wrong to reduce the collapse of socialism in Yugoslavia to a regional demonstration effect, it is, nonetheless, important to recognize that Yugoslavia did feature, albeit in exaggerated form, the very same costs of socialism that existed elsewhere in the region (as also observed by, e.g., Stanovčić, 1989; Goati, 1989). This made the Gorbachev reforms necessarily influential, since Yugoslavia echoed, like its neighbors, the costs of socialism and thus exhibited an understandable receptivity to Gorbachev's message. At the same time, developments within the bloc in general and in the Soviet Union in particular did have the effect of expanding what was considered possible in Yugoslavia. As Adam Przeworski (1982) once argued with reference to Solidarity in Poland, the end of socialism – like any dictatorial order, only more so – begins when alternatives appear on the horizon.

CONCLUSIONS

The purpose of this chapter has been to solve the puzzles surrounding the collapse of socialist regimes in Europe from 1989 to 1990. The most obvious puzzle is: why did socialism collapse? The answer is that two factors were crucial: all of these regimes shared certain institutional commonalities that over time divided the party, empowered the society and undercut economic growth; and the decade of the 1980s exposed all of these regimes to succession struggles, struggles over reform, and a dramatically changed international system. Thus, socialism ended because its institutions redistributed resources, and it ended in 1989–1990 in particular because the political opportunity structure had become unusually open to the possibility of large-scale change.

Regime collapse began in Poland and Hungary because they were members of the Soviet bloc, which rendered these regimes unusually vulnerable, and because they combined, like Yugoslavia (which also underwent regime change early), liberalized politics with disastrous economic performance. Thus, they featured in the extreme the anger, resources, and opportunities for change that are key to regime transition. Both of these transitions, moreover, were pacted, unlike the ones that followed. This would seem to suggest that comparatively robust civil and political societies, severe economic problems, and Communist parties with a strong reformist contingent provide the foundation for pacted transitions (see Bunce, 1998b, for other consequences).

Indeed, this is an argument one could also apply to Spain, where long-term socioeconomic changes combined with the death of Franco and a relative balance of power between the opposition and the rightist forces to produce a pacted transition from dictatorship to democracy. This in turn leads to another insight. The uncertainty surrounding the Spanish experience and the history of violence during regime transitions together provided the foundation for cooperation between old and upcoming elites, just as the uncertainty following these first transitions in Poland and Hungary and the memories participants had of prior jousting between the party and the society seemed to have done the same.

The fall of socialism then moved to the rest of Eastern Europe. All of these regimes lacked the liberalized politics and economics of Poland and Hungary, and they all featured as well weaker civil societies (though, importantly enough, both East Germany and Czechoslovakia – the next two regimes to fall – had histories of political protest and, by bloc standards, relatively sound economic performance). This would seem to suggest that mass mobilization occurred when the regime was hard-line, and when the opposition was deficient in size and organization. Why the process of regime collapse seemed to diffuse to these other countries was primarily because of the structure of the Soviet bloc. All these regimes were redundant in their political and economic problems and, thus, highly receptive to both Gorbachev's message and to the precedents set by Hungary and Poland. These precedents included not just the sudden and peaceful end to socialist rule, but also, just as remarkable, Soviet acceptance of this outcome – if not Gorbachev's outright encouragement.

Finally, it is far from accidental that the collapse of socialism was peaceful in most of the region. It was not just that the party either defected to the opposition or realized that the future was with those who made the quickest peace with the new order taking shape. It was also that Soviet control over the Eastern European militaries through the Warsaw Pact structure – and Gorbachev's refusal to send out the troops – meant that the Eastern European elites encased within the bloc did not have the option of deploying force to save themselves. Where that option did present itself, as in Romania, Yugoslavia, and Albania, the transition from socialism was violent. What is more, it was severely compromised.

LEAVING THE STATE

Nationalism gets its chance when the non-ethnic imperial structures collapse.

Ernest Gellner (1995: 6)

The end of socialism in Europe was quickly followed by the dissolution of three states in the region: Yugoslavia, the Soviet Union, and Czechoslovakia. This was a most surprising set of developments. At a general level, we can observe that, if regime collapse is rare, especially when it occurs peacefully (see Gurr, 1974), then even more unusual is state dismemberment.[1] However, even by the standards of those states that have either reduced in size or ended, the recent dissolution of the Soviet Union, Yugoslavia, and Czechoslovakia stands out as exceptional. In particular, why did two of these three states dismember peacefully, in contrast to the pronounced historical norm of violent state collapse? Particularly puzzling in this regard was the Soviet case, where most of the necessary ingredients for a violent end to the state were present – for example, the pattern there of increasingly violent nationalist mobilization prior to the end of the state (Beissinger, 1995a) and the demonstrated willingness of Mikhail Gorbachev, the Soviet president and party leader, to use force to preserve the union (as in the Baltic states in early 1991).

Equally puzzling is why these three states, all in a single region, ended in rapid succession. While there are historical precedents for multiple and geographically and temporally clustered shifts in state boundaries, these earlier cases of state reconfiguration invariably reflected the impact of in-

ternational factors with evident regional reach – for example, decolonization, foreign intervention, and war termination. In the cases of interest
here, however, such explanations do not apply. In occupying very different
positions in the postwar international order and the regional order as well,
the Soviet Union, Czechoslovakia, and Yugoslavia could hardly be said to
have been equally and similarly affected by international influences, whatever their content. Moreover, even if we posit, say, the Gorbachev reforms
as the international influence at work in these instances, we would face yet
another problem. Why did other states in the socialist region, many of
which were quite well positioned to be strongly affected by the Gorbachev
reforms, manage to survive the transition from state socialism fully intact?

This leads to a third and final set of distinctive features attending the
end of Yugoslavia, the Soviet Union, and Czechoslovakia. These focus on
outcomes. Why was the territorial dissolution of these states complete,
rather than partial (though Serbia and Montenegro remained attached to
lay claim to the title, Yugoslavia)? Why did no less than twenty-two new
states arise – and quickly – in a terrain that had long featured a mere
three? Finally, why have *all* of these new states endured?

These questions are hard to answer from a comparative historical perspective. Demands for secession tend to come from some, not all regions
(as was also the case, we must remember, for Yugoslavia, the Soviet Union,
and Czechoslovakia), and they tend to produce, as a result and only in the
extreme, some territorial leakage, not full-scale dissolution. In this sense,
the Bolshevik Revolution, with its shedding of the Baltic area, was typical
of conjoined regime and state collapse. Moreover, new states, particularly
when formed out of existing states, have usually taken a great deal of time
and conflict to jell. And they tend to do so only under the best of circumstances.

Conditions in the Soviet Union, Yugoslavia, and Czechoslovakia, however, represented in many ways the "worst of circumstances." For instance,
the correlation between national and new state boundaries was far from
perfect in the Soviet Union and Yugoslavia in particular, and the commitment of regional leaders and their followers to independent statehood differed substantially across the republics that made up the Yugoslav, Soviet,
and Czechoslovak federations. Thus, one would have expected that these
three countries would have at most leaked some territory, rather than
simply vanishing; that the process of new state formation would have been
far more contested and prolonged; and that the new states that arose would
have had far more variable degrees of staying power.

PLAUSIBLE ANSWERS

What, then, accounts for these surprising patterns of state dismemberment in the socialist world? In this chapter and the one that follows, I provide an answer that is remarkably similar, in both method and content, to what was presented in the preceding chapter with respect to regime collapse. In particular, I again engage in a series of instructive comparisons – in this case, between the states in the region that ended versus those that survived, and among the three states that dissolved. While the first helps us understand the causes and consequences of state dissolution following regime collapse in the socialist region, the second helps account for contrasts in how these states ended. What these comparative exercises suggest is that precisely the same factors were at work in ending socialist states as in ending socialist regimes. In brief, what appears to have been crucial was the interaction between the long-term consequences of socialist institutional design and the shorter-term effects of the more malleable domestic and international environment of the 1980s.

In this chapter, I address three issues: why these three states ended (whereas others in the region survived), why the process began in Yugoslavia, and why these three states gave way to twenty-two successor states. In the chapter that follows, our attention shifts to explaining the most obvious difference in how these states dissolved – that is, the violent end of Yugoslavia versus the peaceful dismemberment of the Soviet Union and Czechoslovakia.

DIVERSITY AS A CAUSE

We can begin our investigation of the causes of state dismemberment by looking at the intersection between two sets: those characteristics (relevant to the issue of state dismemberment) that Yugoslavia, the Soviet Union, and Czechoslovakia had in common, *and* that, at the same time, distinguished these three countries, in turn, from their socialist neighbors. At first glance, there is one obvious candidate. If we measure national diversity of domestic populations by the size of the second largest national group, then Yugoslavia, the Soviet Union, and Czechoslovakia were the most diverse countries in the European socialist area. This, plus the geographical compactness of the minority population(s), would seem to suggest that these three countries were, all else being equal, unusually vulnerable by regional standards to secessionist pressures (and, for that matter, to more troubled transitions to democracy – see Snyder and Vachudova, 1997).

This line of argument has much to recommend it. It draws the specific constellation of similarities and differences that a robust explanation of socialist state dissolution requires, and it resonates with the literature on nationalism and secession (see, e.g., Bates, 1983; Hechter, 1987; Hechter and Levi, 1979; Hechter and Appelbaum, 1982; Horowitz, 1985). Moreover, the focus on size and compactness of minority populations as two key factors helps account for the extremes within the socialist region – that is, not just the presence of secessionist demands in the Soviet Union, Czechoslovakia, and Yugoslavia, but also their absence in relatively homogeneous Poland and Hungary.

There are, however, some limitations to this interpretation. One is that the postsocialist region as a whole features a number of large and compact minority populations, yet significant variation in their political aspirations and behavior – during socialism and during the process of regime (and state) transition. As examples, we can point to the Roma throughout the region, the Poles in Lithuania, and the Turkish minority in Bulgaria, all of whom have voiced some dissatisfaction at times, but who have been for the most part quiescent. More vocal, but not avowedly secessionist, have been some other groups, such as the Russians within the new states of Kazakhstan, Ukraine, Estonia, and Latvia, and the Hungarian minority in Romania and the new state of Slovakia (see, e.g., Barany, 1994; Gordon and Troxel, 1995; and, more generally, Medrano, 1995). Perhaps the best indication of a low correlation between large and compact minority populations, on the one hand, and secessionist propensities, on the other, is the evident contrast between the behavior of the Hungarian versus the Albanian minority in Yugoslavia. While the former has been quiet, both during and after socialism and the breakup of the state, the latter has been prone to protest – during the last years of the regime and state and again in 1998, largely in response to the violent interventions of the Yugoslav president, Slobodan Milošević. During the wars of Yugoslav secession, however, a truce, albeit tense, existed between the Albanian majority within Kosovo and its Serbian minority, closely allied with the Yugoslav government (and see Treisman, 1996; Solnick, 1998b; Derlugian, 1995, on the quite variable behavior of nations and regions within Russia and Georgia).

Another problem is the failure to explain the considerable variations in which nations mobilized and when. For instance, why did Slovaks mobilize from 1967 to 1968 and Croats from 1971 to 1972, and why did other nations, very similarly situated (such as Lithuania, Latvia, and Estonia), fail to mobilize over the course of much of the socialist era? More to the point, why was the late 1980s – and not some other period – the time when a number of nations mobilized in the Soviet Union, Yugoslavia, and Czechoslovakia, and why did rates of nationalist mobilization differ so much at that time, even when taking size and geographical compactness into account (see, e.g., Beissinger, 1995a, on these variations in the Soviet Union)?[2]

Finally, there is a big difference between secessionist pressures and secessionist outcomes. While diversity and compactness can account for the former (though imperfectly so, as I argued earlier), these factors cannot account for the latter. This is primarily because diversity in and of itself has nothing to say about all those issues surrounding bargaining between the state and recalcitrant regions that determine in large measure whether secessionist movements arise and, if so, whether they succeed. Nor can minority size and compactness explain either why twenty-two and not, say, twelve or sixty states formed in the aftermath of state dismemberment, or why all twenty-two of these new and in many cases highly improbable states demonstrated such staying power.

All of these considerations, however, must be joined with another. Virtually all of the regional challenges to the continuation of socialist and postsocialist states have come from geographically compact minority communities (but with some exceptions – e.g., Istria within Croatia). All this would seem to suggest that such communities are a necessary, but not sufficient condition for nationalist mobilization – an argument that resonates with the literature on secession (see Chapter 1) and that is in keeping with the particular strengths of different systems design (see Ragin, 1998; Dion, 1998).

THE HISTORICAL CONSEQUENCES OF DIVERSITY

This leads to a second plausible factor – and one that builds on the first – that could account for patterns of state dissolution in the socialist world. What Yugoslavia, the Soviet Union, and Czechoslovakia shared, and what differentiated them from others in the region, was a long history of contestation over the boundaries of the state and over the definition and the rights of nations and national minorities. The most obvious indicator of this is the history in all three cases of border changes, including fragmentation of the state along national lines – for example, the disintegration and, ultimately, the reduction in the eventual size of Russia during the Bolshevik Revolution (which was altered again during and after World

War II), and the disintegration of both Yugoslavia and Czechoslovakia during World War II with the invasion of the Germans and their construction of puppet states in both Slovakia and Croatia-Bosnia.

These border shifts testify to a larger theme running throughout the history of these three countries: the centrality of national-regional issues in their political and economic conflicts. For example, looking to Yugoslavia and Czechoslovakia, we can point to the considerable international conflicts surrounding the very formation and resulting structure of these two states after World War I; the continuing relevance for politics and economics of these national-territorial and, indeed, socioeconomic and ideological cleavages during the interwar period; the role of such issues in the collapse of the interwar regimes; and the continuing centrality of the national question in the Communist era, as witnessed by, for instance, the correlation among political, social, and economic inequalities along national-regional lines and periodic outbursts of nationalist protests.[3] Similar observations can be made, moreover, about the Soviet Union. Here, we can point to the decision by the Bolsheviks to use nationalist appeals and nationalist institutions as key mechanisms for the construction of the state and socialism (see especially Slezkine, 1994; Hodnett, 1967); the role of the regions in the struggle for political power following Lenin's death (Harris, 1998); the murder of Beria by his colleagues in response to Beria's flirtation with nationalism as a basis for winning power after Stalin's death; and the purges of a number of indigenous republican leaders from the late 1950s to the early 1960s.

Perhaps the greatest testimony to the importance of nation and nationalism in these three countries, however, involves the following two characteristics common to each during the socialist era. One was the national-federal structure of these systems, which, as argued in Chapter 3, both reflected and reinforced the importance of nations and national diversity in the Soviet Union, Yugoslavia, and Czechoslovakia. The other was more subtle. Like sex in a Victorian novel, which was conspicuous all the more so by its absence, the failure of Communist elites to address the national question, except through their issuing of periodic platitudes, testified in many ways to its overarching political importance. Indeed, even with nations on the streets in the late Gorbachev era, the promised Central Committee plenum on nationalities was put off three times. When finally held, it was little more than a verbal exercise in political circumlocution (see "Natsional'naya politika partii," 1989; and, similarly, see Tito, 1971, for his comments on Croatian nationalism).

All of this points to the inherently contradictory roles of nations and nationalism in the European socialist experience (see Connor, 1972, 1984; Suny, 1993; Vujačić and Zaslavsky, 1991; Verdery, 1991, 1993a, 1993b). Nations were, on the one hand, a fact of political life. Moreover, they were annointed as key players in the construction of socialism. As Victor Zaslavsky (1993: 32–33) has argued for the Soviet case: "The major task of Soviet nationality policy can thus be . . . defined as mobilizing ethnic populations to accomplish Soviet-style modernization, while maintaining internal stability in a country harboring deep ethnic divisions and resentments." Finally, nations were useful in yet another way: they could strengthen political leaders by giving them the opportunity to play groups off against one another and by allowing elites to become in effect final arbiters – as Milovan Djilas (1990) has argued, for example, for Tito (also see Verdery, 1993a, 1993b).

However, at the same time, nations and nationalism were a constant and nagging worry for socialist leaders. From their perspective, the facile formula of national in form and socialist in content could all too easily be translated into national in form *and* nationalist in content. As Tibor Varady (1997: 18) has observed for the Yugoslav leadership:

> It was understood that national homogenization could not be imposed on the territories that made up Yugoslavia, and that multicultural coexistence was the only option. Schools, theatres and media in several languages were not only permitted, but supported as well. At the same time, it was also perceived that nationalism was the most dangerous rival of communism. Whatever was considered nationalistic was persecuted with all the instruments of the authoritarian regime.

All of this leads to an inescapable conclusion. The dissolution of Yugoslavia, the Soviet Union, and Czechoslovakia was the outcome of histories saturated by conflicts, spoken and tacit, over the nation, the regime, and the state *and* the relationship among the three.

Any explanation of the collapse of these three countries must, of course, recognize these historical legacies. This is not just because of their obvious and long-term importance, but also because many of the symbols central to earlier rounds of contestation over the nation and the state reappeared when many of the nations in these three states began to go their separate and quite vociferous ways in the 1980s (see in particular Denich, 1994, on the Yugoslav example). However, this line of argument is, ultimately, unsatisfying. One problem is that it leaves the mistaken impression of a linear story, featuring continuous and growing conflicts among nations within the former Yugoslavia, Czechoslovakia, and the Soviet Union. Instead, the reality for all three cases was different: periodic outbursts of national conflicts interspersed with long periods of either cooperation among nations or isolation from one another (see, e.g., Roksandić, 1991, on the Serbs and Croats).[4]

Like the first explanation that focused on the fact of diversity, moreover, so this historically based explanation of the consequences of that diversity fails to account for some of the key details surrounding the dissolution of these states. History has little to say, in particular, about the quite uneven patterns of nationalist mobilization prefacing the end of these states; about why these states dissolved and did so when they did; and about the rapid formation of twenty-two durable states in their place. For example, if a prior history of nationalist mobilization was crucial to explaining who left and who did not, then the number of new states in the region should have been much smaller. One would have expected the Soviet Union to have leaked, say, the three Baltic states, but to have remained otherwise intact; Czechslovakia to have lost Slovakia; and Yugoslavia to have subtracted Croatia and, perhaps, Serbia and Macedonia. The reality, of course, was full-scale state dissolution and, just as importantly, dissolution that occurred at a particular time.

Both the obvious value, yet the limitations, of using national diversity and national histories to account for the dismemberment of Yugoslavia, the Soviet Union, and Czechoslovakia lead us to a final and more useful distinction among the European socialist states. That is the institutional contrast, developed in Chapter 3, between the national federations of socialist Yugoslavia, the Soviet Union, and Czechoslovakia versus the unitary state structures of Albania, Bulgaria, Romania, and Hungary (again, leaving out the exceptional case of the German Democratic Republic). This distinction has one clear advantage over the alternatives. It summarizes the two earlier variables in efficient fashion, while giving us, in the process, more explanatory reach.

NATIONAL FEDERALISM

As argued in Chapter 3, the national-federal design of the Soviet, Yugoslav, and Czechoslovak states had several important consequences over time, all of which were to prove crucial to the eventual enterprise of dismembering the state. One was that national federalism constructed nations at the republican level – or, in the case of nations that were, for historical reasons, already relatively well defined, to reinforce and elaborate that process (as with, for instance, Slovakia, the Baltic states, Croatia, and Serbia).

Another was to create, again at the republican level, states-in-the-making, complete with their own borders, elites, national communities, and a full array of economic, political, social, and cultural institutions. This in turn gave a distinctly national and spatial content to the process of bargaining over power and privilege within these federations. Thus, like the Soviet bloc, the very process of deciding who gets what in the Soviet Union, Czechoslovakia, and Yugoslavia politicized national-territorial divisions, while giving them economic content in the process.

Third, the fate of the state in these cases was unusually dependent upon the fate of the regime. This was because the party organs dominated the state organs, and because the party functioned as *the* linkage among the constituent economic, political, and social units of the system (since the economy, for example, was based on a sectoral, rather than a territorial model). While party domination on these bases was characteristic of all the socialist systems, federal as well as unitary, it was only in the former where some of the constituent units – in particular, the republics – commanded virtually all the territorial, national, and institutional resources they needed to move (when circumstances so allowed) in distinctive and disparate directions.

Finally, during the 1970s, circumstances did allow. The policy of stability in cadres – which meant that republican elites were frozen in place and resentful of the diminished opportunities for political mobility – created both the incentives and the capacity for these elites to carve out islands of republican autonomy within the federation. Economic decline had the same effect. It left central party elites with fewer resources to control their lieutenants in the periphery; it made it harder for the center to access the resources in the periphery; and it forced republican party officials to seek power and money within their provincial domain rather than going begging in Moscow, Belgrade, or Prague (see Helf, 1994).

By focusing on national federalism and its consequences over time, then, we can understand several features of the dissolution of Yugoslavia, the Soviet Union, and Czechoslovakia – in particular, why state collapse followed regime collapse, in that order and only in these three countries; why the new states that formed in the wreckage of socialism took on the borders they did and did so with such speed; why the successor states numbered twenty-two (though the Serbia-Montenegro exception still needs to be explained); and why all twenty-two successor states have managed to become durable, if not always terribly viable, political and economic units.

The design and impact of national federalism, therefore, provides answers to many of our key questions, and allows us, in turn, to incorporate the earlier arguments while dealing with their deficiencies. However, this account of state dissolution still leaves several related questions on the table. How were nations- and states-in-making at the republican level transformed – and so quickly – into nationalist movements and nation-states? Again, there is a big difference between nations and nationalism, between secessionist pressures and the actual dismemberment of states, and between state formation and the survival of new states. A second question is timing. Why did the socialist states end in the early 1990s and not a decade earlier? Finally, if we recognize that regime collapse in all three cases preceded state collapse, and if we then argue that the necessary condition for state dismemberment was the termination of the regime, then what precisely was the relationship between the end of the regime and the end of the state?

To answer these questions, we need to fold in a second and by now familiar factor into our explanation: the changes in the opportunity structure during the 1980s. As argued in the previous chapter, the postwar international order began to loosen in the 1970s. This was followed in turn by a loosening of socialist regimes during the next decade in response to the coincidence at the time among economic decline, leadership succession, and protracted elite struggles over reform. When combined, these developments undermined the socialist dictatorships while opening them up to new directions in politics and economics.

This process had spatial as well as ideological implications for the federalized socialist states, because of reasons already noted. Given the existence of the republics and their particular and differentiated character, each of the federal systems responded to the expansion of the opportunity structure during the 1980s by, for example, leaking power and economic resources from the center to the periphery and by allowing for, if not encouraging, multiple responses – where nation, territory, institutions, and political administration intersected – to the many problems besetting socialism. As a result, the federalized socialist states were exposed to nationalist movements, the multiplication of political-economic systems within their environs, and countersovereign claims – with all three developments entangled with each other and following the fault lines of the federation. As Vesna Pusić (1992: 248) has summarized, for example, for Yugoslavia by 1990:

> Thus, there were created two serious and possibly insuperable obstacles to reform in Yugoslavia. In the first place, since in one republic communists had power firmly in their hands, and in the other republics the process of reform had already begun and new parties or coalitions had come to power, the political changes in the country as a whole developed simultaneously in two opposing directions. Second, since it was the national communists who were in charge, that is, communists who based their collectivism on the concept of the nation and nationalist ideology, it meant that the nation and nationalist questions had to be the main issues from the outset.

Reform and regime weakening in the federal contexts, therefore, were necessarily accompanied by state-weakening, republican empowerment and nationalist mobilization (see especially Comisso, 1993). Nor was this story of combined regime- and state-weakening, nationalism and political liberalization an unusual one from a historical vantage point. The following observations by two well-known students of nationalism, based on their reading of its historical origins, bring home in succinct fashion the typicality of the socialist experience. Thus, as Miroslav Hroch (1996: 75) has argued, "The basic precondition of all nationalist movements, yesterday and today, is a deep crisis of the old order, with the breakdown of its legitimacy, and of the values and sentiments that sustained it." And, as John Hall (1995: 18) has observed, "Nationalism has habitually and historically involved separation from authoritarian politics."

It was the interaction between national federalism and the opportunities of the 1980s, then, that explains the dissolution of the Yugoslav, Soviet, and Czechoslovak states by the end of that decade. What then remains to be understood – and what serves as the focus of the remainder of this chapter – is the process by which all of this took place. It is through that discussion that we can also understand the particular relationship that developed among socialism, nationalism, and federalism – or, more simply put, between the end of socialist regimes and the end of socialist states.

THE STAGES OF STATE DISMEMBERMENT

We can compare the fragmentation and then the collapse of Yugoslavia, the Soviet Union, and Czechoslovakia by dividing the processes of state dismemberment into three stages. In doing so, however, I must admit that such an exercise glances too quickly over differences among and within these cases (though these differences will be addressed in part here and in detail in the next chapter). At the same time, an exaggeratedly neat temporal progression is forced on developments that were in practice both nested and messy.

To provide a brief overview: in the first stage, the political opportunity structure expanded and politics, economics, and institutions took on a more fluid character. In the second stage, a weakened center, divided elites, and liberalized politics translated into a breakdown in the economic and political ties between the center and the republics; the expansion of political protest along primarily national-republican lines; and the diversification of interrepublic dynamics, as regional party elites fought for their survival by distancing themselves and their republics from the center through particular and varying but usually self-serving combinations of nationalism and reform. In the third and final stage, the collapse of Communist Party hegemony combined with ongoing declarations of republican sovereignty to produce an exit of some and then all the republics from the state. What then followed was the immediate formation of new states along strictly republican lines. Let us now examine each of these stages in greater detail.

LOOSENING THE STRUCTURE

As with its regime counterpart, so the process by which these states ended began in response to the convergence in the 1980s among succession struggles and struggles over economic and political liberalization. In Yugoslavia, this process began in earnest at the very beginning of the decade. This was when the poor performance of the economy had become evident to all Yugoslavs; when Tito, the longtime leader and "final arbiter" of Yugoslav socialism, died; and when new institutions were introduced that created full political equality among the republics and provinces, that allocated to them virtually *all* the decision-making powers vested in the party and the government, and that, as a result, encouraged republican party elites to go in very different economic and political directions. Put simply, then, Yugoslavia at the beginning of the 1980s featured two characteristics apparent to virtually everyone: the economy was in shambles, and the center was reduced to little more than a battleground among warring republican elites. What divided these elites was their radically different positions on economic reform, political liberalization, and the preferred design of the state. *All* the core issues of politics and economics were on the table by the early 1980s in Yugoslavia.

In the Soviet and Czechoslovak cases, the expansion of the political opportunity structure came later and in a more telescoped form with Gorbachev's rise to power, his introduction of both new policies and new institutions at the domestic and regional levels, and his deregulation, as a result, of the regime, the state, and the bloc. What also contributed to the fluidity of Czechoslovak politics in particular and exaggerated, as a result, the impact there of the Gorbachev reforms was Gorbachev's speech in Prague in April 1987 (which involved a defense of his reforms, a hint at their parallels with the Dubcek era, and an explicit recognition of the independence of Eastern Europe) and the comparatively early onset of a succession struggle.

POLITICAL MOBILIZATION AND REPUBLICANIZATION OF POLITICS

While a protracted stalemate in public policy and the distribution of political power best describes Yugoslavia over much of the 1980s and a "refolution" (Ash, 1989) best captures what happened in the Soviet Union and Czechoslovakia when Gorbachev introduced his reforms, the immediate results in all three cases were, nonetheless, rather similar. Thus, the party elite at the center divided; republican elites were cut off from the patronage networks and the economic resources of the center, while being subjected to more competitive pressures from within their locales; and publics mobilized along primarily national lines in response to the organizing power of national federalism, political and economic disarray, and the combination of opportunities and threats provided by a rapidly liberalizing economic and political environment. The end result was that the center weakened, politics and economics were "republicanized," and each of the republics began to follow different trajectories, depending upon how publics, elites, and elites-in-waiting defined and combined reform and nationalism.

In the Soviet Union, for example, public mobilization was in fact encouraged by Gorbachev, especially beginning in 1987, since these popular fronts in support of perestroika were to contribute to the size of his reform coalition while helping him isolate those, such as Ligachev, who wanted less radical reforms. However, the form these fronts took, given the legacies of federalism and the vulnerable position of republican elites, was primarily national. Publics in the Baltic republics took the lead in this process by using nationalism as a base for the development of civil and political society (see especially Ekiert, 1991, on civil versus political society; Karklins, 1993, Lieven, 1993, Senn, 1990, Muiznieks, 1995, on the Baltic mobilizations; and, on the more general relationship among nationalism, local politics, and democracy, see Mann, 1995; deNevers, 1993; Nodia, 1994).

Thus, in the Baltic area, liberal reform and nationalism managed to go together. This reflected, in part, certain historical influences – for instance, the interwar precedents of independent statehood and democracy (with the latter even more transitory than the former) and the well-established equation in the mind of the Baltic peoples of Russian and Soviet imperialism with such objectionable outcomes as dictatorship, denial of sovereignty, and isolation from Europe. Important as well in the Baltic cases were some more proximate factors – in particular, the resonance of Gorbachev's messages about democracy, economic reform, and integration with the West as a single package, along with the eventually and largely conciliatory responses of the Baltic Communist parties to substantial public mobilization around the intersection among democracy, nationalism, and economic reform. Indeed, this overview of Baltic developments applies equally well to what happened and why in Slovenia.

Developments in the other Soviet republics, however, were different

(Beissinger, 1993). Russian and Ukrainian publics, for example, were slow to express nationalist concerns – a reflection, in part, of the overlapping historical development of Russia and Ukraine and, in the Russian case in particular, the blurred boundaries between state and empire (drawing upon Vujačić, 1996; also see Arutiunian and Drobizheva, 1987; Drobizheva, 1992; and, for the Ukrainian case, see Motyl, 1993, 1991, and Von Hagen, 1995). At the same time, the leaders of these two republics were divided on the question of political and economic transformation, and they took the state for granted, while using it at times as a convenient site for political contestation and as an equally convenient weapon in their local and larger struggles for political power.

In Czechoslovakia, the precedents set by the radicalization of Soviet politics and the rapid collapse in 1989 of socialism in Poland, Hungary, and, especially, East Germany, brought hundreds of thousands of protesters to the streets. However, even as the regime was rapidly collapsing, there were differences in how reform and nationalism combined in the Czech versus the Slovak portions of federal Czechoslovakia. It was not just that more Czechs than Slovaks took to the streets; it was also that their publics and the leaders of their Communist parties and their opposition movements had quite different perspectives on what the future should entail. This was in part because of interests – or the likely higher costs of rapid economic reform in the Slovak portions of the state and the probability that the Slovak minority would have less power than its Czech counterparts in a fully democratic order. This was also a function of perceptions – or the different perspectives Czechs and Slovaks tended to hold with regard to the history of their country, the meaning of 1968, and the costs and benefits of the normalization that followed.

Thus, the Czech Communists remained hard-line and internationalist, which led to their quick defeat at the polls in June 1990. By contrast, the Slovak Communists, seeing a different combination of stances as key to their political survival, divided between those who stayed with the party (which then lost at the polls) and those who rejected socialism, rushed headlong to embrace its dominant ideological substitute, or Slovak nationalism, and formed a new and successful party, Movement for a Democratic Slovakia.

At the same time, the Czech portion of the opposition converged quickly around a formula involving the rejection of socialism in its domestic and regional forms, a rapid transition to capitalist liberal democracy, and the maintenance of the federal state. As a result, the Czechs defined nationalism in liberal terms, while ignoring in the process the close historical linkage between liberalism and Czech economic and political domination. What facilitated all this was their shared resentment about 1968 and post-1968 developments. Again in contrast, the Slovak wing of the national front (or the Committee against Public Violence) shared the commitment to being done with socialism and the bloc, while supporting a less rapid and thorough transition to capitalism and a state that was more confederal in its structure and, thus, less dominated than in the past by the Czechs.

Thus, both the Czech and the Slovak opposition movements were nationalist, and nationalism in both cases was tied to anticommunism. Beyond that, however, nationalism had very different implications for perspectives on the regime, the state, the economy, and the nation after socialism. These differences shaped in turn not just the post-Communist trajectories of the two halves of Czechoslovakia, including political party development (see Innes, 1997), but also the capacity of the state to survive in the face of these cumulative and thus increasingly polarized positions. What also played key roles in the dismemberment of Czechoslovakia was the continuation of the Communist era constitution – which spoke in part to the inability of Czech and Slovak leaders to bargain effectively with each other – and the dual structure of the federation. Both legacies of the socialist past made compromise between Czech and Slovak leaders quite difficult during the years immediately following the collapse of Communist Party hegemony. They also provided ample temptations to the two sets of leaders to defect from the state, even when they lacked the support of their respective populations to do so (see Elster, 1995; Wolchik, 1994, 1995, 1997; Cox and Frankland, 1995).

The dynamics of territorial fragmentation, the mobilization of publics into politics, the struggle of republican leaders and the opposition to build bases of power, and the resulting diversity in how reform and nationalism were combined at the republican level were all developments that took their most complex forms in Yugoslavia (see, e.g., Woodward, 1995b; Silber and Little, 1996; Cohen, 1993; Lampe, 1996; Goati, 1989; Gow, 1992; Križan, 1993; Magaš, 1993; Pesić, 1996; Tašić, 1994; Ramet, 1996; and the insightful overviews provided by Irvine, 1997a, and Stokes, Lampe, and Rusinow with Mostov, 1996). Here, the story centered on developments over the course of the 1980s within two republics: Slovenia and Serbia. Like a fractious couple contemplating divorce, but without the benefit of a marriage counselor in sight, Serbia and Slovenia suffered greatly from the fact that their profiles were both very similar and yet very different. In particular, these two republics were the most politically liberalized regions within Yugoslavia (see, e.g., Bolčić, 1983, on strike patterns); their Communist Party leaders were similarly confronted with substantial public protests that featured nationalism as one pronounced and continuous theme (see especially Gagnon, 1994, and Vukomanović, 1995, on Serbian protests); and the Slovene and Serbian parties (along with their publics) were increasingly persuaded that the prevailing design of Yugoslavia was working against their interests (see especially Goati, 1990, on public opinion in Yugoslavia).

In the Serbian case, this perception took a particular twist. With the publication of the Memorandum of the Serbian Academy of Sciences in 1986 (which had been written by a broad range of Serbian intellectuals over the course of three years), the concerns of Serbian political elites, intellectuals, and mass publics were framed through an argument that resonated deeply with Serbian history and Serbian identity. In particular, it was claimed that there was a large, deeply disturbing, and inherently unfair gap between what the Serbian nation deserved versus what it had received (see Tašić, 1994: 60–76). This resulted in the demand for "realization of the full national and cultural integrity of the Serbian people independent of where they [were] . . . located within republics or autonomous provinces" (quoted in Goati, 1990: 75). Thus, in Serbia and, more to the point, for Serbs wherever they lived, the issue was injustice and the need for retribution – an unusually potent set of themes for mass and elite mobilization. By contrast, in Slovenia the issue was more one of process and outcome, though the implication was that Slovenes deserved better in both categories (see Rizman, 1995).

These similarities, however, were joined with a number of differences. In Slovenia, the protesters called for a considerable liberalization of the polity and the economy and, at the least, a confederalization of Yugoslavia and, at most, the departure of Slovenia from the Yugoslav state (with the latter position clearly dominant by 1988). These positions flowed directly from the Slovene political-economic context – for instance, Slovenia's role as the most developed Yugoslav republic and the decidedly liberal thrust of much of the Slovene League of Communists. What also pushed Slovene developments toward rapid and full-scale deregulation of the polity, the economy, and, indeed, the state were certain expectations about the costs of continued membership in the Yugoslav polity – for example, the fear that this would terminate the liberal experiment, while foreclosing the possibility (with 1992 approaching and still claiming to be the immediate future of Europe) of Slovene integration into the European Community (now Union). It was also recognized that independent statehood was at least a possible project, given the homogeneity of Slovenia (in contrast to the other Yugoslav republics); the likelihood that the West (or at least its most important representative, Germany) would tolerate a Slovene state;

and the growing irrelevance of state size in a united Europe and an increasingly liberalized international economy (see, e.g., Benderly and Kraft, 1994; Woodward, 1995a; Rizman, 1995; Vodapivec, 1992). What the Slovenes recognized, then, was what has become a new and often overlooked fact of contemporary political life. As Katherine Verdery (1993b: 44) has summarized: "The size requirements . . . of viable nation-hood are decreasing."

In Serbia, by contrast, the position of the protesters was far more mixed with respect to reform and, at the same time, more supportive of one option that was never entertained in Slovenia at either the mass or elite level: recentralization of the Yugoslav regime and state. This was, for the Serbs, a remarkably efficient and, thus, highly attractive position. Centralization would allow for the orchestration of a coherent response to the crisis engulfing Yugoslavia – an argument that was hard to refute in the stalemated conditions of the 1980s. At the same time, recentralization would serve the political and economic interests of Serbs who had been in effect twice-taxed by the decentralization and diversity of the Yugoslav confederation. Thus, while Serbs constituted nearly 40 percent of the Yugoslav population, their political vehicle and, thus, their political voice – that is, the Serbian republic – was allocated only one of nine votes within the party's collective presidency (since each republic and province, along with the military, was allocated equal voting shares).

What made this situation even more galling was that precisely the same voting share was allocated to Vojvodina and Kosovo – two provinces that were attached to Serbia, much smaller in size, and of a lower administrative rank within the federal system. At the same time, Serbia was poorer than Slovenia and Croatia and lacked their hard currency reserves. However, because of its location at the Yugoslav economic mean, Serbia failed to qualify for transfers of revenues from the richer republics of Slovenia and Croatia through the Socialist Development Fund.

If recentralization was a position that flowed directly from Serbian elite and public interests, moreover, it was also a position that resonated with certain themes in Serbian culture and history. Thus, public opinion surveys show that Serbs were, by the standards of other nations within Yugoslavia, unusually supportive of a strong state. Indeed, in direct contrast to the Croats, Serbs ranked this considerably above economic enrichment in their hierarchy of personal goals (see especially Grdešić, Kasapović, and Šiber, 1989: 13, 103). In addition, what also contributed to Serbian support of centralization was Serbia's history as a victim of imperialist aggression from both outside and within Yugoslavia (with the latter referring to atrocities committed during World War II).

Finally, the Serbian understanding at the time of the formation of Yugoslavia was that a particular trade had been made – a trade that was being increasingly violated over the course of the 1980s, if not earlier. Serbs had given up their independent statehood only under the conditions that a larger political entity would be formed that would encorporate virtually all of the Serbian nation, that would give this largest nation its political due, and that would feature a strong and, thus, centralized state (see especially Banac, 1984, and Tašić, 1994: 31–40; also see Vujačić, 1996; Pesić, 1996; Cohen, 1993; Denich, 1994). While Serbian culture, like all cultures, is fluid and composed of competing symbols (including, in the Serbian pantheon, not just soldier-heroes, but also, as with Marko, soldier antiheroes), the historical memories surrounding the themes of defeat, decentralization, and armed struggle had particular resonance for the Serbs in the Yugoslav context of the 1980s. In Slobodan Milošević's characteristically blunt summary of Serbian culture, "We may not know how to work, but we do know how to fight" (quoted in Vasić and Švarm, 1995b: 16).

Thus, to summarize: while Slovene history during the Habsburg, interwar, and socialist periods tended to emphasize the benefits of decentralization, and while the Slovene position within Yugoslavia in the 1980s made decentralization quite attractive, a similar resonance between past experiences and present interests – though pushing in quite the opposite direction – described Serbs and Serbia as well. Not surprisingly, this sharply etched contrast between Serbia and Slovenia played out in their respective governing parties. Although both Communist parties opted to ride the wave in the streets rather than to move forcefully against it (though Milošević sought to isolate the liberals from the rest), this action had very different meanings in the Slovene and Serbian contexts. The League of Communists in Slovenia came to support the arguments of the students and the intellectuals and, thus, came to oppose socialism and to support a transition to capitalism, liberal democracy, and independent statehood (see Rizman, 1995; Benderly and Kraft, 1994). This was not a difficult decision, in part because of the liberal complexion of the Slovene party, in part because of the homogeneity of the Slovene public and public opinion, and in part, it must be noted, because a secret understanding was eventually reached between the Serbian and Slovene leadership (in the midst of their heated exchanges) that Slovenia would be allowed to exit from the state (see the memoirs by Kadijević, 1993; Jović, 1995a).

On the other side, the Serbian League of Communists was more populated by hard-liners – a product in large measure of the antinationalist purges of the 1970s, which were carried out in Croatia as well (see especially Gagnon, 1994). Party members in Serbia, moreover, were in the midst of a struggle for political power and were facing a continuing crisis of political control over Kosovo and its numerically dominant and increasingly dissident Albanian population. What made the Kosovar crisis all the more difficult for the Serbian leadership and the Serbian public was that Kosovo summarized all-too-efficiently (and in an area of enormous historical significance for Serbs) what was wrong with Yugoslavia. All this led the Serbian party leadership to ally with its angry publics, as in the Slovene dynamics, but to do so by calling for better, not less socialism and for more, not less state.

This also led the party to support the "moderate," Slobodan Milošević, in his struggle for power, first within the Serbian party, and then later "abroad," beginning with his takeover of the Communist parties of both Kosovo and Vojvodina, continuing with his political annexation in effect of Montenegro, and then moving on to the wars in Slovenia, Croatia, and Bosnia. In his struggle for power within the party and in his struggle to control the Serbs on the streets, Milošević had discovered – primarily by accident in a meeting with Serbs in Kosovo Polje in April 1987 – a remarkably efficient issue that could serve both interests simultaneously: Serbian nationalism, defined as resentment over the treatment of the Serbian nation in general and in Kosovo in particular (see especially Tašić, 1994; Stanovčić, 1993; Cohen, 1993, 1997; Silber and Little, 1996).[5]

Thus, what differentiated the Slovene from the Serbian party was not nationalism, because nationalism and even secession, for that matter, were central to the project of their respective political leaders, Milošević and Kučan, by the second half of the 1980s (see especially Kadijević, 1993, on the Serbian case). Nor was the contrast one of the distance separating the party elites from protesters, since in both cases the Communist Party moved toward the public, with nationalism serving as the bridge. Rather, what was different was that nationalism in the Slovene context was linked with reform and an exit from socialism and the state. By contrast, in the Serbian context, nationalism, socialism, and opposition to reform were joined together, and two options were considered for the future of the state: recentralization of the existing state, or, failing that, expansion of Serbia to embrace the totality of the Serbian nation.

CONSTITUTIONAL WARS AND THE COLLAPSE OF THE REGIME AND THE STATE

With the regime in ideological disarray, the state in territorial disarray, and politics increasingly republicanized and "nationalized," the process of state dismemberment then moved on to a third and final stage. This was when the struggle between the center and the republics – or, in Yugoslavia and Czechoslovakia, among the republics as well – focused on the format and the future of the state. This typically involved, for instance, the election of nationalists to republican office (whether Communists or, less frequently in absolute numbers, members of the opposition); a war of laws carried out between the center and the republics; protracted constitutional negotiations that failed to reach a durable compromise; a rewriting of republican constitutions to establish even greater distance from the center; declarations of republican sovereignty – for example, the Russian legislative declaration of June 1990; and the collapse of the regime. What followed in all three cases was the exit of some and then all of the republics from the state (though Montenegro was the exception, remaining bonded to Serbia to form a truncated Yugoslav state).

In Yugoslavia and in the Soviet Union, the key period for these developments was 1989–1991, when competitive elections in the republics brought nationalists to power in most cases. This was also when attempts by the center to reimpose power and reestablish control over the reform process failed in a spectacular fashion – as with the rise and fall of the Marković reforms in Yugoslavia from 1989 to 1990 (Tašić, 1993) and, in the Soviet Union in 1991, the showdown at the beginning of the year in the Baltic states and, later in the summer, the attempted coup d'etat. Finally, this was when the Serbian, Slovene, Lithuanian, and Russian leaders, to name some of the most pivotal players, presided over the drafting of new and secessionist constitutions (with Serbia being the first to do so within Yugoslavia); when the central-level Communist parties gave up their formal rights to a political monopoly and dissolved at the central level; and when negotiations over redefining the federation either broke down (as in Yugoslavia) or produced a document (see Draft Union Treaty, 1991) that then prompted an attempted coup d'etat (as in the Soviet Union). All of these developments then led to the formal ending of these two states, as a number of leading republics, such as the Baltic states and Ukraine within the Soviet Union and Slovenia and Croatia within Yugoslavia, having already declared sovereignty, then held referenda on independence followed by an exit from the state. They were quickly joined in their exodus by Bosnia and Macedonia within Yugoslavia and the remaining republics within the Soviet Union.

In Czechoslovakia, the final stage of state dissolution took place later and thereby extended well into the post-Communist phase. Thus, the differences between Slovakia and the Czech-Moravian lands, which were evident even in the fall of 1989, only deepened in response not just to different definitions of nationalism and reform and the differences in political parties and governing coalitions, but also to the equally divisive and paralyzing effects of the decision to hold competitive elections first and to rewrite the constitution second. This had two implications. One was that it became hard for the president, Vacláv Havel, to intervene in Czechoslovak politics in general and in the growing crisis developing between the two halves of the country in particular. Thus, when Havel pushed for a referendum on the future of the state following the elections in summer 1992, it was relatively easy for Václav Klaus, the prime minister of Czechoslovakia, and Vladimír Mečiar, the premier of Slovakia, to ignore him and to arrogate for themselves in the process the power to determine the future of the state. Here, it is important to recognize that neither Klaus nor Mečiar had majoritarian mandates, and that the votes they did win did not signify by any means votes to terminate the state. Indeed, public opinion in both the Slovak and, especially, the Czech portions of the country, while different on many issues, supported, nonetheless, the continuation of a single state (see Wolchik, 1994).

The other consequence was that those who wrote the constitution were far from being either interest- or national-blind. Thus, the constitution itself, along with parliamentary politics, functioned as the locus of a complex and interrelated struggle between Klaus and Mečiar. This struggle focused simultaneously on the institutional design of democratic Czechoslovakia, the approach to the economic transformation, and the power of the two men in their respective parties and governing coalitions and, thus, in their respective portions of the country.

What made all of this particularly conducive to the dismantling of the state was that the first-order preferences of the Czech and Slovak leaders were very far apart indeed. Klaus wanted a federal state, one countrywide policy on economic reform, and the institutional capacity to orchestrate the economic and political transformation (see, e.g., the interview with Klaus in Blejer and Coricelli, 1995). Moreover, while Klaus had substantial support for his reform project within the Czech lands, he was constrained from moving ahead by Slovak public opinion and Mečiar. By contrast, Mečiar wanted a confederal state, a separation of the Slovak and Czech economic reforms, and a larger and more stable power base within Slovakia – with all three objectives best served through veiled threats to take Slovakia out of the federation. These differences, however, led to a fairly straightforward agreement in second-order preferences. Thus, once the summer 1992 elections produced different outcomes in the two portions of the state and a stalemate on reform, Klaus moved quickly to a position supporting the end of the state. This would meet his economic and political concerns and allow him, in the bargain, to be the "Leninist" – that is, the dominant political force shaping socioeconomic change – that he wanted to be. Mečiar, however, was stuck. He had little choice but to cooperate with Klaus and to convert what had always been a strategic threat into the reality of state division. Thus, the two leaders spent the fall of 1992 bargaining away the state, and Czechoslovakia formally divided into two entities on January 1, 1993.

YUGOSLAVIA AS THE FIRST

The process by which these three states dismembered, therefore, followed roughly the same pattern – in large measure because of the homogenizing effects of socialism, national federalism, and regime transition. Simply summarized, the process began when crises over power and reform weakened the regime, mobilized publics, "republicanized" the state, and "nationalized" political protest. Within the context of the socialist federations, then, conflict was defined in both ideological and territorial terms. As a result, struggles within Yugoslavia, the Soviet Union, and Czechoslovakia centered quickly on the future of not just the regime but also the state. This was in contrast to developments elsewhere in the postsocialist region, where conflict centered on ideological issues, and where the character of the regime, economic and political, became the sole focus of political struggle.

The similarities in these three stories of state dismemberment, however, mask two obvious differences that need to be addressed. One was in the timing of state dissolution. Yugoslavia was the first of the socialist states to unravel. Why this was the case is relatively easy to explain, given certain characteristics of Yugoslav economic and political developments from the second half of the 1970s through the 1980s. For example, this was the country that stood out within the region as having the most liberalized and most "regionalized" politics and economics (see, e.g., Bolčić, 1983: 129, on variations in social indicators by republics and provinces, and Bičanić, 1995); that witnessed the sharpest drop in economic performance from the 1970s to the 1980s; and that had featured the longest and most raucous debates over economic and political reforms – debates that were dominated from the beginning by republican leaders whose major interests were their own political survival first, the needs of their republics second, and the future of the Yugoslav regime and state a distant third. At the same time, it was in Yugoslavia where the International Monetary Fund, in response to heavy hard-currency debts, had imposed stabilization measures that by the first half of the 1980s had unleashed a constitutional war among the Yugoslav republics – a war that set the stage in many respects for the real war that eventually followed (see especially Woodward, 1995a).

What also distinguished Yugoslavia was that it was here where, with the death of Tito, the first major socialist succession of the decade took place. Thanks to a series of decisions in preparation for a post-Tito era, moreover, the resulting struggle for power was played out within a new institutional context that reduced the Yugoslav central government and the central League of Communists, already quite limited in their powers, to the simple sum – literally in terms of vote allocations – of their republican and provincial parts. Indeed, the extraordinary decentralization of Yugoslavia also took an economic form. For example, by November 1986 the republics had gained full fiscal sovereignty (see Woodward, 1995a: 74).

As a regime, a state, and an economy, Yugoslavia was unusually well positioned to disintegrate after the death of Tito in 1980 (see, e.g., Golubović, 1988; Goati, 1989; Stanovčić, 1989; Županov, 1983; Bolčić, 1989; Gligorov, 1992; Ramet, 1985).[6] Although few doubted the survival of the Czechoslovak and Soviet states, even by, say, the beginning of 1990, most informed analysts did wonder, at least five years before that, whether the Second Yugoslavia, like the first, was doomed to become history (to borrow from Lampe, 1996; also see P. Ramet, 1985; Rusinow, 1988).

While it is easy to explain why Yugoslavia dismembered first, however, it is far more difficult to account for a second obvious contrast – again, between Yugoslavia, on the one hand, and the Soviet Union and Czechoslovakia, on the other. That is the contrast between the peaceful division of the Soviet and Czechoslovak states versus the wars that engulfed Yugoslavia. This difference, which is quite difficult to explain and constitutes the final issue to be addressed in this book, will be the subject of the next chapter.

CONCLUSIONS

If the story of regime collapse in the socialist world was one of subversive institutions interacting with subversive opportunities, then the story of state dissolution following regime collapse was largely the same. Just as the structure of socialist regimes functioned over time and quite by accident to homogenize publics, divide elites, and undercut the party's control over itself and over the society and the economy, so the structure of socialist federations constructed a fifth column within its own environs – or, in this context, increasingly well defined, differentiated, and autonomous nation-states at the republican level within what were supposed to be single nation-states. Thus, both of these institutional playing fields of socialism – or the regime in general and the national-federal states – redistributed political power and economic resources from their core, however defined, to their periphery. And the same dynamics seemed to have taken place as well within a third institutional constellation of European socialism: the Soviet bloc. There, the Soviet Union as the core leaked power and money to the Eastern European periphery.

The more uncertain and elastic environment of the 1980s – produced by the confluence of economic crises, leadership succession, protracted struggles over reform, and a loosening of East-West boundaries – merely exaggerated the redistributive dynamics at work in these three arenas of socialism. As a result, the regime, the bloc, and the national-federal states all weakened, and successors to these constructs, already endowed with resources, rushed in to fill the void. Thus, all the socialist regimes ended when the party fissured and (in most cases) publics protested; the bloc ended when the Eastern European Communist regimes collapsed and then emptied the Soviet bloc; and the Yugoslav, Soviet, and Czechoslovak states dissolved when the regime collapsed and republics began to secede from the state. The redistributive pressures built into socialist institutional design, therefore, shifted from a dynamic that had been informal, tentative, and uneven to one that was formal, full-scale, and permanent. And with that, the socialist experiment – as a regime, a bloc, and a federation – was over.

This explanation of state, as well as regime and bloc dissolution, has several important implications. One is that the only difference between the regime story, on the one hand, and the state and bloc stories, on the other, was whether the collapse of the system was purely ideological or at once ideological and spatial – that is, a change in the organization of political power or a change in not just the organization but also the physical boundaries of political power.

A second implication flows from this. While analysts have been quite ready to refer to the collapse of the Yugoslav, Soviet, and Czechoslovak states as the direct outcome of nationalist revolts, they have been less willing to see the end of the Soviet bloc and socialist regimes in nationalist terms (but see Taras, 1993a). However, the similarities in institutional context and in causes and consequences would seem to suggest that the end of the regime and the bloc, like the end of the state, was a product of a process that was at its heart nationalist. Mark Beissinger's (1996: 100–

101) observations about nationalism, therefore, are as relevant to socialist regimes, domestic and international, as to socialist states:

> Nationalism is not about ancient enmities or even always about ethnicity, but, rather, about authority over a set of objects in politics, about the drawing of the physical, human, and cultural boundaries of the state and the life chances people believe are associated with the definitions of boundaries.

In the socialist context, therefore, nationalism was as much about regime destruction and regime construction, whether domestic or international, as it was about the more familiar terrain of state subtraction and state building. And this should not be all that surprising. When viewed from a longer-term historical perspective, just as nationalism has often been an indicator as well as a cause of transitions from dictatorship to democracy (a point often overlooked in studies of recent democratization), so the rise of democracy, at least in the Western experience, went hand in hand with the rise of the nation.

Finally, an obvious theme in this book has been that socialism was a self-destructive system. However, it was self-destructive only up to a certain point. While socialism in its various institutional guises undermined the hegemony of the Communist Party, the state (where it was federal), and the Soviet bloc (which was an international version of federalism), socialist institutions also had, at the same time, a quite different set of effects. They were responsible for organizing politics in disorganized times. This meant, for example, giving publics the resources they needed to surmount collective-action problems in times of regime unraveling (see Bunce and Chong, 1990; Lohmann, 1994); providing the resources the "dependent" regimes in Eastern Europe required to exit from both socialism and the bloc; and, finally, doing the same for the republics, once leaving the state became possible and desirable, if not necessary. In this sense, socialist institutions were both destructive and constructive. They created receptacles for both exit and reentry.

6

VIOLENT VERSUS
PEACEFUL STATE
DISMEMBERMENT

Culture is often not what people share, but what they choose to fight over.
Eugene Weber (quoted in Suny and Eley, 1996: 9)

The past several decades in Yugoslavia may not have been a fully enjoy-able present, but they have become a respectable and even enviable past.
Tibor Varady (1997: 18)

In the preceding chapter, the primary task was explaining why the Yugo-slav, Soviet, and Czechoslovak states ended, whereas other states in the region, so similar in history and circumstances, managed to survive. To-ward that end, I focused on what these three states had in common – and what differentiated them, in turn, from their socialist neighbors. This com-parison produced a relatively straightforward argument. National federal-ism produced over time a "dis-integration" of the Soviet, Yugoslav, and Czechoslovak states along republican lines. With the expanded opportuni-ties for major change in the 1980s, "dis-integration" in all three instances translated quickly into actual disintegration, and the state and the regime departed from Europe in virtual tandem.

The task in this chapter is quite different, though the methodology remains the same. Of interest here is explaining *variations*, not similarities, in the process of state dismemberment, with a focus on the most glaring contrast among our three cases: the violent end of Yugoslavia versus the peaceful dissolution of Czechoslovakia and the Soviet Union. Our central concern now, therefore, is identifying those factors that would appear to influence whether states end amicably or violently. And a key test of the power of that explanation is whether it manages to pair the Soviet Union and Czechoslovakia against Yugoslavia.

At first glance, this would seem to be the moment when we should discard the institutional focus that has served as the foundation for the arguments developed thus far in this book. After all, the three socialist states that unraveled have a common institutional heritage, given both socialism and national federalism. However, as I argue here, institutional design nonetheless remains at the center of the explanation. In this instance, what seemed to have mattered were differences in the institutional *details* of socialism and federalism in Yugoslavia versus the Soviet Union and Czechoslovakia.

As with the previous chapter, so in this one I begin the investigation of variations in state dismemberment by examining some competing lines of explanation. As we will discover, while these arguments about culture, leadership, nationalism, and federalism have all been used with seeming success to explain how one or another of the three states ended, they are less convincing when subjected to a comparative and, hence, more stringent test. What does seem to explain patterns in the dismemberment of these three states – and what serves as the focus for most of this chapter – are three factors in particular, all of which are institutional in nature: the degree of decentralization of the federation; the political power versus the institutional resources of the dominant republic, and the relationship between the military and the party-state.

CULTURAL-HISTORICAL EXPLANATIONS

One plausible account of why these states dissolved differently emphasizes cultural diversity and its historical consequences. It has been argued with respect to the Yugoslav case, for example, that a history of conflict among constituent nations, as occurred most notably during the interwar and wartime periods in that country, and the existence of a large diaspora population, as was the case in socialist era Yugoslavia with respect to Serbs within Croatia and Serbs and Croats within Bosnia, provided two key preconditions for the violent dismemberment of that state: historical enmities and a record of heated and prolonged disputes about state boundaries. Of course, such legacies assumed particular importance, once the Yugoslav regime and state began to disintegrate (see, e.g., Kaplan, 1993;

Larrabie, 1990–1991; Zimmerman, 1995; Lampe, 1996; Cohen, 1993; Hayden, 1992, 1995a; Vukomanović, 1995; Van Evera, 1994; Brubaker, 1995, 1996).

These observations about culture in general and its role in Yugoslavia in particular have obvious merit. This is especially the case, given, for instance, the central role of historically defined cultural symbols in the expression of both Serbian and Croatian nationalism, and given as well the aggressive behavior on the part of the Serbian and Croatian leadership and the Serbian and Croatian minority populations during the process of regime and state dissolution.

However, cultural accounts leave us with at best a partial explanation. First, as observed in the previous chapter, if we look more closely at the Yugoslav situation, we see a much more variegated picture of interethnic relations than these arguments seem to imply. The history of "international" relations within Yugoslavia features, among other things, long periods of either limited or quite peaceful interactions among those very nations that in 1991 went to war with each other. As a Bosnian translator observed with some irony when speaking to Tadeusz Mazowiecki (the former Polish prime minister and for a time United Nations special envoy to Bosnia): "Maybe we were living with people who hated us, and we never noticed" (quoted in *Gazeta Wyborcza*, September 2, 1995: 2).

Indeed, in the socialist period in particular – which spanned no less than forty-five years, we must remember – relations among the constituent nations of Yugoslavia were peaceful; interethnic marriage rates, particularly in Bosnia, were high; and the percentage of the population claiming to be Yugoslav grew over time (see, e.g., Roksandić, 1991; Donia and Fine, 1994; Hodson, Sekulić, and Massey, 1994; Friedman, 1997).

This speaks to a more general point that has been repeatedly made by both historians and anthropologists (see especially Wolfe, 1982; Verdery, 1991; Danforth, 1995). History is important, but always subject to constant and contested interpretations – not just by historians, who are in the business, after all, of reinventing, as well as reinterpreting the past, but also by intellectuals, political leaders, and mass publics responding to their personal needs, their life experiences, and the exigencies of the moment. At the same time, culture is fluid, and the symbols defining and defending culture are ever changing. Thus, while the "revenge of the past" (Suny, 1993) was important in what happened in Yugoslavia, what is just as important – there as elsewhere, since the Balkans are no more mired in their history than other places (see Todorova, 1994) – is explaining the following. Why do politicians use the past as they do and when they do? Why do some historical symbols seems to resonate more than others and at certain times? More generally, why is there much variance across time and space in the construction and the power of historical messages and cultural symbols?

Perhaps a brief comparison with a country outside the region will render these observations more concrete. If a painful past is necessarily invoked during times of regime transition, then how can we explain the Spanish case where, following the death of Franco, Spanish elites and elites-to-be rejected a variety of historical symbols that would have played up the class and national divisions of the civil war and the Franco period and opted, instead, for historical symbols that spoke to, if not imagined, a united Spain engaged in a common political project? Put more bluntly: a painful past can serve as a pretext for cooperation, as in Spain, or conflict, as in Yugoslavia (on the Spanish case, see Share, 1982; Edles, 1998; Conversi, 1993).

Moreover, while Yugoslav history features ample evidence of what is more correctly termed "recent national hatreds" (and not the cliché, "ancient ethnic hatreds"), a similar history, albeit not quite as extreme, can be identified for both the Soviet Union and Czechoslovakia. Here, I refer, for example, to the anger of the Baltic peoples in response to Soviet acquisition of the Baltic states during World War II. One can also cite the heated conflicts between Czechs and Slovaks that occurred as a consequence of Czech political, economic, and cultural dominance during the interwar period and over much of the socialist era as well (see, e.g., Gitelman, 1992; Karklins, 1993; Senn, 1990; Lieven, 1993; Henderson, 1994; Leff, 1988; Rychlik, 1995; Prucha, 1995; Bartlova, 1995; Butora and Butorova, 1993; Wolchik, 1994, 1995). If a sharply etched contrast between Yugoslavia versus the Soviet Union and Czechoslovakia is a necessary condition for a robust account of violent versus peaceful state breakup, then the historical patterns of interethnic conflict and cooperation in these three cases do not seem to provide it.

Another cultural factor that is plausible and that has been used to explain in particular the violent end of Yugoslavia is the problem of incongruent boundaries defining nations versus emerging states (see Brubaker, 1995). Thus, in the Yugoslav case, it has been suggested that the dismemberment of this state produced violence, because of the existence of a large Serbian minority community outside of Serbia. This was a problem that, in a period of regime transition and state weakening, encouraged the aggressive behavior of Serbia and Serbian minorities within both Croatia and Bosnia – behavior that was reinforced, if not invited (depending upon one's interpretation), by the provocative words and actions of the equally ultra-nationalist regime in neighboring Croatia (see especially Hayden, 1992,

1995a; and on Croatian public opinion, Grdešić, 1992; Irvine, 1997b). However, if this cultural factor is so important, then how can we explain the absence of similar behavior on the part of Russian leaders and Russian minorities outside of Russia? After all, like Serbia, Russia was the largest republic within the federation; Russians, like Serbs, were overrepresented at the top of the state's military structure; and Russians, like Serbs, constituted significant minorities in those republics abutting their Russian homeland. For example, with the dissolution of the Soviet Union, twenty-five million Russians were left stranded outside of Russia, with the great majority of these in neighboring Ukraine and Kazakhstan (see Harris, 1993).

What makes this even harder to reconcile with the Yugoslav experience was the existence of threats to the political rights of Russian minorities in Estonia and Latvia following independence – two nation-states that were formed by ethnically based nationalist movements, that bordered Russia, that had large Russian minorities relative to population size, and that were highly vulnerable to Russian threats because of energy and market dependence. Thus, while the imperfect correlation between national communities and state boundaries necessarily complicates the process of state division, it does not necessarily lead to war. Other factors, apparently, intervene.

POLITICAL EXPLANATIONS

In analyzing the reasons behind the violent collapse of his erstwhile state, Vojislav Stanovčić (1993), a Yugoslav political scientist, has drawn two succinct conclusions. One is that there was a built-in tension between federalism and dictatorship, and this produced, as he put it, less the condition of federalism than a form of feudalism along republican lines. His other observation is that "Yugoslavia was destroyed by its political leaders" (also see Zimmerman, 1995; and for a nuanced and quite historically rich argument along the same lines, see Lampe, 1996; Silber and Little, 1996; Cohen, 1993; Burg, 1995; Magaš, 1993; Lukić and Lynch, 1996).

Both of these observations are powerful and to the point. The first is undoubtedly true – for Czechoslovakia and the Soviet Union, as for Yugoslavia. Indeed, the same argument was implied in the analysis presented in the previous chapter and in Chapter 3, where I examine the costs of national federalism within a socialist and dictatorial context. The second argument, focusing on leadership, is also undoubtedly true and applies equally well to the Soviet Union, Yugoslavia, and Czechoslovakia. Given their applicability to all three cases, however, neither of these arguments can explain, in and of itself, the differences in the processes by which these three states ended. Moreover, to focus on leadership is to beg the question.

The real issue is *why* the leaders of Yugoslavia and its constituent republics behaved in different ways than their counterparts in Czechoslovakia and the Soviet Union. Particularly important in this regard was the contrasting behavior of the leaders of the dominant republics: Yel'tsin of Russia, Klaus of the Czech Republic, and Milošević of Serbia. When all is said and done, what mattered in the most proximate sense for how these states ended was whether the leader of the dominant republic embraced reform and accepted the end of the state (which describes both Yel'tsin and Klaus) or rejected reform and made noises about defending the state, while preparing at the same time to expand his republic's borders in the event of dismemberment (Milošević). These questions, then, and not the fact of leadership culpability, are what need to be addressed.

NATIONALISM

The other political argument focuses on nationalism. It has been argued for the Yugoslav case in particular that violence was a function of the development of Serbian, Slovene, and then Croatian nationalism. In particular, it has been suggested with respect to Serbia that violence grew out of what happened when the head of the Serbian League of Communists, Slobodan Milošević (who subsequently became president of Serbia and, then, in 1997 president of the former Yugoslavia), searching for new sources of political power in a time of economic crisis and regime disintegration, used nationalism and its powerful message of Serbian suffering at the hands of other national groups within Yugoslavia in order to mobilize political support (see, e.g., Cohen, 1997, 1993; Zimmerman, 1995; Kaplan, 1993; Silber and Little, 1996). It was the explosive interaction between nationalism and regime collapse, then, that produced the war in multinational and multireligious Yugoslavia.

The problem with this argument is that nationalism played a central role in the Soviet and Czechoslovak stories as well, yet did not have the same consequences for interrepublican and intrarepublican violence. This is because, as was highlighted in the preceding chapter, nationalism is capable of taking a wide variety of forms, connecting with a wide variety of ideologies, encouraging a wide variety of elite behaviors, and producing, as a result, an equally diverse set of political outcomes. This is even so, moreover, when, as in the Soviet, Yugoslav, and Czechoslovak cases, the

social, political, and economic contexts of nationalism appear to be so
similar.

The various forms, functions, and consequences of nationalism can be
seen, for example, if we look more closely at Boris Yel'tsin and the Russian
case and compare this with Milošević and Serbia.[1] For the ex-Communist
Yel'tsin, the key issue from 1989 to 1991 was strengthening his own base
of power, while weakening Gorbachev's, such that Yel'tsin could succeed
Gorbachev as the leader of the Soviet Union. The context, however, was
that nationalist movements, based in the republics, were developing
throughout the Soviet Union, but were far less in evidence in the core –
that is, in the Russian republic (which was in direct contrast to Serbia).
All of these considerations led Yel'tsin to construct a coalition that was
rooted in the Russian republic (especially after Yel'tsin was elected chair-
man of the Russian republican soviet by its members in May 1990, and
then president by the Russian republican electorate in June 1991), but
that extended outward in horizontal fashion to existing and emerging leaders in other Soviet republics. Thus, by late 1989 Yel'tsin became a team
player, if not a leader, in such popular republican games as challenging the
legal precedence of the center (or the war of laws); rewriting republican
constitutions in order to lay claim to both distinctiveness and sovereignty;
resisting central demands for revenue transfers; introducing republic-level
tax systems and, in some cases, republican ministries of foreign affairs; and
promulgating a series of bilateral treaties between republics that recognized republics as sovereign states and that dealt with a range of economic
and human rights issues.

Yel'tsin's coalition with the other republics was premised on three
arguments. One was that the socialist experiment was bankrupt, as was
Gorbachev's ambivalent attempts to reframe that experiment through major reform. Another was that center-periphery relations within the Soviet
Union had to be redrawn through a significant expansion of the powers of
the republics (in general, but, more specifically, of course, Russia or the
RSFSR). Finally, Yel'tsin supported a sharp break with the socialist past
through a rapid and full-scale transition from socialism to a liberal democratic order.[2] All three arguments were mechanisms through which
Yel'tsin could achieve his most cherished aim, supplanting Gorbachev, and
all three pointed straightforwardly to one strategy: constructing horizontal
alliances at the republican level against the center – and, not accidentally,
against its foremost representative, Gorbachev.

All of this gave Yel'tsin's nationalism a very different cast than what
one saw with Milošević in Serbia, despite the overarching similarity be-

tween the two cases with respect to the role of nationalism as a mechanism for mobilizing political support in a time of regime and state unraveling. First, Yel'tsin and Milošević had different targets. In Serbia, the key target was, first, the autonomous provinces of Kosovo and then Vojvodina, and then the republics – most notably, Slovenia, to be followed by Croatia and Bosnia. By contrast, in Russia the primary target was socialism, Gorbachev, and, thus, the center as a politically efficient summary of the first two.

At the same time, Yel'tsin's brand of nationalism was framed in center-periphery and not ethnic terms, and it was, if anything, contraction-ist in its geographical implications, rather than expansionist (though Yel'tsin's preference ordering was maintenance of the Soviet state, domi-nated by him, followed by an independent Russia, also dominated by him). In both cases, the end result was to encourage Yel'tsin to form coalitions with other nationalist leaders, even in those republics that had significant Russian minorities, rather than define these leaders, as was the case with Milošević, as threats to the national project.

Finally, nationalism in the Russian republican context was linked to rejection of socialism and the embrace of democracy – a linkage that may or may not have fit Yel'tsin's personal ideology, but, without question, served his political needs. By contrast, in Serbia nationalism was a mecha-nism for safeguarding the ancien regime – or, at the least, its political leader (Gagnon, 1994, 1994–1995). Thus, it was the way nationalism was framed and used and the extent to which the personal political needs of the leader were served by combining nationalism with reform that were the key variables distinguishing the Russian from the Serbian political leadership and, ultimately, peaceful versus violent dismemberment of the Soviet and Yugoslav states.

This leads us to an important aside. The variable definitions and roles of nationalism in the Serbian and Russian contexts serve as evidence for two observations about socialism and nationalism. First, just as socialism was both an antinational and an international project, so it was, at the same time, a profoundly national and, in diverse contexts, "inter-national" project (Connor, 1984; Verdery, 1991, 1993a, 1993b; Harsanyi and Ken-nedy, 1994; Slezkine, 1994). Second, while nationalism is generally thought to narrow the scope for political action, since it creates boundaries between legitimate and illegitimate participants and between acceptable and unacceptable goals, it also functions, at the same time, to widen the possibilities for action. This is because the nationalist message can be so easily combined with other messages, liberal and illiberal, centralist and decentralist, state-serving and state-destroying.

NATIONAL FEDERALISM

This leaves us with a final line of explanation: a focus on institutions. In his analysis of the development of nations in the Soviet Union and the breakup of the Soviet state, Rogers Brubaker (1996) has argued that the federal structure of this system during the socialist period contributed in important ways to the peaceful passing of both the regime and the state (but see Gligorov, 1992, for virtually the same argument, but opposite conclusions). His logic is inescapable. National federalism removed from the political field many of those issues and developments that have else-where fanned conflict when secessionist movements arise, when states confront the threatening prospect of losing territory, and when new states form along national lines. Thus, what was subtracted from the Soviet story by virtue of national federalism was, for example, a powerful center bent on maintaining the state and using its full coercive powers to destroy any and all secessionist challenges; the heated debates within nationalist movements and between them and the state over the question of where to fix the boundaries of the new political entities; and the dissension that arises within nationalist movements, once the political project shifts from challenging the territorial reach of the state to building a new regime and state (on divisions within social movements, see especially the rich historical studies of Luebke, 1997; Medrano, 1995).

It is true, as the discussions in Chapters 3 and 5 highlighted, that national federalism had the advantage of not just building nations and states within the state, but also in easing, as a result, the transition from one state to a number of new ones. However, while this argument seems to fit circumstances in not just the Soviet Union, but also Czechoslovakia, it can hardly account for Yugoslavia and its violent demise. Indeed, if well-established regional boundaries, highly resourceful republics, and nations with strong identities are so crucial to peaceful decomposition of the state along republican lines, as Brubaker seems to suggest, then it was in Yugoslavia, far more than in the Soviet Union and Czechoslovakia, where one would have expected the most trouble-free transition from one to many states. After all, it was there, and not in the Soviet Union and Czechoslovakia, where a decentralized federation had been long in place and had produced, even before the turmoil of the second half of the 1980s, unusually strong nations and unusually well-defined states-in-the-making.

Brubaker's analysis, therefore, like the earlier explanations of peaceful versus violent state dismemberment,[3] exhibits one key problem. In the absence of multiple cases and controls, the argument is neither well developed nor well tested.

This does not mean, however, that we should dismiss the role of institutional factors. Instead, what we need to do is to look more closely at patterns of institutional design – that is, at variations among these countries within the overarching similarities of socialism and national federalism. Once we do so, we can see some important contrasts in socialist institutions in Yugoslavia versus those in the Soviet Union and Czechoslovakia. And these differences are directly relevant to violent versus peaceful dismemberment of the state.

FEDERALISM VERSUS CONFEDERALISM

While all three of these socialist states were national-federal in form and this explains, along with the expansion of opportunities for systemic change in the 1980s, their common fate of dismembering along republican lines, their federal structures exhibited, nonetheless, several key differences. One core contrast was between actual federalism in the Soviet Union and Czechoslovakia, characterized by the existence of shared power based on territorial-administrative divisions, versus what could only be termed confederalism in Yugoslavia, or the domination of republics over the center.[4] Confederalism in Yugoslavia developed in response to a number of factors – for example, the passage of a new and highly decentralizing constitution in 1974; the decision after the Soviet invasion of Czechoslovakia in 1968 to allow the republics to have their own territorial defense forces; the growing segmentation of the Yugoslav market, including the banking system, along republican lines; and, finally, the death of Tito in 1980 and the introduction of collective decision-making units at the center that were based on equal votes allocated to each republic and province (along with the military as a "ninth" republic-province within central-level party organs).

As a result, Yugoslavia featured by the second half of the 1970s a clear pattern that was to characterize the political economy of that system until its end: an ever weakening economic and political center that was forced to work through the republics and their leadership in order to make and implement virtually all policies, to gather revenues, and to establish connections with the citizenry. This is the precise definition, we must observe, of confederalism (see Elazar, 1982, 1993; Riker, 1964). This meant, not surprisingly, that the Yugoslav republics were very strong. They had accumulated by the beginning of the 1980s the resources necessary to act as virtually independent economic and political agents (on the decentralization of Yugoslavia, especially from the 1970s onward, see Woodward,

1995a, 1995b; Bookman, 1990; Rusinow, 1988; Burg, 1983; S. Ramet, 1984; P. Ramet, 1985, Flaherty, 1989; Dubravčić, 1993).

The formal end of the Yugoslav state, then, was preceded for at least a decade by a process in which the state, precisely and ironically in strict accordance with ideological precepts, had withered away. Economic, political, and cultural sovereignty, therefore, had been parceled, and all three forms of sovereignty resided in the republics that made up the Yugoslav confederation – or what Sabrina Ramet (1984) aptly termed the Yugoslav international system. Thus, while struggles over power and reform both prefaced and caused a sudden and rapid decentralization of the Czechoslovak and Soviet states, a decentralized context was already well established in Yugoslavia by the time long-existing policy priorities and power networks came into serious question.

This had several important consequences for the process by which the Yugoslav state eventually ended. First, with the center eliminated as a key economic and political player, "domestic" politics and economics in Yugoslavia was in practice the politics and economics that went on within each of the republics and provinces. Second, with political power and economic resources locked in at the regional levels, the republics had both the means and the incentives to pursue distinct political and economic trajectories – and, not surprisingly, they did so. Finally, minus a center, bargaining within Yugoslavia became strictly horizontal – that is, interrepublican in form.

Thus, to focus on republican elites in particular, we can conclude with the following. What confederalism meant in Yugoslavia, even by the early 1980s, was that republican leaders were powerful; they were pitted against each other and had a long record of conflicts with each other; they represented quite different economic and political, as well as national constituencies; and they adopted, as a result, political and economic preferences that were widely divergent from each other. All this, plus the death of Tito, abysmal economic performance, and prolonged struggles over power and reform within and across the republics, ensured that Yugoslavia would become the first socialist federation in the region to dismember. All this meant as well that the process of state disintegration in Yugoslavia would be, by regional standards, unusually entangled with regime disintegration, unusually long, and unusually conflictual.

THE DOMINANT REPUBLICS

A second key difference among these federal states was in the institutional endowment of the dominant republic – or Serbia within Yugoslavia, Russia within the Soviet Union, and the Czech lands within Czechoslovakia. During the socialist period, neither Russia nor the Czech republic was in fact allotted the same institutional status as the, purportedly, "lesser" republics making up their federations. In particular, both of these leading republics were denied their own Communist parties, their own academies of sciences, their own media, their own ministries, their own secret police organizations, and the like (see especially Dunlop, 1993a, 1993b; Leff, 1988; Wolchik, 1991). Instead, their only connection was to the all-union, or central institutions of the party and the state – a connection open, as well, to all others in the system and tied to socialism, not the nation.

This asymmetric federalism reflected the impact of several considerations – that Russians and Czechs were the numerically dominant group, and not minorities, within their countries; that they had, as a result, no special "needs" and, thus, a weak case for institutional "boosting"; and that they were, if anything, *the* representatives of the center and socialism. This meant, in combination with their sheer size, that these republics were understood to require in effect institutional constraints, not empowerment. The analogy drawn by Yuri Slezkine (1994) for the Soviet Union, then, seems to apply equally well to Czechoslovakia during the socialist era. If we imagine each of these countries as an apartment building and their titular nations as the communal apartments within that building, then the Czechs, like the Russians within their federation, functioned in effect as "the hallways."

From this vantage point, it is hardly surprising, therefore, that Russian national identity was far less developed and far more confused with Soviet identity than the identities of, for example, the titular nations of the Baltic states, Armenia, and Georgia. As the historian Yuri Afanas'ev once responded to a question concerning his own identity as a Russian:

> This is difficult to say. I am Russian, certainly. I have been educated and brought up as a Russian. But I am more a Soviet, perhaps even a European, because it does not seem either necessary, useful, comfortable or even polite to be in the first place a Russian. (quoted in Laba, 1996:7)

The confusion between Soviet and Russian identity, along with institutional weakness and the absence of a clear historical tradition of statehood (see Vujačić, 1996), helps explain why Russian identity was so weak (see Drobizheva, Juk'man, Polishchuk, and Saboskul, 1992), and, just as importantly, why Russian nationalist mobilization during the Gorbachev era was the proverbial dog that did not bark (see Beissinger, 1995a). Indeed, by 1990, both eyeing circumstances in the other Soviet republics and joining in the battles against the center (including formal declaration of Russian sovereignty in June of that year), Russian politicians began to complain about the costs of institutional deficits. As Boris Yel'tsin bemoaned:

> If a clear violation of the Soviet of the Russian Federation takes place, then the [Russian republican] Supreme Soviet as the highest legislative organ of Russia must defend itself. But with what? It has no army, no KGB – what is it to defend its sovereignty with? It must do so with its laws. (quoted in Dunlop, 1993a: 31)

These worries led Russian leaders to take action on two fronts. They proposed a series of new, indigenous Russian institutions, and they converted all-union institutions into Russian ones (see especially Dunlop, 1993a; Mikheyev, 1996: 80–82). While the Czechs only did the same, once the state was in the process of formal dissolution, they did share precisely the same burdens as Russia. They lacked an institutional foundation for national identity, and they lacked as well a state tradition. This in turn meant that the Czechs, like the Russians, did not tend to mount nationalist movements, especially once socialism departed from the scene. Nor did they see their protests in the streets in 1989 as nationalist. Rather, it was defined as anti-Communist – not unlike the few demonstrations that took place in Russia during the late Gorbachev era.

However, if the Russian and Czech republics were institutionally weak, they were politically strong. During the socialist era, Russians and Czechs dominated their respective federations, not just in numerical terms, but also in terms of their representation in important economic, political, and military institutions. What we find for Russia and the Czech lands during the socialist era, therefore, is a contradictory state of affairs. As Gail Lapidus and Edward Walker (1995: 80) have observed for the Russian case:

> The position of Russia within [the] . . . federation . . . was an anomalous one. On the one hand, Russia was the imperial center, and Russians were the beneficiaries of this position. At the same time, the conflation of Russia with the Union deprived Russia of both the institutional and the cultural attributes of national statehood.[5]

There was, in short, a gap for the Czech republic, as well as for Russia, between political power and institutional resources. Looking ahead in our analysis, this gap played a key role in nudging developments within Russia and the Czech lands toward a particular type of nationalism. This was a form of nationalism that rejected the regime and socialism, but did not require in any way a reexamination of the national question; that was free of the convenient substitution of nationalism for communism that took place in many of the "lesser" republics (either through the rebirth of Communists as nationalists, or through the rise from below of a nationalist and anti-Communist movement); and that was able, as a consequence, to embrace both economic and political liberalization as valid and attractive ideological substitutes for socialism.

This in turn produced a particular set of positions on the state question. Continuity of borders was preferred, not just because it was the status quo and would maintain existing patterns of Czech and Russian domination within their states, but also because border changes were irrelevant to the main issue: regime transition. However, for precisely the same reasons, the nationalism of Russia and the Czech lands could accept, if necessary, the establishment of new state borders along existing republican lines. This was particularly the case if the partition of the state enhanced the prospects for full-scale liberalization of politics and economics in Russia and in the Czech lands.

The Yugoslav story provides a sharp contrast. Especially by the second half of the 1970s, Yugoslavia featured *equality* among the republics. Thus, the Serbian republic had precisely the same economic, political, social, and cultural institutions as existed in Slovenia, Croatia, Bosnia, Montenegro, and Macedonia. This meant that the resources of nation and state building, then, were far more available to Serbia and its leaders than to Russia, the Czech lands, and their respective political leadership. Moreover, Serbia, unlike Russia and the Czech lands, had a tradition of independent statehood – and, what is more, one that was established in the battlefield and that had long served as the foundation for Serbian national identity, if not pride.

At the same time, Serbia was denied the political power that the Russian and Czech republics enjoyed. While Serbs were in fact overrepresented in the officer corps of the military and in the secret police, they were underrepresented in *all* of those institutions responsible for making day-to-day decisions within Yugoslavia. This underrepresentation is evident, if we measure it by the gap between the Serbian weight in the population versus the voting shares of the Serbian republic within the party and the government. Put another way, it is only in Yugoslavia where we find political bodies at the top of the system during the socialist period that were based strictly on one republic or province (and its titular nation), one vote, rather than on other principles that might have recognized the size of Serbia and the Serbian population and, thus, worked more in Serbia's political favor. This imbalance, moreover, affected economics as much as politics.

The underrepresentation of Serbia and Serbs can also be viewed from the standpoint of perception. For Serbs, what mattered most, perhaps, was the gap between their political representation and the Serbian presumption of their right to be the first among equals. This presumption reflected the impact of a variety of historical factors, including Serbia's prior history as a state, Serbian sacrifice of that state to the formation of a larger Yugoslav constellation after World War I, and Serbian success when bargaining over state formation in defining that new and larger entity as unitary, centralized, and dominated by Serbia, complete with the Serbian royal family (see Banac, 1984; Vujačić, 1996).

As a consequence, it is not surprising that Serbs were resentful of Yugoslav developments following the adoption of the 1974 constitution, since their status and power within the federation, already too limited in their view, declined sharply with decentralization and the establishment of full equality among the republics and provinces. Nor is it surprising that the crisis in Kosovo, which began in 1980 (and kept reappearing), angered Serbs and quickly became a touchstone for the rapid development of Serbian nationalism. Kosovo was a province having great symbolic meaning for Serbs, given both its impressive collection of Serbian churches and other cultural artifacts, and given as well its role as the site where Serbia had been defeated by the Ottoman Empire in 1389. At the same time, contemporary developments within Kosovo summarized all too efficiently all that had gone wrong with the Yugoslav experiment – given, for example, the allocation of equal votes to Kosovo and Serbia; the declining proportion of the population that was Serbian (which was interpreted to be a function less of differential birthrates than harassment); and the increasingly restive nature of what had become a very large Albanian majority.

What appeared in Serbia during the socialist era, then, was a pattern opposite to that found in the Russian and Czech republics: considerable institutional resources at the republican level joined with considerable limits on political and economic influence within the federation. Again, looking ahead, it was that particular combination of strengths and weaknesses – or the joining of resources with resentments – that opened Serbian leaders and publics to a version of nationalism that was the mirrored opposite to that found in the Russian and Czech republics. In particular, while the grievances underlying Russian and Czech nationalism focused on the costs of socialism, the concerns of the Serbs targeted two issues: the form of the state and the maltreatment of the nation. The issue of socialism, therefore, was not at the center of the picture.

At the same time, the solution to these grievances also varied. For Russian and Czech nationalists, the goal was to end socialism, establish a democratic and capitalist regime operating within a federal state, and, failing federalism, accede to the dismemberment of the state along strictly republican lines. This alternative had two advantages. The Czechs and the

Russians could keep the central institutions as their own, and they could pursue their liberal agenda, unencumbered by their less liberal and at times recalcitrant neighbors in the "near abroad." By contrast, the solution for Serbian nationalists was reforming socialism, recentralizing the state, and, failing that, establishing in the wreckage of the state a new and Greater Serbia (and see Modrić and Djula, 1994, on "ethnic cleansing").

Thus, the violent end of Yugoslavia reflected not just the fact that the dominant republic there had a particular brand of nationalism that differed from its Russian and Czech counterparts with respect to grievances and goals. It was also that the Serbian leadership's second-order preferences were conducive to war in the event of state dismemberment, whereas the second-order preferences entertained by the Russian and Czech leadership, again in the event of state dismemberment, were not.

This leads us to a final institutional factor that distinguishes Yugoslavia from the Soviet Union and Czechoslovakia and that contributed in important ways to whether these states ended violently or peacefully. That factor is the contrast in the structure, the mission, and the role of the military.

SOCIALIST MILITARIES

States can use words, laws, money, and/or armies to protect their boundaries against secessionist pressures. All three of the federalized socialist states used words, laws, and money to defend themselves. Only in Yugoslavia, however, did the military (the Yugoslav National Army, or JNA) play a central role in the dismemberment of the state. This occurred, initially, through military intervention to save the state – as when the JNA sent in tanks in response to the Slovene removal of federal signs along its borders and Slovene occupation of border outposts and customs offices. Later, as in Croatia and Bosnia, the JNA again intervened on the basis of a similar rationale. In these cases, however, the JNA had allies within the republics: the secessionist Serbian minorities within both of these republics (along with the free-riding Croatian minority in Bosnia).

By contrast, the military stood on the sidelines while the Czechoslovak state was dismantled. In the Soviet Union, the military was deployed, but in minimalist, short-term, and rather halfhearted fashion – as in the Baltic states in early 1991 and as with the participation of segments of the military in the attempted coup d'etat in August 1991. However, when the Soviet state was formally dismantled in December 1991, the military was not a participant. Indeed, throughout the fall of 1991, the Soviet military had consistently resisted invitations to become more involved (see Dunlop, 1993a).

The contrast, therefore, is between an activist military in Yugoslavia, which contributed significantly to the violent dismemberment of that state, versus a passive military in Czechoslovakia and the Soviet Union, which contributed in both cases to a peaceful end to these states. The question then becomes: why the difference in these three socialist militaries?

One distinction that can be drawn is in the structure of these institutions. The confederal character of the Yugoslav party and state had created an unusually confused chain of military command. While the Soviet Union also presented some problems in this regard (see, e.g., Rice, 1987; Nichols, 1993; Kolkowicz, 1967; Colton, 1979; Holloway, 1989–1990; Busza, 1994), as did Czechoslovakia (because of changes in the Warsaw Pact following the invasion of Czechoslovakia – see Jones, 1981), the Yugoslav case represented an extreme variation on a general socialist problem (see especially Perlmutter and Leogrande, 1982; Barany, 1993). In particular, in Yugoslavia authorization to deploy military force at home and abroad could come, variously, from the state and the party collective presidencies (separately or together), from the prime minister, from the minister of defense, and/or possibly from representatives of the military at the highest levels of the party and the state (see, in particular, Gow, 1992; Remington, 1996).

To this must be added two related points. One is that the JNA had close connections in particular with one republic: Serbia. This reflected, among other things, Serbian historical connections to the military, the convergent interest of the military and the Serbian republic in maintaining a centralized and socialist state, and the overrepresentation of Serbs in the officer corps of the JNA.

The other is that only in Yugoslavia do we find the existence of territorially based militias that were under the control of the republics and that had unclear linkages – in terms of function as well as command and control – to the central military, let alone the central political structure. This proved to be crucial in the process of state building at the republican level and in the leakage of weaponry to minority populations. It was also important in the brief skirmishes in Slovenia, where the wars of secession began and where the Slovene territorial defense forces were pitched against the JNA.[6]

When combined, all of these factors point to a simple conclusion: the potential for praetorian politics was very high indeed in Yugoslavia. What further contributed to such a possibility was the legitimacy accorded the

JNA as a domestic political actor. Again, the contrast with the Soviet Union and Czechoslovakia is sharply etched. In Yugoslavia, the military's mission was defined as much in domestic as in international terms. This reflected such factors as the historical role of the military in defending the Yugoslav state and Yugoslav society against fascism and in building support for socialism from the ground up during World War II; the interdependence following the revolution between the legitimacy of the regime and socialism, on the one hand, and the legitimacy of the military, on the other (see especially Gow, 1992); the political influence accorded the JNA as a consequence of its role as one of the few institutional representatives of the center and, thus, of the Yugoslav idea; and, finally, the fusion of the domestic and international functions of the military, given the equal weight placed on domestic and foreign threats to the survival of Yugoslavia and Yugoslav socialism.

Because of these and other factors, then, the JNA was a powerful domestic political player throughout the socialist era in Yugoslavia. This was indicated, for example, by its direct representation at the highest level of the party apparatus (beginning with the Croatian crisis in the early 1970s), and by a twenty-year history of domestic interventions – for example, in the Croatian crisis of the early 1970s, in Kosovo in 1981 (where martial law was declared for the first time in postwar Yugoslavia), in Slovenia in 1988 (albeit primarily political in form), and, again, in Kosovo in 1989 (see especially Vasić and Švarm, 1995b; Hadžić, 1994).[7]

It is fair to say, then, that socialist Yugoslavia was held together by three forces: Tito, the party, and the army. When Tito died and the party became fully republicanized by the early 1980s, all that was left to defend both the regime of socialism and the state of Yugoslavia – and the only organ that defined its mission in precisely those terms – was the military. The military, in short, came to be the only counterweight to the decentralization and the interrepublican conflicts over reform and power that dominated Yugoslav politics during the 1980s. And the military was, for the same reasons, easily threatened by developments during that decade – not just the political and economic turmoil of that period, which, characteristically, threatened both the state and socialism, but also the reduction in the military's legitimacy and resources, given direct and unprecedented criticisms of the military in the liberalized atmosphere of Slovenia in the mid-1980s, on the one hand, and, on the other, cuts in its defense budget, beginning in the second half of the 1970s (see Woodward, 1995a: 63, 66–67; Gow, 1992; Vasić and Švarm, 1995b).

The involvement of the military in the process of Yugoslav dismemberment, then, was not surprising. There was a long history of such interventions, and the process of secession challenged the dual mission of the military to defend the state and socialism. As Miloš Vasić and Filip Švarm (1995b: 12) have summarized:

> The process of the destruction of Yugoslavia can be understood best through the history of the ruination of the military; one without the other cannot be understood. Confronting choices between watching over communism or the state, the military managed to lose both.

The Czechoslovak case could not be more different. There, the military was kept separate from civilian life in general and domestic politics in particular. This was typical of those Eastern European militaries that were fully integrated into the Warsaw Pact structure – a point that was duly noted in Chapter 4, when I analyzed the reasons behind the peaceful collapse of communism in the Soviet bloc. In the case of the Soviet Union, the military was also subservient to civilian authority – a practice that was rooted not just in decisions taken by the Bolsheviks after the civil war and the demobilization that followed, but also in the long expanse of Russian history prior to the socialist epoch. In contrast to, say, Latin America, dictatorship in Russia has long been premised on civilian control over the military.

In addition, the role of the Soviet military was clearly defined in international and not domestic terms, as one would expect for a highly professional military situated within a long-established regime and state and concerned with all those issues involved in building and then maintaining global power status. Indeed, it was this mission and the ways in which the war in Afghanistan and the Gorbachev reforms produced a divided and immobilized, rather than a divided and interventionist military, that allowed the Soviet military to function as a bystander while leaders of the Soviet republics began to divy up the state (see, e.g., Holloway, 1989–1990; Meyer, 1991–1992; Lepingwell, 1994). Finally, unlike Yugoslavia, the overrepresentation of Russians in the officer corps was not combined with a dominant republic rich in institutions. Thus, Yel'tsin, with his political base in the RSFSR, lacked the institutional capacity to deploy the military in order to achieve his aims, even if he had so wanted.

THE GAMES OF STATE DISMEMBERMENT

Despite the commonalities of socialism and federalism, then, there were, nonetheless, three key differences in the design of Yugoslavia versus the Soviet Union and Czechoslovakia – differences that affected in important ways how these states came to an end. In particular, the Yugoslav federation was far more decentralized than its Czechoslovak and Soviet counterparts. This produced what was by Soviet and Czechoslovak standards an unusually weak center, and republics that were unusually strong, distinctive, and combative.

At the same time, the dominant republic within Yugoslavia, or Serbia, was rich in institutional resources, but impoverished with respect to political power – a pattern precisely opposite to that found in the dominant republics of the Soviet Union and Czechoslovakia, or Russia and the Czech lands, respectively. This produced two kinds of nationalisms that had enormous implications for how the state ended. One, as in Serbia, was ethnic in content; based upon a convergence between strong national institutions and considerable national resentments; and committed to socialism within a recentralized state, or, failing that, within a new state significantly larger in size than the existing Serbian republic. The other form of nationalism, as in Russia and the Czech lands, was primarily civic in emphasis; constrained in its nationalist agenda by weak republican institutions and a tradition of political dominance; and committed, above all, to ending socialism and constructing a liberal order in its place. As for the larger state context within which this transition would occur, the preference of both Czech and Russian political leaders was for either building a genuinely federal system, or, if that were out of the question, new states that corresponded precisely in their borders to the existing lines demarcating the republics.

A final institutional contrast was that the Yugoslav National Army was the guardian of socialism and the state; it had long functioned as a central player in the domestic politics of socialist Yugoslavia; and it continued to do so, once the regime and state began to unravel. By contrast, both the Soviet and the Czechoslovak militaries were, by mission and practice, outward-looking, not inward-playing. This tradition continued, once the regime and the state began their exit from the political stage.

How, then, did these institutional differences affect the actual process of state dismemberment? Much of the answer to that question has already been provided – in this and the previous chapter. However, one useful way of summarizing these developments in a manner that is both parsimonious and comparative is to treat the dissolution of the Soviet, Czechoslovak, and Yugoslav states as a game. Indeed, what is striking about such an exercise is that the assumptions underlying the notion of a game – which are often violated in games constructed by social scientists – are in fact met in these three instances of state dissolution (see Morrony, 1994). Thus, it can be argued that there was in fact a limited number of key players in each of the three cases – in particular, Mikhail Gorbachev and Boris Yel'tsin in the Soviet case; Sloboban Milošević, Franjo Tudjman (the leader of Croatia), Milan Kučan (the leader of Slovenia), and the JNA in the Yugoslav case; and Václav Klaus and Vladimír Mečiar (the leaders of what came to be the Czech Republic and Slovakia, respectively). At the same time, the preferences of these players are easy to construct and easy to rank, given what has already been argued in this chapter and the one that preceded it. Finally, in all three cases the state ended following bargaining over the design and the future of the state.

From the perspective of gaming, we can argue that the peaceful end of the Soviet Union and Czechoslovakia was a product of two factors, each of which flowed directly from their institutional conditions during the socialist period. First, the military was excluded from the game. Second, because of the particular combination of political power, yet institutional deficits within the Czech and Russian republics, the leader of each of these two dominant republics defined nationalism in a manner that minimized resentments toward other nations, and that focused, instead, on the following preferences: the rejection of socialism; support of a transition to capitalism and democracy; and support of the continuation of the state, albeit one that was genuinely federal in its functioning.

With regard to the final preference, which was, unlike the first two, negotiable and not fixed, a second option was entertained – that is, in the event of state breakup, support for dismemberment along strictly republican lines. What made the fourth option necessary was the behavior, or at least the strategic threats, of the other republics making up the federation. What made it tolerable for both the Russian and Czech leadership was the bonus of getting control over the institutions of the center in the bargain, and getting what would be, in all likelihood, an easier and more rapid transition to capitalism and democracy, given the exit of those regions likely to stall, if not sabotage the liberal agenda. Thus, while the ideal outcome was liberal democracy and capitalism in an integrated state, the second most attractive outcome was liberal democracy and capitalism in a reduced state. In this sense, the end of both the Czechoslovak and Soviet states was peaceful, because the leader of the dominant republic in each of these cases could still get what he most wanted.

Within these similarities between the Soviet and Czechoslovak cases, however, there were several differences – differences that, nonetheless, contributed as well, albeit in contrasting ways, to the peaceful end of these two states. Let us turn, first, to the Soviet case. What helped that state dismember peacefully, in addition to the reasons already noted, were the following characteristics peculiar to the Soviet context: the sheer size of the

Russian Federation, which made losing the larger entity more palatable; the guarantee, highly attractive to Yel'tsin, that Gorbachev would be finally defeated, not because he was deposed, but, rather, because the country he led was in effect deposed; and the halfway house represented by the Commonwealth for Independent States, which allowed Russia to have a forum within which to express its regional dominance, while also allowing the leaders of the other republics, with their varying commitments to independent statehood and their varying fears of rupture with Russia, the attractive option of being at the same time independent of, yet still connected to, Russia.

Finally, the very structure of struggle during the Gorbachev era had the complicating effect of diversifying the domestic trajectories of the republics, which meant, in effect, a dispersion of republican preferences. At the same time, however, there were important compensatory pressures that overrode these differences – in particular, the incentives for interrepublican cooperation as a result of their shared opposition to the center in general and Gorbachev and his approach to reform in particular. It was the latter that dominated the former, and that produced ratification of a series of bilateral treaties between Russia and other republics in the year and one-half preceding the end of the state. These treaties assured the lesser republics of continued access to the Russian economy in exchange for legal guarantees concerning the security and the rights of Russian minority populations. As a result, cooperation, not conflict dominated the game of Soviet state dismemberment, and Russian fears about the nationals in the "near abroad" – which could have challenged Russian acceptance of state dismemberment or tempted Russia to expand on its republican borders – were put to rest.

Yel'tsin's strategy of allying with the other republics and using interrepublican treaties to cement those alliances, therefore, had four consequences. One was intentional: to isolate and, thus, weaken Gorbachev and thereby empower Yel'tsin. The other three were accidental: to speed the process of state dissolution along republican lines; to enhance the prospects for Russian acceptance of state dissolution; and to guarantee, as a result, that the end of the Soviet state would proceed peacefully.

The division of the Czechoslovak state was different in the sense that there was no center in this instance that could function, as in the Soviet Union, to override the political and economic differences between the republics and to forge, as a result, interrepublican cooperation. Instead, such cooperation evolved in the Czechoslovak context through rather different channels. One key factor was the absence, in direct contrast to both the Soviet Union and Yugoslavia, of large minority populations residing outside of the republic-states. Another, again in sharp contrast to the other two cases, was the relatively limited differences in socioeconomic terms between the two halves of Czechoslovakia – reflecting, in large measure, the success (obviously more in economic than political terms!) of regional redistribution as a mechanism for state integration and political stability in the years following the crisis of 1968, with its defining features of reform communism, Slovak nationalism, and the Soviet invasion (see Brada, 1994; Kaiser, 1994).

Finally, and again distinct to Czechoslovakia when compared with the Soviet Union and Yugoslavia, was a more proximate factor of importance that was the end result in effect of the other two: the existence of relatively limited differences in the preferences of the two leaders responsible for dismantling the state: Václav Klaus and Vladimír Mečiar (and see Wolchik, 1994, 1995, 1997, on why the Czechoslovak game was two- rather than three-person, or, more precisely, why President Václav Havel was excluded). Both of these leaders rejected socialism, and both favored economic and political liberalization (though democratization was another question, especially for Mečiar). Moreover, both were backed in their views by public opinion in their respective portions of the country (see Wolchik, 1994). Where they differed was in the details. Klaus wanted fast economic reform and one federalized state, whereas Mečiar wanted slower economic reform and, for reasons of domestic political support within Slovakia, a confederalized state (with the latter demand often embedded in a larger and not-so-veiled threat of actual divorce). What this meant was that, while first-order preferences did not match, second-order preferences could, and, given the electoral results of the mid-1992 elections, eventually did. Thus, Klaus could get the economic reform he wanted and maintain political power in the Czech lands, and Mečiar could do the same in Slovakia. Whereas neither the public nor the president, Václav Havel, wanted to divide the country, such a division made sense because of the congruent political and economic interests of the two adversaries, Klaus and Mečiar. In this way, the Czechoslovak state ended, but without virtually anyone, including Vladimír Mečiar, who really championed that outcome.

In many ways, Klaus, exactly like Yel'tsin, settled for less state, but, by shedding the periphery, gained more reform and, arguably, more power. And for precisely these reasons, the dismemberment of Czechoslovakia at the end of 1992, like the end of the Soviet Union a year earlier, was a velvet rather than a violent divorce.

The game of state dismemberment in Yugoslavia was different on all counts. First and most obviously, the military was a player. Second, Yugoslavia combined in many respects the worst of both the Czechoslovak and Soviet worlds, but without any of their compensatory assets. Thus, like Czechoslovakia, the bargaining process was interrepublican, and, like the Soviet Union, the differences among republics and, thus, among their leaders, was substantial. As a result, the Yugoslav game was one in which republics were very different, but lacked the incentives to identify common ground. Conflict, in short, was built into the game of dismemberment, and this conflict, if anything, expanded, when moving down the scale of republican elite preferences. Finally, the combination of resources and resentment in the dominant republic produced a form of Serbian nationalism that actually widened the differences among republican leaders with respect to the future of socialism, the state, and reform. This guaranteed that the state would end, and increased the likelihood that the process would be violent.

What guaranteed that violence would be central to the Yugoslav story of state breakup were three factors. Two have already been noted: the particular focus of Serbian nationalism, along with its capacity to reproduce a similar form of nationalism in Croatia; and the role of the JNA as an extension, at first accidental and then later quite deliberate, of Serbian national interests. The third was the presence of large Serbian minorities in both Croatia and Bosnia. This was, it must be emphasized, a factor that was less important in and of itself (as the Russian case reminds us) than through its interaction with those institutional characteristics, already noted, that distinguished Yugoslavia from the other two socialist federations.

Thus, the institutions that made Yugoslavia unique among the socialist federations in eastern Europe were precisely what guaranteed that the end of this state, unlike the end of the Soviet Union and Czechoslovakia, would be violent. However, it is worth noting at the same time that Yugoslavia's story, while unusual for the region, is, from a larger comparative perspective, typical – and typically tragic.

CONCLUSIONS

The institutional design of socialism, therefore, did not just subvert the regime and the state. It also played a crucial role in shaping *how* regimes and states ended. Thus, to combine the arguments presented in this chapter with those in the previous two chapters, we can draw the following conclusions.

First, socialist regimes collapsed in large measure because their design undermined over time both economic performance and the political and economic monopoly of the Communist Party. Second, the socialist federations, along with the Soviet bloc, also collapsed because of the institutions that had long defined them, and because the monopolies upon which they were based had been similarly deregulated. Third, what differentiated regime from state and bloc collapse was, simply, whether the setting during the socialist era featured one national-territorial unit, as with the regime, or more than one, connected in radial fashion to the center, as with the bloc and the socialist federations. Finally, what accounted for whether the process of dissolution was peaceful or violent was, again, institutional design. In the case of the socialist regimes, what mattered was, simply, membership in the Soviet bloc. In the case of the federal states of the Soviet Union, Yugoslavia, and Czechoslovakia, the explanation was more complex. In particular, what seemed to be crucial was the decentralization of the federation, the power versus the institutional resources of the dominant republic, and the mission and the role of the military in the domestic political arena.

INSTITUTIONS AND OPPORTUNITIES: CONSTRUCTING AND DECONSTRUCTING REGIMES AND STATES

Institutions constrain not only the ends to which behavior should be directed, but the means by which those ends are achieved. They provide individuals with the vocabularies of motives and with a sense of self. They generate not only that which is valued, but the rules by which it is calibrated and distributed.
Roger Friedland and Robert R. Alford (1991: 251)

From mid-1989 to the close of 1992, state socialism collapsed in Eastern Europe and then in the Soviet Union; the Soviet bloc emptied and then formally dismantled; and the Yugoslav, Soviet, and Czechoslovak states dismembered. In a mere three and one-half years, virtually every defining feature of the postwar European landscape – and, thus, of the postwar international order – had been dramatically and irretrievably altered. To put the matter succinctly: there was, quite suddenly, one superpower instead of two; one Germany, not two; and one Europe (at least in the making) in the place of two. If the new Europe was reduced in these respects, however, it was also expanded in others, as twenty-two new states arose from the wreckage of Yugoslavia, the Soviet Union, and Czechoslovakia. Thus ended the remarkable forty-six-year run of stable state boundaries in Europe. With the war in Yugoslavia from 1991 to 1995, moreover, what also came to a close was the equally remarkable postwar "long peace," a product in part of those stable state boundaries (see Gaddis, 1986; but see Bunce, 1993).

These dramatic events bring to the fore a number of important questions. Why did both the Soviet bloc and the European socialist dictatorships collapse, and why did they do so when and how they did? Particularly surprising in this regard was both the regionwide character of regime collapse and the largely peaceful means by which both the domestic and the international regimes of socialism ended.

Equally puzzling are the following: why did the Yugoslav, Soviet, and Czechoslovak states end and, again, end when and how they did? Why were these three states replaced – and so quickly – by such a large number of new and unexpectedly durable successor states? Why did the dissolution of Yugoslavia occur through violence and the dismemberment of the Soviet Union and Czechoslovakia through a peaceful process, despite their commonalities of socialism, federalism, cultural pluralism, and regime transition? Finally, what was the relationship among the collapse of socialism, the bloc, and the state – a relationship strongly suggested by the temporal and geographical proximity of these developments?

APPROACH

The purpose of this book has been to provide answers to these questions. I have done so by constructing several cross-country comparisons, each of which was tailor-made – through its particular combination of similarities and differences – to address the issue at hand. Thus, when I was interested in explaining why socialist regimes ended and why this development was regionwide, I compared all of the European socialist dictatorships with each other, searching for those similarities that could, plausibly and theoretically, account for their common demise. Although such an approach is strong in identifying necessary conditions, particularly when the number of cases is so large (or nine in this context), it can be less helpful in specifying sufficient conditions (see, e.g., King, Keohane, and Verba, 1994; Dion, 1998; Ragin, 1998). For that, one needs to vary outcomes, which in this study was accomplished by comparing socialist regimes with other dictatorships (sustainable and disintegrating) and with themselves at earlier points in their history when they seemed to be both stable and durable. By expanding the terrain of comparison and by introducing a diachronic element into the analysis, I was able to speak directly and precisely not just to the questions of why socialism ended and did so on a regional scale, but also why it collapsed when it did.

When the focus shifted to *variations* in how and when socialist dictatorships fell, I again compared all of these regimes with each other, but looked in this case for the differences among them that could explain contrasts in the timing and process of regime dissolution. What made this comparison so useful was that I was able to control for both many likely causes *and* the same outcome for nine countries, yet have, nonetheless, significant variation in the dependent variable – or the process of regime transition.

The final set of concerns addressed in this study centered on state dismemberment. Here, I introduced two more sets of comparisons. One involved identifying what the Soviet Union, Yugoslavia, and Czechoslovakia had in common and what differentiated them in turn from other states in the region that had also been socialist but that had managed to undergo regime transition with their borders intact. This exercise allowed me to locate answers to the question of why the Yugoslav, Soviet, and Czechoslovak states ended. Because these three states ended differently, however, I introduced yet another (and final) comparison – in this instance, among the three states that dissolved. What interested me here was why the Soviet Union and Czechoslovakia disintegrated peacefully and Yugoslavia through war. The goal, therefore, was to isolate those characteristics which the Soviet Union and Czechoslovakia had in common, which were absent or took a different form in Yugoslavia, and which were directly related to violent versus peaceful state division. What made this comparison so illuminating was that it followed the earlier comparison establishing similarities, distinct within the region, among these three states. Thus, various plausible causes for violent versus peaceful state dissolution were thereby eliminated in a comparative context that featured another, overriding similarity: the outcome, common to Yugoslavia, Czechoslovakia, and the Soviet Union, but distinct within the post-Communist region, of state dismemberment.

Through a method that might be termed cascading comparisons, I sought answers to the variety of questions posed by the collapse of socialism, the Soviet bloc, and socialist states. All of these comparisons were informed by one guiding premise. The universe of possible explanations – always too large in any comparative enterprise, no matter how well controlled – had to be limited. This I did by developing an approach that brought together in streamlined fashion many of the factors identified as crucial in the literature on nationalism, secession, revolution, and social movements. This approach emphasized the interaction between two factors. The first, more long-term in nature, was the institutional design of socialism – as a regime, a state, and a regional bloc – and the impact of these institutions over time on the incentives, the resources, and the identities of key players. The other, more proximate to the collapse of these systems and these states, entailed major changes in the political opportunity structure brought on by such developments in the 1980s as leadership succession, intraelite struggles over economic and political reforms, and shifts in the structure and the stability of the international system. These two factors, or the interaction between the institutional logic of socialism and a growing elasticity in its domestic and international environment, provided a powerful explanation of why, when, and how socialism, the bloc, and the Soviet, Yugoslav, and Czechoslovak states disintegrated.

What made this account all the more compelling, moreover, were two additional considerations. This explanation worked for *all* of the puzzles addressed in this book – an outcome satisfying in itself but particularly so, given the seemingly close linkages with respect to time and geography among these nonetheless different developments of regime, bloc, and state dissolution. At the same time, the focus on institutions and opportunities proved to be superior to a variety of alternative lines of argument – arguments suggested by both theoretical work on nationalism, revolution, and secession and by a series of studies of the region that were single country and/or single issue in their focus.

In the remainder of this chapter, I summarize the arguments presented in this book and then draw some of their implications for issues central to both global trends and scholarly debates in comparative politics. Thus, I use this study, supplemented by other research, to rethink certain aspects of the role of institutions in politics, the meaning and the causes of revolution, the origins and consequences of nationalism, and the place of history and institutions in domestic and international regime transitions. This discussion will lead us, in turn, to a final methodological issue that spans all of these subjects of study: the role of area knowledge versus theory in comparative inquiry.

CENTRAL ARGUMENTS

All socialist regimes featured three core characteristics: an ideological commitment to rapid transformation, a fusion of politics and economics, and domination by a single and highly penetrative party. These systems, therefore, featured an extraordinarily powerful party-state and a weak and dependent society. This description applies as well to the structure of the Soviet bloc and socialist federations, albeit with a change in the identities of the key units. Thus, just as the Communist Party dominated domestic societies, so within the Soviet bloc the Soviet Union dominated Eastern

Europe, and within the socialist federations the center dominated the republics.

As detailed in Chapters 2 and 3, however, the longer-term impact of socialist institutions was quite opposite to what party elites intended. This was largely because the very design of these systems functioned over time to divide and weaken the powerful, homogenize and strengthen the weak, and undercut economic performance. As a result, the rate of economic growth declined; upper levels of the party had reduced economic control over the lower levels; the Soviet Union leaked money to Eastern Europe; and the center within socialist federations leaked economic resources to the republics. At the same time, because of fusion between politics and economics in socialist dictatorships, power was redistributed along with economic resources. Thus, socialist societies became more autonomous and more powerful when bargaining with the party-state – a pattern that was replayed within both the Soviet bloc and the socialist federations, with the client states and the republics in these cases gaining leverage when bargaining with the Soviet Union and the center, respectively.

The strong, in short, grew weaker, and the weak stronger. By its very design, then, socialism had deregulated itself – over time and by accident. This, in turn, called the very survival of the regime, the bloc, and the federal states into question. Economic growth and the maintenance of the party's economic and political monopoly – and the monopoly of the Soviet Union within the bloc, and the center within the federations – were, after all, the necessary conditions for the continuation of socialism as a domestic and a regional order.

The events of the 1980s functioned in effect to formalize this process of deregulation. What happened at that time was a regionwide succession crisis prompted by the deaths of three long-serving leaders: Tito, Hoxha, and Brezhnev. While Tito's, Hoxha's, and Brezhnev's deaths unleashed major struggles over power in Yugoslavia, Albania, and the Soviet Union, respectively, the Soviet succession, because of the bloc's structure and membership, had regional reach. As a result, *all* of the states in the eastern half of Europe were strongly affected, if not destabilized, by succession struggles. These developments combined in turn with several others: a protracted and bitter intraelite struggle over economic and political liberalization (which reflected the interaction between economic crises and successions that involved not just a change in leaders, but also a change in political generations and coalitions), and, in the international realm, a loosening of both national and state boundaries in Europe as a consequence of détente and the Helsinki process. With the domestic and regional environments of European socialism already fragmented, these factors produced by the end of the 1980s an interrelated collapse of the regime, the Soviet bloc, and the federal states. This was the case, moreover, whether radical reforms were introduced, as with Gorbachev in the Soviet Union, or avoided through a prolonged intraelite stalemate, as in Yugoslavia and Poland throughout most of the 1980s.

Thus, it was the interaction between institutions and opportunities that explains why socialist regimes ended and did so when they did, and why regime collapse was quickly followed by the disintegration of both the Soviet bloc and the federal states — with the former breaking up along the borders of the member states and the latter along the borders of the constituent republics. All that differed with respect to the collapse of these three arenas of socialism, then, was whether the process was just ideological, as with regime transition, or both ideological and territorial, as with the end of both the bloc and the federal states.

The dissolution of socialism, the bloc, and socialist states, therefore, can be described in four ways. It was a process that was at once abrupt and long in the making. At the same time, it was a process that spoke to the power of socialist institutions — in defining, defending, and, ultimately, destroying the system. From yet another perspective, it was a process that was remarkably similar in its dynamics, whether the result was hiving off society from the regime, Eastern Europe from the Soviet Union, or republics from the state. The key factor in all three cases was redistribution of political power and economic resources — from the first to the next tier of the system.

Finally, the collapse of socialism, the bloc, and the state can be described as a process that was in each of these institutional contexts *nationalist* to the core. This was because socialist institutions had forged communities of common feelings, and these communities had developed over time the desire and the capacity to challenge the legitimacy of the larger ideological and spatial community within which they were were embedded — whether the particular form this took was societies poised against the party-state, Eastern European countries poised against the Soviet Union, or republics poised against the center. The collapse of socialism, the bloc, and the state, therefore, was not just a matter of regime- and state-rejection; it was also a matter of national liberation. Whether the result was a liberal or an illiberal regime and whether the bearers — or the interpreters — of nationalism were anti-Communists, Communists, or ex-Communists do not detract from this conclusion. Nationalism, constructed in large measure by socialism and as ideologically wanton in the socialist context as in others, was responsible for bringing down the regime, the bloc, and, in the federal cases, the state. At the same time, it was also nationalism that was responsible for substituting new regimes and newly sovereign states in their place – whether the latter involved new borders, as with the republics that became states, or the same borders, as with the Eastern European countries that liberated themselves from Soviet domination.

RELATED ARGUMENTS

In the process of explaining why socialist regimes and states dissolved and, what is more, dissolved when they did, I also examined a series of related issues. One was why the collapse of socialism was regionwide. Part of the answer has already been furnished: the commonalities of socialism put all of these regimes in effect in the same listing boat, and the turmoil of the 1980s assured that the boat would sink. Thus, despite their many differences from each other before and during socialism, the Soviet bloc regimes, Albania, and Yugoslavia all suffered in similar ways from the redistributive dynamics of socialism, and they were all exposed during the 1980s to a substantial loosening of the political and economic, domestic and international environments within which they were located.

However, this leaves open the question of diffusion and demonstration effects, as well as the impact of Gorbachev. Here, I argued that all three were important. The structure of the Soviet bloc had created geographically proximate and identical regimes, and it guaranteed that struggles over power and reform in the Soviet Union would travel westward, would become more radical and destabilizing in the process, and, finally, would tend to loop back to the east.

If diffusion was important, moreover, so were demonstration effects. The collapse of socialism in Poland and Hungary and the willingness of Gorbachev to stand by while that happened changed the calculus of protest significantly in the more hard-line regimes in Eastern Europe that bordered these countries – in particular, East Germany and Czechoslovakia. Once mass protests broke out in these two countries, the others to the south of them followed suit (and see Martiniello, 1995, for effects on Western Europe as well).

Finally, Gorbachev was crucial – in introducing a series of reforms that undercut the cohesion and the power of the Eastern European parties, in pressing Eastern Europe to follow the Soviet precedent while withdrawing the Soviet military umbrella, and in not just watching socialist regimes unravel to the west of him, but also throwing his support to reformers within these parties and, in many cases, to the opposition forces as well.

He did all this because his overriding concern was saving Soviet socialism and protecting his reforms and the domestic-international coalition on which those reforms and his own power were based. In trying to rescue socialism in one country, however, Gorbachev lost both socialism and the country.

This leads us to another set of issues addressed in this study – in this case, focusing on variations in when and how socialism and socialist states ended. One of the most unusual aspects of this process was its generally peaceful character. While many recent transitions from dictatorship to democracy have been peaceful, this was in large measure because the changes involved were so modest and had been preceded by both a significant softening of the dictatorial environment and expanded integration with the West (see especially Fishman, 1990; Edles, 1998). The end of socialism, however, involved a simultaneous and radical transformation of the polity, the economy, the society, and the relationship of the state to the international system. The collapse of socialism, therefore, was revolutionary – a point that will be addressed later in more detail. But a peaceful revolution is a contradiction in terms. How, then, can we explain why socialism went in most cases with a whimper, not a bang, and why, as in Yugoslavia, Romania, and Albania, regime collapse was more typically violent – and, to add further to the puzzle, less, not more disruptive of the status quo than the other, more peaceful transitions elsewhere in the region?

The answer takes us back, once again, to institutional design. *All* the regimes that ended peacefully were full-scale members of the Soviet bloc, and all those that ended violently were either on the fringes of the bloc (or Romania, with its deviant foreign policies and the absence of Soviet troops within its borders) or outside (as with Yugoslavia and Albania). Why the bloc mattered so much on this issue was because control over domestic militaries resided in Moscow and nowhere else, and because it was up to Gorbachev, therefore, to either deploy troops to defend socialism or keep them in the barracks. While he played a bit with the former in the Baltic states in early 1991,[1] he did not give the go-ahead in Eastern Europe in 1989. Thus, after using his reforms to weaken Communist Party control in Eastern Europe (as in the Soviet Union), Gorbachev then deprived his allied parties of the capacity to defend the little remaining power they had. By contrast, in Yugoslavia, Albania, and Romania, control over the military – and, for that matter, over the security forces as well – resided at home. Threatened leaders in these three countries took quick and predictable advantage of that fact.

Another variation that appeared as socialism and socialist states in the eastern half of Europe unraveled was in timing. In particular, why were the Polish and Hungarian regimes the first to go, despite the fact that it was in the Soviet Union where radical reforms were being introduced? Moreover, why did the collapse of socialist states begin in Yugoslavia? In the first instance, I argued that the structure of the bloc made the Eastern European regimes particularly weak, and that the combination of economic crises and a liberalized political environment, unique to Poland and Hungary, made these regimes all the more vulnerable.[2] In the second instance, I suggested that the decentralization of Yugoslavia, the severity of its economic difficulties, the death of Tito as the first major succession of the region in the 1980s, and the introduction of a new institutional framework immediately after Tito's death all worked to dismantle the Yugoslav regime and state long before such developments could even begin to materialize in a formal way in the Soviet Union or Czechoslovakia.

A final variation investigated in this study, which served as the focus of the previous chapter, was the contrast between the wars of secession in Yugoslavia and the peaceful division of the Soviet Union and Czechoslovakia into their republican parts. Here, we returned once again to the institutional line of argument, pointing out in this case, within the similarities of national federalism, some institutional differences that distinguished Yugoslavia from the Soviet Union and Czechoslovakia. In particular, Yugoslavia was different from the other two regime-states, because it was confederal, not federal; because the dominant republic, or Serbia, combined a full array of republican institutions with severely limited political influence within the federation (which was a pattern opposite to that of the Russian and Czech republics); and because the Yugoslav military had long been a powerful domestic actor whose mission was to protect the regime and the state, not just from foreign but also from domestic enemies (again, in contrast to Czechoslovakia and the Soviet Union, where the military was removed from domestic politics and, moreover, not so easily deployed).

When combined, these distinctions contributed to violence in Yugoslavia, because they ensured that the focus of conflict over the format and the future of the regime and the state would be horizontal and not vertical; that republican leaders would have quite divergent interests that could not be resolved; that the leaders of the dominant republic would combine nationalism with statism, territorial expansion, and opposition to reform; and that the military would become enmeshed in the processes of regime and state dissolution. Simply put, then, the problem in Yugoslavia was interrepublican conflict, Serbian expansionism, and military engagement.

By contrast, Czechoslovakia and the Soviet Union were optimally set up, primarily by accident, to avoid war in the event of state breakup. The republics in these two federations could find common ground – whether by forming a coalition against the center, as in the Soviet Union, or, as in Czechoslovakia, by using state dissolution as a mechanism for resolving somewhat different republican positions on economic and political reform. Moreover, the leaders of the dominant republics in both cases defined nationalism as anticommunism. Finally, because of the structure of the Warsaw Treaty Organization, the military was excluded from the processes of regime and state dissolution in both the Soviet Union and Czechoslovakia. Thus, while neither Boris Yel'tsin of Russia nor Václav Klaus of the Czech lands favored an end to the state, this outcome nonetheless met their most cherished concerns: to leave socialism, to build a new order, to defeat their main rivals, and to maintain at the least their regional bases of political power.

QUESTIONS OF INTERPRETATION
NATIONAL FEDERALISM

These, then, represent the primary conclusions of this study. Before we move on to their larger implications, however, we need to pause for a moment over a few questions that have been left hanging. One has to do with the interpretation of national federalism. In Chapters 3 and 5, I argued that the national-federal structure of the Soviet, Yugoslav, and Czechoslovak states seemed to explain their dismemberment, once the regime collapsed. This argument followed from two straightforward observations. One was that the structure of national federalism worked to build nations (or reinforce such processes, if nations were already formed), along with protostates at the republican level. The other was that the only states that dismembered in the region were those that had been national-federal during the socialist period. This would seem to lead to an inescapable conclusion: national federalism was central to the story of state dismemberment in the socialist world.

However, this explanation leaves open the possibility of another and more parsimonious interpretation. Could we dispense with the federal side of the argument and account for the end of these three states by emphasizing, simply, the national side? This interpretation is plausible, given the following observations. The three socialist states that ended were the most nationally diverse of any in the region – as indicated, for example, by the size of their second largest national group; many of the nations in each of these cases were geographically concentrated and, thus, optimally positioned to form solidaristic groups promoting a nationalist agenda; and it was precisely those compact nations that did mobilize and tear the state asunder.

The socialist experience, unfortunately, does not allow us to disentangle so easily the effects of nation versus federalism. This is because the comparison drawn in this instance – in direct contrast to the other comparisons drawn in this study – is flawed, given the correlation between diversity and federalism and, at the same time, the absence in eastern Europe of nonnational federal states along the lines of, for instance, the United States and Germany. The real world of socialism, in short, has deprived us of the kinds of controls that would be optimal.

However, there is some suggestive evidence that points to the importance of the *interaction* between the national and the federal sides of the equation and, thus, the importance of national federalism as the explanatory factor. First and most obviously, the new states that did form did so along republican lines. These states, moreover, have demonstrated surprising staying power – despite, for instance, their often heterogeneous populations; the absence, particularly in the Soviet and Yugoslav cases, of a high correlation between national and new state boundaries; and periodic challenges to new borders from within and outside these states (on the particular case of the Russian Federation, see, e.g., Stern, 1994; Treisman, 1997; Solnick, 1996, 1998b). The institutional legacies of federalized socialism, in short, have been unusually powerful – before and after state dismemberment.

Another piece to this puzzle is provided by patterns of nationalist mobilization during and after socialism. As Mark Beissinger (1995a) has argued for the Soviet Union, nationalist mobilization was far more common when nations had republics – than, for example, when they had lower-level administrative units or when they were deprived of any administrative identity. Indeed, this generalization seems to hold, even when we take geographical compactness into account, and even when we shift our attention from patterns of nationalist mobilization in the Soviet Union to such patterns in the new federal state of Russia (see Treisman, 1997). Additional evidence is provided by other states in the region, new and old, that are unitary in structure, but that have minority populations – for example, Estonia, Latvia, Ukraine, and Kazakhstan, with their sizable Russian minorities; Bulgaria with its Turkish minority; and Slovakia, Romania, and rump Yugoslavia with their large Hungarian minority populations.

What stands out from this comparison – and what is supported as well by the behavior of the Roma (Barany, 1994) – is the following. While certain factors seem to contribute to nationalist mobilization (for instance, the size and compactness of minority communities and the existence of legal and other forms of discrimination), these factors do not produce the levels of mobilization we find in federalized contexts (see, e.g., Gordon and Troxel, 1995). Institutional resources, in short, seem to matter a great deal. They explain differential rates of nationalist protest both within federal states and between these states, on the one hand, and unitary, but culturally diverse states, on the other.

Further insights into the role of nation versus federalism is provided by the experiences of states outside the postsocialist region – though even here the real world fails to cooperate fully, since national federalism, for example, has been invariably joined with regimes that are democratic, not dictatorial. What this survey suggests is the following. There is no question but that virtually all secessionist movements have a national, as well as a geographical base, which speaks to the power of the nation as an organizing symbol and to geographical concentration of the nation as a prime facilitator of the development of group solidarity. Moreover, it is obvious that secessionist movements develop outside of federal systems – as the continuing struggle between Tamils and Sri Lankans, for example, testifies (see Brass, 1985; Premdas, Samarasingha, and Anderson, 1990). Thus, while the nation in some sense seems to be a necessary condition for secession, federalism does not.

However, on the other hand, it is clear that the nation and federalism, where the boundaries of the first correlate with the boundaries of the second, seems to be a combination that contributes significantly to strong pressures for autonomy, if not flirtations with outright independence, as the recent histories of Belgium, India, Canada, and, earlier, Pakistan testify (see, e.g., Bossuyt, 1995; Martiniello, 1995, 1998; Brass, 1985; Sinha, 1998; Lijphart, 1996; Meadwell, 1994; Meadwell and Martin, 1996). At the same time, in the absence of federalism, geographically concentrated minorities seem to be less prone to either want to leave the state or, if that is desired, to succeed in doing so.

Perhaps the best way to draw a conclusion on this issue is to look at the Spanish experience, a case that affords us an unusually helpful comparison because of the similar circumstance of secessionist pressures arising during a transition from dictatorship to democracy (see Conversi 1993, 1994a, 1994b; Žic, 1994; Medrano, 1995). Several factors have been advanced to explain why Spanish elites, following Franco's death, managed to hold the state together. For example, Juan Díez Medrano has made a persuasive argument for important differences in the socioeconomic development of the Basque and Catalan regions, in the ideology of the leaders of the nationalist movements situated in these two regions, and in the degree of conflict within these two national groups. These differences seemed to have affected, in particular, what was demanded and what constituted a satisfactory response by the center. They also enhanced the bargaining power of the center and its capacity to keep secessionist pressures at bay.

Another explanation has focused on electoral sequencing (Linz and Stepan, 1992; more generally, 1996). Here, the argument is that, because Spanish elites held national before local elections following Franco's death, they provided incentives for parties to develop broad constituencies that cut across minority group lines – an argument that resonates with the work on consociational democracy within divided societies and, more generally, with analyses emphasizing the importance of institutional design for the survival of multinational states (see, e.g., Lijphart, 1996; also see Horowitz, 1985).

Both of these arguments have obvious merit, although the latter is less persuasive when applied to the three socialist cases. In particular, all three of these states divided, yet only in Yugoslavia do we find local elections preceding national elections (and, given their outcomes, preventing in effect the sheer possibility of national elections – see Grdešić, 1992, on the 1990 Croatian elections). However, one argument that has not been proposed – and one that emerges, once we cast our comparative net more widely – is a distinctive aspect of Spain that contrasts nicely with Yugoslavia, the Soviet Union, and Czechoslovakia and that brings us directly back to the question of nation versus federalism. Whereas Spain began its transition to democracy as a unitary state, the three socialist federations obviously did not. That was important for the future of the state, because the Spanish center in effect had room for compromise – or the granting of regional autonomies – whereas the three socialist federations had significantly less to offer their recalcitrant republics. Put another way, regional autonomies functioned as a halfway house between a unitary and a dismembered state; no such halfway house, with its capacity to appease a variety of constituencies, was available to an already federalized or, as in Yugoslavia, an already confederalized state. This, plus the power of national federalism in building nations and constructing protostates and, at the same time, guaranteeing that the republics would be both dissident and diverse from one another (arguments elaborated in Chapters 3, 5, and 6), would seem to point to the following conclusions with respect to the relationship between nation and federalism as variables.

First, national minorities within a state, particularly when they are geographically compressed, are potentially secessionist. Second, their propensity for secessionist demands – or at the least demands for greater autonomy – will increase under the following, less common conditions: when national minorities are well endowed with institutional resources; when they have leaders and political boundaries already in place; and when the political environment becomes more malleable (see Conversi, 1993, 1994b).[3] Finally, whether secessionist pressures produce an actual departure of the region from the state will depend on the willingness and the capacity of the regime to defend the territorial integrity of the state – through force and/or through the provision of a compromise that manages to preserve the state while meeting some of the concerns of the secessionist region. From this perspective, we can then see why the three socialist states ended, why Spain did not, and why the marriage of nation and federalism in the socialist world, once the regime weakened, proved to be an unusually combustible combination insofar as the survival of the state was concerned.

Thus, what seems to have been important about national federalism was that it was *both* national and federal. This conclusion can be augmented in turn by three other brief observations. In many cases, the nation in the eastern half of Europe would not have gained such a sense of identity and cohesion were it not for the institutions of federalism. Second, perhaps the most important difference among the dominant republics within the Yugoslav, Soviet, and Czechoslovak federations was in institutional endowments. Serbian nationalism drew strength and direction from Serbian institutions, whereas Russian and Czech nationalism had no such opportunities. This proved to be crucial in whether and how nationalism combined with reform – and this in turn affected the role of the dominant republic in the processes of regime and state dissolution.

This contrast leads to a more general point. It was the combination of nation and federalism within the larger context of socialism and its particular dynamics that gave republican elites within these federations a distinctive position on nationalism, reform, and the state, and that set republics on quite varied political and economic trajectories – before and during the processes of state and regime collapse. Thus, the federal side of national federalism contributed not just to homogeneity *within* the republics, but also to diversity *among* the republics, and it was the latter that made a single-state project untenable, especially in turbulent times, and, for that matter, a single-regime project untenable as well. Just as we see new states throughout the region, so these new states in turn feature very different regimes. And both developments speak to the power of the national and the federal legacies of socialism.

INSTITUTIONAL DETERMINISM

The other issue posed by the conclusions I have drawn focuses on institutional determinism. Put bluntly: did the institutional design of socialist regimes and federal socialist states preclude any outcome aside from their eventual collapse?[4] On the one hand, it is easy to dismiss such an interpretation. In particular, institutional determinism ignores the importance of the political opportunity structure in altering the environment from one of weakened regimes and vulnerable states to one where regimes and states dissolved. Whereas the former describes a relatively common situation, the latter is much more unusual – as the incidence of protest versus revolution reminds us. Put another way: weak states and weak regimes can limp on for a very long time indeed. Thus, as I emphasized throughout this study, the developments of the 1980s were a necessary (albeit not sufficient) condition for what followed.

Moreover, a purely institutional interpretation, while central to most of the issues we addressed, was less helpful with respect to answering some questions – for instance, why the parade leaving socialism started in Poland and Hungary. In addition, there is the undeniable impact of the decisions taken throughout the region in the second half of the 1960s – that is, to open up to the global economy, to place limits on economic and political liberalization, and to stabilize cadres. All three decisions, which speak to the power of socialist elites and the impact of their decisions, made a bad economic and political situation worse. These decisions also ensured that the succession crises and the struggles over policy that took place in the 1980s would have unusually powerful consequences throughout the socialist area. This was because ruling parties were already fissured along vertical and horizontal lines; because republican claims to autonomy and sovereignty were already well grounded; because society had gained significantly in its bargaining leverage; and because these earlier reforms had produced a regionwide economic crisis, albeit one that varied in intensity from state to state. The decisions made in the 1960s, moreover, did vary across the region – as the contrasts between, say, reformist Hungary and hard-line Romania, or between the opened economy of Poland and the closed economy of Czechoslovakia, during this period make abundantly clear. This leads to a final challenge to an interpretation along the lines of institutional determinism. Elites had choices and made them.

However, there are very good reasons to couch our arguments in a relatively deterministic framework. If the decisions socialist leaders made in the 1960s were so important in rejecting options that would have better served the system and its reproductive capabilities, these decisions were also to a large extent the *product* of the very institutional logic of the system itself. Indeed, one could argue that the choice in the 1960s was to save the system in the short term by rejecting reform, rather than to dismantle it quickly through the introduction of such reforms. Elites did have choices, then, but these choices were heavily conditioned by the institutional framework within which they operated.

Thus, in response to the question of institutional determinism, we would have to argue that these systems were fated to end – whether in the 1960s or in the 1980s. However, timing did matter. If the end had come in the 1960s, it would likely have led to a bloodbath. This was in part because of the greater asymmetries in the 1960s than in the 1980s between the top and the bottom levels of the party, between the party and the society, between the center and republics, and between the Soviet Union and Eastern Europe. These asymmetries would have prolonged the process of dissolution, and, as the painful example of Yugoslavia throughout the 1980s attests, generated more violence in the process. What would also have contributed to violence was that domestic control over the military and the security forces in Eastern Europe was still largely in place in the 1960s. Thus, Communist elites would have had ample opportunity to defend their hegemonic but eroding positions. The failure of the Prague Spring, then, was indeed a turning point, as Mark Kramer (1998) has so persuasively argued. However, it may have been in some respects a blessing in disguise. Regime and state dissolution is rarely so graceful as what we saw in 1989–1992. What happened in Yugoslavia is, unfortunately, the historical norm.

We can now turn to the final issue that will be addressed in this book. As observed in the introductory chapter, the collapse of socialism and the state provides us with an ideal window for viewing both contemporary trends in the world at large and current debates in comparative politics. In the remainder of this chapter, I look at both by using the arguments in this book, sometimes augmented by other analyses, to revisit the study of institutions, nationalism, revolution, and regime transition. This chapter and the book ends by examining briefly a final issue that spans all of these subjects and many others: the place of place in comparative inquiry.

INSTITUTIONAL ANALYSIS

Whether claiming to be new or a return to fundamentals, whether concerned with the historical evolution of institutions or more short term in emphasis and rooted in the literature on public choice, institutional analysis has come to occupy an increasingly prominent place within the disciplines of political science and sociology (see, e.g., Levi, 1997; March and Olson, 1984; Moe, 1984; Searing, 1991; Eggertsson, 1990; North, 1981; Powell and Di Maggio, 1991; Steinmo, Thelen, and Longstreth, 1992). While representative of this trend, this study nonetheless offers some modifications in some of the current thinking on this subject.

First, like most approaches in the faddish social sciences, institutional analysis has had a history of being "in," "out," and then "in" again. The role of institutional studies in Communist systems, however, has been far more consistent – and consistently prominent over time. While this says something about the obstacles in an authoritarian setting to applying, for instance, behavioral approaches, this also points to one advantage specialists in Communist studies had. Because these systems were so ever present, or so "all-thumbs," as Charles Lindblom (1977) once put it, one could hardly escape their institutional messages. This was the case whether living within these systems or analyzing them from the outside.

More generally, this study supports a perspective on institutions that reinforces the position of those who have argued for the importance of looking at institutions in a historically sensitive and empirically detailed way (Solnick, 1998a; Kaminski, 1992). In practice, this means viewing institutions as films, not snapshots. Thus, while we could explain, for example, the end of socialist regimes and states by looking at the more proximate and turbulent developments of the 1980s, we would be left with a rather shallow account – because we could not understand within this limited framework why the successions of that decade had so much impact; why economic and political liberalization came to dominate the elite agenda; why publics and many Communist elites, whether within states as a whole or within republics, were so willing and able to break with the regime; and why there were variations in when and how regime collapse occurred. Indeed, once we move beyond the obvious questions of why these regimes and states ended, "thin" institutionalism ceases to be of much use (see Peter Katzenstein's comments, in "The Role of Theory," 1995: 10–15).

Recognizing the importance of history and details also means acknowledging that institutions can appear to have one set of consequences, but in practice and over time, quite different, if not opposing ones. Thus, a major theme in this study has been the self-destructive nature of socialist institutions. These institutions did not just put some of these states and most of these Communist parties "out of business" (and some of these parties into business!); they also fashioned through the very process of self-destruction radically different alternatives to the existing order. This explains why these systems ended, or at least why the Communist Party in all cases lost its political and economic hegemony, *and* it also explains why the transition to the new order was in many cases so remarkably fast. There was, in short, a new system waiting in the wings (and see Greskovits, 1998, on socialism's demobilizing benefits for economic reform).

The importance of historical sensitivity can also be seen in another lesson to be drawn from this study. That lesson is that the devil is in fact often in the details – or, more in keeping with the notion of political architecture, that God is in the details (to borrow from Mies Van der Rohe). Thus, for instance, while one could point to the obvious commonality of national federalism in explaining the dismemberment of the Yugoslav, Soviet, and Czechoslovak states, this could not account for the differences between violent and peaceful state dismemberment. For that we had to dig much deeper into socialist-era institutions.

At the same time, however, it must be recognized that details can sometimes get in the way. For example, in Chapters 2 and 3 we reexamined what most scholars have taken to be quite different and distinctive socialist playing fields – the Soviet versus the Yugoslav model of socialism, and socialist federations versus the Soviet bloc – only to discover remarkable similarities among them in their institutional design and dynamics. Thus, all socialist regimes, domestic and international, federal and unitary, state socialist and self-managing pluralist, were subject to the same kinds of difficulties over time with respect to economic performance and redistribution of political power and economic resources. From this perspective, a general model of European socialism emerged in this study, and this model only needed one additional, territorially defined layer of units to be retrofitted to apply equally well to the Soviet bloc and socialist federations.

This leaves us with several concluding observations about the political place and impact of institutions. One concentrates on the issue of interests. Most would agree that institutions define interests and that interests play a key role in shaping political behavior. Indeed, this is the foundation not just for institutional studies, but also for structuralist and most behavioral analyses of politics (see especially Levi, 1997; Hall, 1997). However, while in most cases it makes sense to move from these observations to the argument that political actors can be reduced to, simply, interest maximizers, this assumption is of limited use, once we begin to worry about predicting preferences, let alone behavior. This is not just because other motivations often come into play, or because interests can be misperceived or misrepresented. It is also because interests and, thus, preferences and behavior are so situationally defined and so ever changing, depending upon shifts in circumstances. This in turn means that the focus on interests, which serves the purpose of streamlining the analysis, seems to lead us back into the political thicket. Thus, to argue that institutions define interests and that actors are interest-driven is to explain in fact very little. It can only be the point of departure for studies that, by necessity, must collect a lot of data elsewhere (also see Bates, Figueiredo, and Weingast, 1998).

This is particularly the case in transformational periods where power is fluid, where the most fundamental political and economic issues are on the bargaining table, and where short-term signals are as convoluted as they are critical (Bunce and Csanádi, 1993). The best example of this in our study is the significant variance in the positions and the behaviors of Milan Kučan (Slovenia), Slobodan Milošević (Serbia), Václav Klaus (the Czech Republic), Vladimír Mečiar (Slovakia), and Boris Yel'tsin (Russia). Each one of these leaders wanted to preserve if not expand his power, and each one was confronted with a roughly similar situation of a regime and a state in the process of dissolution. However, there was considerable variance in the stances each of these leaders took on the key issues of the day – that is, on the nation, the state, and the regime (understood as both political and economic). The variance, moreover, was not just across leaders but also across time. Yet each of them succeeded, it must be noted, in realizing much of what was desired. For example, they all managed to hold on to power. But how informative is it to say that they maximized their interests and that their behavior was rational?

This gets us back to an earlier point. Without a historically grounded and empirically detailed understanding of institutional context, we would be left with an empty argument that simply said that all of these leaders were pursuing their interests. And if we took institutions as simplistic behavior motivators, we would be unable to explain why pursuing interests in what appeared to be the same institutional context led to such different preferences and such different actions – and, significantly, with relatively similar payoffs. What constitutes rational behavior and what produces variations in payoffs, then, can only be determined by knowing a lot of less-than-obvious details – details that, of course, are subject to competing interpretations.

If institutions define interests, at least in a rough sense, so they shape identities. This is the case, whether we focus on the nations that arose to take political power in the republics within the federal states or on the nations that already had states and that liberated themselves from their regimes and, in the Soviet bloc case, from the larger socialist international order within which they were embedded. Key to this process of forming nations was both differentiation from others and the homogenization that came from the institutional dynamics of socialism as a regime, a federation, and a bloc.

This leads to our final observation. It is tempting to think of the revolutionary changes that took place in the Soviet Union and Eastern Europe as cases of institutional collapse. From this perspective, the temptation is to draw a thick line – between the institutional past of socialism and the rise of new institutions from the debris of socialist regimes and states. However, what was striking in our story was the role of institutions in providing some structure and some certainty in unusually fluid and uncertain times. For example, national federalism in the socialist context created order in disorganized circumstances by virtue of having built nations and states at the republican level and, through that, constructing what became receptacles for rebellion and, ultimately, for state building.

This, in turn, reminds us that the lines between old and new institutions are blurred, even in periods of rapid change. Ivo Andrić (1945: 136), in his powerful historical novel about Bosnia, *Bridge on the Drina*, has brought this point home when writing about the reaction of the townspeople to the shift in occupying forces from the Ottoman Turks to the Austrians:

> But in the homes, not only of the Turks but also of the Serbs, nothing was changed. They lived, worked and amused themselves in the old way. Bread was still mixed in kneading troughs, coffee roasted on the hearth, clothes steamed in coppers and washed with soda which hurt the women's fingers. . . . But on the other hand the outward aspect of the town altered visibly and rapidly. Those same people, who in their own homes maintained the old order in every detail and did not even dream of changing anything, became for the most part easily reconciled to the changes in the town and after a longer or a shorter period of wonder and grumbling accepted them.
>
> Naturally here, as always and everywhere in similar circumstances, the new life meant in actual fact a mingling of the old and the new. Old ideas and old values clashed with new ones, merged with them or existed side by side, as if waiting to see which would outlive which. People reckoned in florins and kreutzers but also in grosh and para, measured by arshin and oka and drams but also by metres and kilos and grams, confirmed terms of payment and orders by the new calendar but even more often by the old custom of payment on St. George's or St. Dimitri's day. By a natural law the people resisted every innovation but did not go to extremes, for to most of them life was always more important and more urgent than the forms by which they lived.

When applied to the issues of concern in this book, this passage has a simple message. We can hardly understand the exit of socialism and socialist states without analyzing the role of the socialist past and socialist institutions in shaping those developments and a lot of what followed (and, for similar arguments, albeit explaining different sets of behaviors, see, for instance, Luong, 1996; Crowley, 1994; Burawoy and Kratov, 1993; Ekiert, 1996, 1998). Indeed, a thorough, but far from parsimonious account, would force us to go even further back. Thus, it was not that socialist institutions collapsed, and new ones emerged from the rubble. It was rather that the new institutions were built by the old ones and represented a melding of new and old. If property in postcommunism can be character- ized as recombinant (Stark, 1996), then so can politics, culture, and social life (Grabher and Stark, 1997).

NATIONS, NATIONALISM, AND SECESSION

The literature on the rise of nations and nationalist movements is divided into three interpretative groups: primordialists, constructivists, and instru- mentalists (see Young, 1993; Esman, 1994). The arguments presented in this book strongly support the constructivist position. This follows from the role of national federalism, the Soviet bloc, and, more generally, social- ist institutions in building (or deepening) national consciousness and unity, in poising these nations against a common enemy, and, finally, in giving these nations the institutions, elites, boundaries, and, ultimately, incentives and opportunities they needed to mount nationalist movements, to liberate themselves from regimes and states, and to construct new re- gimes and sovereign states in their place.

What socialism, the Soviet bloc, and federalism did, then, was to homogenize, focalize, antagonize, and mobilize – whether the nations in- volved in this process were, say, Poles within the Soviet bloc, Slovenes within Yugoslavia, Lithuanians within the Soviet Union, or Slovaks within Czechoslovakia. That all the socialist regimes collapsed, that the Soviet bloc divided on national-state lines, and that all the republics became states (with the exception of Serbia and Montenegro forming a single unit) – these all point in unison toward the fundamental similarities among all the socialist playing fields, whether domestic or regional. These also point, at the same time, to the power of socialist institutions in building nations, counterregimes, and counterstates.

Does this mean, however, that a constructivist approach tells us all that we need to know about nations, nationalism, and secession? The an- swer, as this study has repeatedly demonstrated, is no. If that were the case, for instance, then all the regimes within the Soviet bloc should have collapsed simultaneously; all the republics within the federations should have mobilized at the same time and at the same rates and should, as well, have pursued the same end of leaving the state; and all the federal states in the region should have ended at the same time and in a similar way. In practice, of course, there was variance along all of these dimensions – though within a larger context, we must remember, wherein all the regimes did end as did all the federal states and in a very brief period of time. While some of this variance can be explained by delving more deeply into intitutional design (as with the issues of the sequencing of regime collapse in Eastern Europe in 1989 and the contrast between violent versus peaceful state dismemberment), some of it can only be accounted for by going outside the institutional framework. Thus, those nations that were quickest to mobilize tended to exhibit two characteristics: a prior history of statehood and/or a long liberalized political environment.

Where, then, does this leave explanations that are grounded in primordial and instrumental lines of reasoning? It is clear that the first was of limited importance. While it is true that the nations that mobilized were in almost every case based on communities defined by language and/ or ethnicity, it is also true that there was significant variation in not just the timing of such mobilization, but also whether nations, even defined in this way, mobilized at all. One would be hard-pressed, for example, to argue that Russians and Ukrainians are "less primordial" than, say, Serbs, Slovenes, or Slovaks, yet the first two were late and lackluster mobilizers, whereas the final three were early and energetic. Moreover, we are reminded here of an earlier point. Whether nations had their own administrative units *and* whether this built upon an earlier history of institutional resources both played a key role in shaping rates of nationalist mobilization, as well as defining the relationship between nationalism and reform (see Vujačić, 1996; also Beissinger, 1995a).

By contrast, it is clear that the instrumental line of argument is very helpful, particularly when in the course of these events the issue for elites shifted from one of how much reform to one involving their political future and that of the regime and the state. As Susan Woodward (1995a: 380) has summarized for Yugoslavia: "Nationalism became a political force when leaders of the republics sought political support as bargaining chips in federal disputes." Institutions, therefore, while important, particularly in building nations and states and structuring the game of bargaining, must be joined with political leaders if we are to understand nationalism.

Let us provide some brief examples, building on the earlier observations about Yugoslavia. When Milan Kučan helped lead Slovenia out of Yugoslavia, he was doing so in large measure because embracing Slovene nationalism and its close connection to liberation from socialism and the state served his interests as a reform Communist attempting to preserve his power in circumstances that made commitment to socialism and to Yugoslavia a form of political suicide. Similarly, the actions of Slobodan Milošević were also important, not just for developments within Serbia, but also outside it. He pushed Serbian nationalism in a certain direction and, far from accidentally, maintained in the process his political preeminence within Serbia.

The role of political leadership in general and its instrumental uses of nationalism in particular, then, were very important. This is even more obvious once we add Croatia to the Serbian-Slovene comparison. All three of these republics were well endowed with national institutions. Moreover, Croatia and especially Serbia in particular had historical claims to statehood. However, the Croatian party leadership, unlike its Serbian and Slovene counterparts, was slow to seize the issue of nationalism – in part because Croats were not out on the streets as they were in Slovenia and Serbia, in part because the leadership of the Croatian party had since the early 1970s been largely Serbian in background, in part because nationalism had proved dangerous in the past, and, finally, in part because the reformist wing of the party was very weak and the Croatian political context hard-line. Put succinctly, Croatia was different because Croatian party leaders considered it quite risky to deploy nationalism as a mechanism for maintaining political power. However, the Croatian example also reminds us that the important "first cut" in the story of nationalism, regime collapse, and state dismemberment was very much a constructivist and not an instrumentalist one.

Nationalism, however, cannot be reduced to institutions and elites, though both tell a lot of the story. It is also about the fears and hopes of publics in a time of transformation and considerable uncertainty. It is no accident, therefore, that the collapse of the Soviet, Czechoslovak, and Yugoslav regimes foreshadowed the collapse of these states, or that nationalist mobilization accompanied the collapse of these regimes. Although institutional and instrumental lines of argument are important, so is political elasticity. And though elites are important, so are the publics on the streets, and both respond to a world composed of new threats and new possibilities. This suggests in turn the value of treating nationalist movements as a type of social movement and, therefore, reflective of the interaction among anger, resources, and political opportunities (see McAdams, Tarrow, and Tilly, 1997; Beissinger, 1995a).

If nationalism is a passionate process, however, it is also, in a curious way, a dispassionate one. As we saw throughout this study, nationalism was capable of combining with all sorts of political objectives, ideologies, and behaviors. Thus, Boris Yel'tsin could be a nationalist and support capitalism and liberal democracy and the continuation of the state, albeit in a more decentralized form; Milan Kučan could be a nationalist, embrace liberalism, but oppose, at the same time, Slovenia's continued membership in the Yugoslav state; and Slobodan Milošević could be a nationalist, oppose capitalism and democracy while playing a double game of seeming to support the continuation of Yugoslavia, albeit in a more centralized form, while preparing for its demise and the expansion in the process of Serbian borders. Even more curious is the fact that all three leaders were very high-ranking members of the Communist Party (with Yel'tsin only resigning in mid-1990).

This leads to a more general point. While it is true that nationalism is an ideology (see Banac, 1984), it is also true that it is an extraordinarily flexible one with respect to issues of regime, state, and economy. Thus, it is wrong to associate nationalism, as some tend to do, with certain kinds of political projects – for example, the once common association (now out of fashion) of nationalism with democracy (see, e.g., Mann, 1995; Hobsbawm, 1992; Nodia, 1994; Karklins, 1993). It is also wrong to assume that nationalism only applies to minority politics, or that nationalism is always joined with authoritarianism, xenophobia, and war. If we review the developments analyzed in this book, for example, we can observe that nationalism sponsored not just the terrible wars in Yugoslavia, but also the peaceful division of the Soviet Union and Czechoslovakia and the peaceful liberation of Eastern Europe from the Soviet bloc. Nationalism, in short, can serve a variety of political functions, and it has its positive and its negative sides – depending on how it combines with other ideologies.

As Donald Horowitz (1992: 10) has reminded us, "Ethnicity has meant conflict and violence, but it has also meant kinship and community." Nationalism, therefore, plays both an integrative and a disintegrative role. And even within the process of disintegration, nationalism can forge new possibilities for integration of the nation into a larger political, economic, and cultural unit. As Mojmir Križan (1993: 140) has observed, "The European-friendly nationalism of the Slovenes is in another sense a contradiction: nationalism can only thrive through the provincialism of the Slovenes, but the process of Europeanization creates the opposite."

Let us now move from general observations about nationalism to some specifics of secession. This study confirms several arguments in the work on secession; that is, that the process is rooted in virtually every case in the nation and that nationalism comes to the fore when the regime and the state weaken (on these points, see, e.g., Horowitz, 1985; Conversi, 1993,

1994a, 1994b; Hechter, 1992; Hroch, 1995; Gellner, 1995). However, at the same time, this analysis suggests that we may need to refine our understanding of secession. First, institutions, far more than such factors as disjunctures between the state and capital, tensions between political representation and economic development, and regional variations in the level of socioeconomic development seem to explain the rise of nationalist movements and secessionist pressures – both within the republics in federal states and within states in the Soviet bloc (on these alternative arguments, see, e.g., Horowitz, 1981, 1985, 1992, 1995; Gourevitch, 1979; Pi-Sunyer, 1984; Medrano, 1995). Second, while international factors played a role in secession, primarily with respect to either increasing tensions among republics, as in Yugoslavia (Woodward, 1995a), or with respect to creating unusually weak regimes and unusually strong and assertive societies, as in those Eastern European regimes encased within the Soviet bloc and within a larger international economic order, international factors, nonetheless, had little impact on the success of secessionist movements in the formerly socialist world. Instead, success seemed to have been a function largely of regime collapse and the structure of socialist federations.

Finally, this analysis both confirms and questions the utility of thinking of secession as a game (see especially Hechter, 1992). On the one hand, it is true that the division of the Soviet Union, Yugoslavia, and Czechoslovakia was the outcome of bargaining, that the number of players central to the outcome was in practice limited, and that the violent versus the peaceful dismemberment of these states could be predicted on the basis of four simple variables: the distance separating republican elite positions (or the potential for cooperation versus conflict), the presence or the absence of a viable center, the intervention of the military, and the orientation of the dominant republic in particular. In this sense, then, a game-theoretic approach is quite helpful (see, e.g., Bates, 1997).

However, to get to the point of specifying leadership preferences – and, most importantly for our cases, their first- and second-order preference rankings – it was necessary to know an extraordinary amount about what happened (Bates, Figueiredo, and Weingast 1998). For example, the disintegration of Yugoslavia would be greatly misunderstood if it were to be assumed that Milošević's position was as he publicly stated – that is, support of the continuation of the state. Moreover, what is striking about all three cases of state dismemberment in the socialist world was that preferences of the key players were shaped and reshaped as the game continued. Indeed, the number of players involved also changed rapidly – for instance, Ukraine's sudden entrance into the Soviet game in early December, 1991 (which proved decisive for the end of the Soviet state); the

exclusion of Václav Havel, the Czechoslovak president, from the Czechoslovak game (which also proved to be decisive); and the inclusion of the
Yugoslav National Army in the games of Yugoslav dismemberment (along
with its complicated role as a defender of the regime, the state, and Serbian
minorities – all of which mixed in different ways at different stages of the
conflict). Thus, to speak of the games of state dismemberment is more to
employ a metaphor that helps highlight what happened than to expand in
any way either our explanatory power or our insights about secessionist
dynamics.

REVOLUTION

Were the events analyzed in this book revolutions? The difficulty of answering this question is that they do not fit very well with common definitions of revolution (see, e.g., Skocpol, 1979; Tilly, 1993; Goldstone,
1991; Goodwin, 1988). On the one hand, like most revolutions, they
originated in a conjoined political and economic crisis that reflected in part
the growing costs of the domestic structure of dictatorship; they produced
a rapid collapse of the old economic, political, and social order; they were
characterized by deregulation of the system to the point where sovereignty
became competitive; they involved mass mobilization against the regime;
and their end product was a new political, social, and economic order
(albeit in varying degrees, as with revolutions – see Foran and Goodwin,
1993). However, unlike most, indeed virtually all social revolutions, the
collapse of socialist regimes and states took place through a largely peaceful
process. Indeed, where violence was present, the revolution was less, not
more revolutionary in its consequences. At the same time, the old elite
survived and in some cases did quite well – for example, by remaining in
power without interruption (albeit stripped of the political hegemony it
once enjoyed), by returning to power as social democrats within a democratic context and after serving for a time as a loyal opposition, and/or by
shifting their base of operations from the political system to an economy
undergoing rapid privatization (see, e.g., Wasilewski and Wnuk-Lipinski,
1995; Lane, 1997; Lane and Ross, 1995; Bunce, 1998c).

Despite their divergence from the historical norm, however, the fall of
socialism and the collapse of states in the eastern half of Europe would still
seem to qualify as revolutionary events (see Goodwin, 1988; Goldstone,
1991; Tilly, 1993). This is because what matters is less how these processes
of change occurred than the nature of the changes themselves. In particular,
what is striking about the collapse of these regimes and these states is that

they all took place very quickly – which testifies to the kinds of sharp and sudden breaks with the past that are usually understood to be revolutionary in character. Just as important is that the changes that did occur seemed to have been decisive – as indicated by, for example, both the near absence of backtracking over time (with liberalized regimes, for example, either staying so or becoming more so) and the failure of even those regimes in the region that remained dictatorships to reimpose the socialist model. Finally, revolutionary change usually refers not just to the pace and permanence of change, but also to its direction. Here, what stands out about the revolutions in the eastern half of Europe was the sheer ideological distance they traveled. As Branko Horvat (1982) has argued, socialism was constructed in quite deliberate fashion as the exact inverse of capitalist liberal democracy. To build capitalism and liberal democracy from the ruins of socialism – and to do so in such quick fashion in at least some of these cases – points to the kinds of radical changes implied in the term "revolution."

Indeed, one could argue that the changes that have taken place in much of this region since communism collapsed are greater than the changes that were ushered in by the victory of the Communists in their revolutions. In the latter, socialism represented in many ways an exaggeration of the past, given, for instance, the traditions of authoritarian rule, fused political-economic systems, and import-substitution economics. By contrast, the transition to capitalism and democracy has represented a sharp break with that past. This observation is most apt, of course, for those cases where shock therapy and shock democracy have tended to go together – for instance, in the Baltic states, Poland, Hungary, the Czech Republic, and Slovenia. And all of this happened without the extraordinary human costs of the earlier transition to socialism, though this more recent transition, to be sure, has generated its own set of costs (see Greskovits, 1998). But how could it be otherwise? Planned capitalism is hardly easy on publics, any more than planned socialism – especially when the former follows the latter.

Precisely because they were atypical in so many ways, moreover, the revolutions in the eastern half of Europe can help us rethink certain aspects of revolutionary dynamics. A case in point is mass mobilization. What was striking about the events of the fall of 1989 in East Germany and Czechoslovakia (and, before that, in Poland in 1980–1981) was both the sheer numbers of protesters that materialized overnight and the remarkable willingness and capacity of those protesters to work together – and peacefully – toward a common and radical goal. The obvious question that this poses is the following. How were mass publics in Eastern Europe able to surmount the familiar constraints on collective action – constraints that, it must be remembered, have usually limited, even in revolutionary situations, both the size of public protests and the ability of protesters to act in concert?

Several answers have been offered to account for massive mass mobilization in Eastern Europe – for example, arguments involving information cascades (Lohmann, 1994), coordination games (Bunce and Chong, 1990), and a large-scale and sudden correction of long-falsified preferences (Kuran, 1992). While all three lines of argument make some sense, they lack one necessary piece that completes the picture and that returns us to the importance of institutions. That piece is the formation of similar preferences among publics and its contributions to the resources available to protesters.

As argued in Chapter 2, the design of socialist regimes was distinctive in its capacity to homogenize publics. This reflected the economic, political, and social monopoly of the party – a monopoly that produced extraordinary similarities in the social, economic, and political experiences of socialist publics; that predisposed the party to "bundle" and, for that matter, "bungle" policy changes, personnel changes, and, thus, crises; and that allowed publics to identify a common source for everything that happened. What all this meant for socialist publics was that they shared a common location in the system, a common set of costs when the system performed badly, a common definition of the enemy, and, thus, both a common set of interests and a common and, in part because of that, ample supply of resources. Publics in socialist systems, therefore, were unusually and ideally situated to surmount many of the well-known obstacles to collective action.

This proved to be particularly important when the performance of these systems declined, when elites were divided and contentious, when publics shared a national identity, and when the costs of protest had either been limited in the past (as in Poland) or underwent, as in 1989, a dramatic decline. In those circumstances, with a weakening of the regime, publics had the desire and the capacity to protest – and to do so in large numbers and at the same time.

Thus, it was the design of the system, long before the appearance of such proximate factors as information cascades, coordination games, and the like that shaped not just the rise of contentious politics but also the remarkable form it took when socialism began to unravel. In the absence of such remarkable harmonization of preferences and resources, as in most revolutionary situations, publics protest, but they tend to do so in smaller numbers and in a manner that more closely resembles parallel play than what seems to be implied by the term "collective action."

All of this points, in turn, to a more general observation. Patterns of mass mobilization reflect in part the structure of the old regime, even as it is falling apart. To echo an earlier point, institutions seem to structure behavior, even when they are being dismantled. Thus, the emphasis on the collapse of the old order in most theories of revolution – an emphasis that leads analysts to focus on the present, while discounting the past – needs to be revised. Even on its deathbed, the institutional past seems to determine to some degree how the old order ends. It does so by shaping both the boundaries and the focus of protest. Thus, it was not just that the design of socialism produced large-scale demonstrations that focused on the regime. It was also, keeping in mind the many arenas of socialism and their consequences, that the institutional past rendered all of these protests national in form, erected specific geographical boundaries around protest activity, and defined the targets of collective action – that is, not just the regime in all cases, but also the state for the republics within federalized systems and the Soviet Union for the Eastern European nations encased in the Soviet bloc.

If the institutional past shaped patterns of mobilization, moreover, it also shaped state responses to protest. Here, I refer to the contrast between violent versus peaceful dismemberment of socialist regimes and socialist states, and the role of socialist institutions in accounting for those contrasts.

Thus, it would seem to be a mistake to treat revolutions as a simple sequence, wherein the old order collapses and the new one takes its place. To this point, we can add several other lessons provided by the recent end of socialism and socialist states. First and most obviously, the arguments in this book support an earlier emphasis in studies of revolution – that is, on the importance of nationalism. In fact, it was nationalism, broadly construed, that played a key role in allowing publics to act in concert. In this sense, nationalism was not just a state of mind and a focus for political action; it was also a resource. This point was recognized, moreover, by both publics and elites in the socialist world – with the former empowered because of nationalism, and the latter, deprived of power and desperate, ever more interested in using nationalism as a means of either shoring up socialism or serving as its substitute.

Second, revolution in the socialist world was not just an ideological process (as is the common focus); it was also a spatial one (which is less commonly noted – but see Walton, 1984; Tilly, 1993; Motyl, 1987). In this sense, the revolutions that brought down socialist dictatorships were remarkably similar to the classic revolutions of the past. They were about political authority and its boundaries, which in practice meant that they were aimed at both the regime and the state.

Third, the process by which socialism and socialist states ended suggests that we may need to blur a few more boundaries that have long divided scholarship – in this instance, between rebellions and revolutions and between great reforms and revolutions. The interesting question posed by the socialist experience, therefore, becomes the following: why do rebellion and reform sometimes slide into revolution? Central to the answer to this question would have to be the institutional structure of the old order in interaction with the expansion of opportunities for change.

This in turn suggests a final observation. Rebellion, reform, and revolution are all members of the same family – that is, social movements. Indeed, what is striking about rebellion, reform, and revolution is that investigations of these three subjects, long isolated from each other and distanced as well by terminology, nonetheless converge around a similar argument: the importance for all three developments of institutions interacting with changing opportunities. It is precisely these two factors, of course, that occupy the center stage in the study of social movements (see Tarrow, 1994). It is, therefore, hardly surprising that these two variables have been central as well in this particular study of social movements – or, should I say, this study of rebellion, reform, and revolution.

REGIME TRANSITIONS

INTERNATIONAL

If the changes in Eastern Europe and the Soviet Union were revolutions, they were also regime transitions – with transition understood to connote the peaceful movement from one mode of organizing political power to another. From this perspective, the collapse of socialism and socialist states involved a number of transitions rolled into one (which is in part why these events were revolutions). Here, I refer not just to the fact that leaving socialism has meant the construction of a new political *and* economic system, and, thus, a new social system as well. I also refer to what could be termed the sum total of the events analyzed in this book – that is, the transition from one international order to another.

If we focus, first, on the international transition, we can make the following observations. First, the story we have told is primarily a domestic one. Although international factors were important, they influenced, rather than caused, what happened. Put another way: they speeded up, but did not produce, regime and state dissolution in the eastern half of Europe – for example, by making a bad economic situation worse, given liberalization of trade in the East during the 1970s, the petrodollar crisis, and the resulting accumulation of massive hard-currency debts (as in Poland, Hungary, Romania, and Yugoslavia); by conferring greater legitimacy to nationalist and secessionist demands because of changes in international norms; and by expanding East-West interactions through Ostpolitik, détente, and the Helsinki Final Act, all of which exposed publics and elites in the eastern half of Europe to a highly attractive economic and political alternative to socialism. In a more proximate sense, moreover, one can point to two other international influences that were important, but, again, not in any real sense causal: the role of the Soviet bloc in exaggerating the effects of the Gorbachev reforms as they traveled from Moscow to, say, Warsaw, Budapest, Berlin, and Prague, and the role of German recognition of Slovenia and Croatia in finalizing (but, again, not deciding) the fate of the Yugoslav state (see, e.g., Woodward, 1995a; Crawford, 1996).

Thus, attempts to explain the collapse of the postwar international order from the vantage point of realism are, quite simply, wrongheaded (Mearsheimer, 1990). To leave out domestic factors is to try to solve a mystery, minus the plot, and, for that matter, minus the modus operandi. Instead, what makes the most sense is not just including domestic factors in the account (which many specialists in international relations have done – see, e.g., Deudney and Ikenberry, 1991–1992; Snyder, 1990; Lebow, 1995; Evangelista, 1998), but, I would argue, privileging them. When all is said and done, socialism failed because its very structure as a domestic regime produced a deregulation of the system – a process that necessarily destroyed socialism, given its dependence on economic and political monopoly, and that had enormous implications for not just the survival of these regimes, but also for the survival of the Soviet bloc, some of the socialist states (if they were federal), and, ultimately, the postwar international order. The rot of socialism, in short, began at home and then spread outward.

In accounting for the end of socialism and the state, this book has taken a particular stance on the question of why the cold war ended. In doing so, this study also has several implications for the study of international relations in general. One is the apparent value of analyzing large-scale changes in the international system as the product of the interaction between domestic and international reform, an interaction that helps make sense, for example, not just of the recent collapse of the postwar order but also important shifts in the international system during the nineteenth century (see Bunce, 1993).

The other implication flows from the striking similarities between the structure and the dynamics of the Soviet bloc, on the one hand, and the socialist federations, on the other. These similarities call into question a distinction habitually drawn between domestic and international politics, a distinction that has been responsible for the divergent approaches taken in these two fields of study. That is the contrast between structured authority relations in the domestic realm and anarchy in the international realm. This study suggests that there are conditions where domestic dynamics come to resemble international dynamics, and vice versa. This is particularly the case when these systems meet each other in effect halfway – that is, when domestic systems are in the process of fragmentation and international regimes (as with the Soviet bloc) have taken on a hierarchical structure.

More generally, this points to the logic of blurring the distinction between comparative and international politics when thinking about the various ways in which political authority is, can, and should be organized. Indeed, this is precisely what seems to be happening in work on the European Union – an ideal site for rethinking the boundaries between the domestic and the international organization of politics, the economy, and, indeed, identities (see, e.g., Risse-Kappen, 1996).

DOMESTIC

The global wave of democratization, which originated in Portugal and Spain in the first half of the 1970s, has produced a rich literature comparing recent transitions to democratic rule – in the "South," or Latin America and southern Europe, and, more recently, in the "East" as well, or the former socialist world (see, e.g., O'Donnell, Schmitter, and Whitehead, 1987; Linz and Stepan, 1996). Most of these studies have been influenced in significant ways by one approach in particular: transitology.

Like most approaches in the social sciences, so this approach downplays the impact of certain factors, while emphasizing others. Thus, what matters to the transitions school is what might be termed "proximate politics" – or the mode of transition (whether pacting or mass mobilization), the dynamics of bargaining between authoritarian elites and their democratic challengers, and the design of democratic institutions. Of less concern in these explanations has been such factors as the nature of the authoritarian past and its institutional characteristics, and the role of that past, along with economics, nationalism, and the international system, in shaping the dynamics of recent democratization.

What is also assumed in most of these studies is that recent democratization has particular characteristics that both differentiate this process from earlier rounds of democratization and that produce certain overarching similarities among new democracies. Thus, for instance, recent democratization is quick and amenable to crafting, not slow or evolutionary in its development. At the same time, all new democracies are defined primarily by where they are going rather than where they have been (see especially Przeworski, 1991). Where they are heading is influenced, in turn, by the capacity of their leaders to manage three tasks: breaking with the authoritarian past, constructing democratic institutions, and eliciting the support, or at least the acquiescence, of authoritiarian elites. These distinctive and common attributes of recent democratization, moreover, lead to a final assumption. New democracies, whatever their origins and trajectories and wherever their regional location, can be profitably compared with each other.

This book has involved comparisons within one region in particular, eastern Europe, with respect to the first stage in the transition story – the breakdown of authoritarian rule. As such, this study, along with recent work on postcommunism, can help us rethink, if not amend, our understanding of recent transitions to democracy. One issue that emerges from such an exercise is to question the explanatory factors emphasized by transitologists. While minimized in most studies of the South, factors such as economic decline (and redistribution), the international system (including norms, demonstration, and diffusion effects), mass protest (see Tarrow, 1995), and, especially, nationalism loomed large indeed in this study of the departure of socialist dictatorships from the European stage.

Even more fundamental to the eastern European story was another factor downplayed in analyses of recent democratization – the socialist past. As argued throughout this book, what mattered primarily about the socialist past was the institutional design of these dictatorships. That design sealed the fate of socialism, much as transitologists see institutional design influencing the prospects for democratic consolidation. Through their propensity for deregulation, moreover, socialist institutions ensured that the successor regimes, economic and political, would be liberalized, if not fully liberal, by comparison. As already observed, socialism was both destructive and constructive, and it was in its latter role that socialism, ironically, opened up the possibility of a liberal future for eastern Europe – a future, we must remember, that had virtually no historical precedent in that region, in contrast to most of Latin America and southern Europe. In this peculiar way, then, socialist dictatorships, because of their form and functioning, made a significant break with the authoritarian past both desirable and possible.

If socialism destroyed itself and shaped possible and logical postsocialist trajectories, moreover, it also structured the actual agenda of the successor systems – and, what is more, gave that agenda what was by comparative standards a distinctive cast. Thus, postcommunism has merged the issues of nation, state, and regime. By contrast, questions surrounding nation and state formation were resolved long before this most recent round of democratization in Latin America and southern Europe (albeit with some exceptions), and transitions to democracy in that context are, as a result, relatively uncluttered by such complications. Moreover, to build capitalism and democracy, along with the construction of new relationships between the state and the international system, is to engage in a far more all-embracing and, thus, radical project than what one finds in either Latin America or southern Europe.

These striking differences between democratization in the East versus the South are only magnified, moreover, once we recognize yet another distinctive characteristic of the East. Twenty-two of the twenty-seven states in the post-Communist region are new. Indeed, if we treat the Soviet bloc as an empire and expand our definition of new states to include those that are newly sovereign, then this number increases to embrace virtually every country in the post-Communist region, save Albania. By contrast, *none* of the new democracies in southern Europe and Latin America are either new or newly sovereign states.

How this agenda has shaped the politics, economics, and culture of postcommunism, moreover, testifies as well to the long shadow cast by the socialist past. This is the case whether we look, for example, at economic reform (see Burawoy and Kratov, 1993; McFaul, 1995, 1997; Stark, 1992), democratization (Ekiert, 1998), patterns of mass protest (Ekiert and Kubik, 1997; Crowley, 1994), or the design of political institutions (Easter, 1997; Luong, 1996). To repeat an earlier point, then, socialist institutions organized politics and economics in disorganized times. In this way, the uncertainties of the future were framed in significant ways by the socialist past – or what Václav Havel (1998: 42), the Czech playwright-president, has recently characterized as that "time of certainties," however "small-minded, banal and suicidal for society."

The power of the socialist past – and the ways in which that past has placed a distinctive stamp on postcommunism – brings to the fore three related questions of central concern to the comparative study of democratization. First, does the weight of socialism after socialism mean that the transition to democracy in eastern Europe will be more prolonged, more difficult, and more mixed in its outcomes than such transitions in the South (see Linz and Stepan, 1996)? The answer seems to be mixed. On the one hand, multiple and simultaneous transitions would seem to constitute an enormous burden, as would the weakness, because of socialism, of civil and political society and the absence in most of eastern Europe of a democratic past (see especially Krygier, 1997). On the other hand, eastern Europe has several important assets, particularly in its northern tier.

For example, there is the tradition during socialist rule (albeit not in every case, as we discovered in Chapters 4 and 6) of civilian control over the military (see Barany, 1997) – a tradition that contributed to the peaceful revolutions of 1989–1992 and that is lacking not just in Latin American history but also even in contemporary Latin American constitutions (see Loveman, 1994). Other advantages include exceptionally high literacy rates, a relatively egalitarian social structure at the transitional point of departure, incorporation into European multilateral institutions that provide incentives for developing capitalism and democracy (though unevenly so – see Bunce, 1998d), and, finally, and most unexpectedly, the felicitous, not disastrous combination of rapid political and economic reform (on this point, see Bunce, 1994, 1998b, 1998c; Greskovits, 1998; Fish, 1998). Whether those factors or the more well-chronicled constraints on post-Communist democratization will prove to be decisive remains to be seen.

A second question is whether, in view of the striking differences between the East and the South, we can accept the idea, central to transitology, of a set of tasks common to all recent transitions to democracy. Here, I would argue, once again joining the arguments in this book with other research, that transitologists are in fact correct in their summary of democracy as an enterprise involving everywhere breakage with the past, construction of democratic institutions, and co-optation of authoritarian elites. However, where the East and the South differ, and where the socialist past comes directly into play, is the range of strategies effectively available to meet (and to juggle) these objectives and the particular payoffs attached to strategic options (see Bunce, 1998c). For example, because the socialist past was so powerful, breakage rather than bridging, as in the South through pacting, was the approach that produced the most rapid and full-scale transition to democracy in eastern Europe. This is the case, moreover, whether we examine the transition to capitalism, the transition to democracy, or the transition to a new relationship between the state and the international system. Similarly, the relationship between democratization and economic reform is quite different in the South versus the East. In the South, economic reform is at odds with democratization, and that is one major reason why most transitologists counsel a sequencing of democratization first and social and economic reforms later (see especially Linz and Stepan, 1996; Przeworski, 1991; Maravall, 1993; Haggard and Kaufman, 1995). By contrast, what we find in the post-Communist world is an affinity between the two. Just as fast-track democracy invariably goes with fast-track capitalism, so slow progress on the political front varies with slow progress on the economic front.

The final question follows from the first two. Is the comparison between democratization in the East versus the South viable and valuable? My response is that such comparisons are both problematic and yet illuminating. They are problematic, because of the differences already noted – differences structured in the final analysis by the institutional design of socialist dictatorships. If nothing else, then, these differences suggest that there are many ways to leave dictatorship and many ways to get to democracy, as well as many ways to get sidetracked in the process. And these ways seem to follow a certain logic, in this instance regional, that reflects the interaction between the tasks of transition and the authoritarian heritage.

However, interregional comparisons are also helpful. They alert us to factors we might otherwise ignore – for instance, the benefits for eastern European democracy of the tradition of civilian control over the military and the burden, common to both Latin American and eastern European democracies, of a weak rule-of-law tradition (see, e.g., Krygier, 1997; O'Donnell, 1997). Such comparisons also force us to look at variations in strategies and payoffs as a consequence of the historical and, thus, the contemporary context of transformation; they allow us to test the limits of generalizations; and they teach us a certain humility when claiming to generalize about new democracies. Finally, they force us to confront an issue at the very heart of the study of democratization and, more generally, comparative politics: that is, whether countries or regions are in fact so distinctive that they render their inclusion in a larger comparative exercise impossible (see Przeworski and Teune, 1970).

AREA STUDIES VERSUS COMPARATIVE POLITICS

It is precisely this issue – the place of place in comparative inquiry – that has prompted a recent and rather acrimonious debate about what constitutes "good social science" (see, e.g., Shea, 1997; Bates, 1997; Hall and Tarrow, 1998). This debate is, of course, a replay of earlier rounds of "academic reform." What is different about the current version is that it was prompted in large measure by two specific developments, one in the real world of politics and the other in the theoretical world of political scientists and sociologists. Here, I refer to the downfall of communism, on the one hand, and the rise of rational choice, on the other.

With the collapse of communism, specialists in Soviet and Eastern European studies, along with others presumed to be members as well of the "area specialist" club, became the target of a series of criticisms launched by "comparativists." In particular, it was suggested that the failure of scholars to predict the collapse of socialism reflected not so much the inherent difficulty of predicting large-scale change or the serious data limitations built into the study of socialist dictatorships as quite another factor: the inherent limitations built into all work done by "area specialists" as a consequence of what was presumed to be their entrenched hostility to theory, their absorption with minutiae, their disinterest in comparison, and their isolation from larger theoretical trends in political science and sociology. At the same time, the growth area within the discipline was rational choice – an approach that was parsimonious in its assumptions and explanations and that minimized the need for detailed area knowledge. When combined, therefore, rational choice became the "other" of area studies, and the key choice for social scientists became one of selecting between two starkly contrasting alternatives: being a comparativist, and thereby committed to theory in general and parsimonious explanation in particular, or being an area specialist, committed to knowing a single place in great detail and to elaborate, single-case explanations.

My response to these characterizations and charges and the acrimonious debate they have produced can be stated succinctly. First, as this book, I trust, illustrates, one does not have to choose between knowing places and using theory. Rather, good and useful work in comparative politics rests on a more subtle and interrelated set of objectives. In particular, one needs to know places, engage in systematic comparisons, proceed with these comparisons on the basis of theory, and emerge from all this with a relatively parsimonious explanation. What undermines comparative study is the absence of one or the other of these four concerns. In this sense, the binary choice between area studies and comparative politics is both artificial and misleading.

Second, it follows from the arguments presented in this book that region does matter – not as a geographical concept (though the location of eastern Europe does explain a lot of its historical development – see, e.g., Szucs, 1983; Bunce, 1998a), but, rather, as a convenient summary of a constellation of characteristics that are shared by countries clustered together in space and that differentiate these countries in turn from others located elsewhere (see King, 1996). However, having asserted the importance of region, I must note several qualifications. One is that the impact of region, far from being fixed, depends on the research question being addressed. Thus, while regional factors in this study could account for the similar outcome of regime collapse in the eastern half of Europe, they could not account for variations in, say, how regimes ended or whether states dismembered. Moreover, for the regional factor to have meaning, we needed to compare socialist dictatorships with other dictatorships, as we did in Chapter 2. Another qualification is that the very nature of socialism rendered region in this instance an unusually meaningful term, whether analyzing developments during the socialist period or after. In most situations, however, region – or country, for that matter – is a less accurate, efficient, or helpful way of summarizing variables. Finally, whether region is meaningful is always an empirical question. Thus, to argue for the importance of region or country is to take on a burden of proof – not just in demonstrating distinctiveness, but, just as importantly, in demonstrating *how* that distinctiveness translates into specific economic, political, and social outcomes. To assert that place matters, then, only makes sense once how it matters is specified.

Finally, this book testifies not just to the importance of the socialist past in shaping the exit from socialism, but also the importance of another past – that is, the field of what used to be termed Soviet and Eastern European studies. As the notes in this study indicate, the story of the end of socialism and the state could never have been constructed (or substantiated) without all those investigations that were conducted during the so-called dark ages of the field, when socialism was king and specialists were king watchers, if not at times king guessers. Communist studies, in short, did some things right – often using, I might add, an abundance of theory and comparisons, usually in conjunction with a wealth of data but sometimes, because there was no recourse, as a filler for missing data. In this sense, the study of the Soviet Union and Eastern Europe during the socialist era was no different from other area *and* comparative studies.

NOTES

CHAPTER 1

1 In this book, the terms "the Soviet Union" and "Eastern Europe" are used when referring to those countries in the eastern half of Europe that were socialist dictatorships during the cold war era. When referring to this area after the collapse of socialism from 1989 to 1990, I use the term "eastern Europe." Thus, the presumption in this study is that the designation eastern Europe includes Russia – as it has for several centuries, except for the interruption of the cold war era.

   Another term, "socialism," also needs some clarification. Rather than use the term "state socialism," which has traditionally referred to socialist regimes based on the Soviet model (thereby excluding Yugoslavia), I have opted to use, interchangeably, a variety of terms – socialist regimes, the European socialist regimes, socialist dictatorships, and the like – when referring to the countries that made up the Soviet Union and Eastern Europe during the cold war era. In using these various terms, however, I do not mean to imply either that these regimes represented the only possible form of socialism in theory or in practice, or that socialism was or is an inherently dictatorial political project.

2 On the end of socialist regimes, see, e.g., Lewin, 1988; Rutland, 1992; O'Neil, 1996; Solnick, 1998a; Bernhard, 1993; Kubik, 1994; Brown, 1991; Ekiert, 1996; Thomas, 1997; Levesque, 1997; Stokes, 1993; Verdery, 1996; Kuran, 1992; Bolčić, 1983, 1989; Golubović, 1988; Kuzmanović, 1995.

3 This is in part because the field of Communist studies, even as these regimes were passing from the scene, was sharply divided with respect to areal focus – between those who worked on the Soviet Union and those who focused on Eastern Europe and, within the latter, between specialists on the Soviet satellite states and specialists on "deviant" Yugoslavia. As for Albania, its isolation meant that little work was done on this regime (see Glenny, 1997).

4 For analyses of state dismemberment in the former Communist world, see, e.g., Dunlop, 1993a; Laba, 1996; Gorbachev, 1993; Yel'tsin, 1994; Stanovčić,

1993; Cohen, 1993; Magaš, 1993; Gow, 1992; Silber and Little, 1996; Woodward, 1995a; Tašić, 1994; Simić, 1995; Musil, 1995a; Henderson, 1994; Lukic and Lynch, 1996).

5 It can be argued, however, that the European Union functions under certain circumstances to integrate cultural minorities – or at least to reduce their incentives to press for statehood. This argument has been made, for example, for the Basques and the Catalans in Spain, and it might be a valid point when applied to Belgium as well.

6 One way to account for the breakup of these states is to treat them as empires and argue that: (1) they were multinational in their political-cultural composition; (2) they lacked, as a result, legitimacy; and (3) they broke up through the familiar process of decolonization (see, e.g., Dawisha and Parrott, 1997; Parrott, 1997). While it is true that these states blurred the boundaries between state and empire as a consequence of having territorially compact national minorities, it is also true that they featured several typical and defining characteristics of states. These include their geographical contiguity, historical precedent for existing boundaries, formal political equality among constituent units and nations, and full ideological penetration. By the final point, I refer to the fact that these states featured a single ideological framework, in contrast to the discontinuities in ideological systems within empires. These characteristics lead me to conclude that little is to be gained by treating them as empires. Instead, Yugoslavia, the Soviet Union, and Czechoslovakia were states that were distinctive within the socialist region, because they were national-federal and not unitary in their structure.

7 This is less the case for the boundaries that formed in the wake of decolonization – though even here, as the Indian experience with decolonization reminds us, boundaries were contested and reframed. What seemed to have mattered in these cases – and what was to provide continuing problems postindependence – was the power of the political-administrative boundaries set by the colonial powers. In our cases, a similar argument will be made, with the emphasis shifting from the boundaries of the state to the boundaries of the republics that made up these three federalized socialist states. Indeed, the power of these administrative residues even seems to extend to the process of regime building (see, e.g., Luong, 1997; Treisman, 1997).

8 As will be evident throughout this book, these variations are relevant not just in differentiating among socialist states, but also, in our cases in particular, within these states. Thus, the process of regime disintegration was very different in Slovenia versus Bosnia; in Lithuania versus Ukraine; and in the Czech lands versus Slovakia. Indeed, it was the variation in these developments by republic within Yugoslavia, the Soviet Union, and Czechoslovakia – and the resulting differences by republic in political dynamics, elite coalitions, and the like – that explains in part the disintegration of these states and their reinvention along republican lines.

9 It is important to note here that states end in practice under one of two conditions. One, which will not be the concern of this book, is "from the outside." This is where a significant shift in the distribution of power in the international system – usually during or after major wars – leads powerful states to construct a new state system and, in the process, to refigure the boundaries of weaker

states. Obvious historical examples include the Polish partitions of the late eighteenth century, as well as the more recent examples, of, say, the reduction of Hungary and the expansion of Romania after World War I. The other method is "from the inside." This is where pressures from within the state (which are entangled, to be sure, with pressures and resources originating outside the state) function at the least to call existing state boundaries into question and, at most, to redraw those boundaries or extinguish the state entirely. It is this process, involving domestic conflicts over territory and authority between the center and one or more regions, that is the subject of this book.

10 As we will see throughout this study, the socialist context complicates considerably our understanding of the process, as well as the indicators, of state collapse. This is in part because of the extraordinary fusion of regime and state in these systems (which meant in effect that regime collapse carried with it the distinct possibility of state collapse); in part because of the segmentation in form and function of both regime and state in federalized socialist systems; and in part because of the difficulties in pinpointing the collapse of the state's coercive monopoly. With regard to the final point, we must note the considerable variation among our cases in the capacity *and* the willingness of the state to defend itself and to use the military to do so – ranging from the absence in effect of a state defense in Czechoslovakia to the quite complex cases of the Soviet Union and Yugoslavia. In the Soviet case, for example, the state's defense of itself took quite varying forms over the course of 1991 – for example, selected and limited military intervention in the Baltic area in the winter, followed by division within the military ranks in August, followed in turn by the formal and peaceful division of the state at the end of the year with the military standing on the sidelines. Yugoslavia presents a different though equally complex picture of the state and the military, given that the Yugoslav National Army represented the center, but also represented Serbian national interests. Thus, its intervention in the processes of secession both protected and destroyed the state.

11 Michael Hechter (1992) has distinguished, for example, between fragmentation, where the center begins to disappear and political authority is reallocated, and secession, where the center remains a political player and bargains with its periphery. However, because the boundaries of the state still exist under both circumstances, because even weakened states still tend to have certain powers (such as the military), and because state elites, at least in a historical sense, have tended to take quite variable positions on a reduction in state boundaries, the use of the more general category of secession for all processes that involve a potential or actual subtraction of a region from the state seems to make more sense.

12 For institutional analyses, see, e.g., Steinmo, Thelen, and Longstreth, 1992; March and Olsen, 1984; Searing, 1991; Linz and Stepan, 1996. For representative studies of revolution and social movements, see Tilly, 1993; Tarrow, 1994; McCarthy and Zald, 1987; McAdams, Tarrow, and Tilly, 1997; Foran and Goodwin, 1993. Finally, for work on nationalism and secession, see, e.g., Anderson, 1991; Hobsbawm, 1992; Hroch, 1996; Hechter, 1977, 1987, 1992; Bates, 1983; Young, 1993; Horowitz, 1981, 1985, 1994; Brubaker, 1996; Beissinger, 1993, 1995a, 1996; Roeder, 1991.

CHAPTER 2

1 This must be qualified for both Yugoslavia and Poland, where there was a large, private agricultural sector. However, for both of these cases, the weight of the private sector in the overall economy was limited, such that the public sector accounted for approximately 80 percent of all goods and services produced.

2 The exception here is Yugoslavia, which, in the 1960s, began a shift from planning to markets (see especially Milenkovitch, 1971; Comisso, 1979; Woodward, 1995b). However, as I argue in Chapter 3, the market in Yugoslavia was heavily politicized and regionally segmented, which reflected the interaction between political decentralization and the political-economic monopoly of the League of Communists. In this sense, Yugoslav socialism is better understood as a variation on state socialism rather than a competing model.

3 One cost of atomization, in combination with the larger characteristics of dictatorship, became apparent in negotiations to end the war in Croatia and then Bosnia. As Paul Szasz, a specialist in international law and an advisor to many of these negotiations recently put it to me, a key problem in trying to stop the fighting was that the players from the region had no understanding of what bargaining meant. Their idea was simply to declare what they wanted rather than to rank preferences, calculate trade-offs, search for workable compromises, and, more generally, engage in direct exchanges while seeking areas of intersecting interests. This reflected not just weak commitment to finding solutions, but also inexperience with the very notion of decisions as the outcome of bargaining processes.

4 The one exception to this generalization was Yugoslavia, which, beginning in 1965 with market-oriented reforms and integration into the global economy, produced growing levels of unemployment (see Woodward, 1995b). This was a problem for the regime, especially since levels of unemployment tended to vary substantially by republic.

5 It is interesting to note here that many of the very same factors that brought socialist publics together have been used to explain why certain types of workers – for example, miners and shipyard workers – tend to be unusually prone to strikes and demonstrations (see, e.g., Kerr and Siegel, 1954).

6 This brings to mind a story once related to me by Maciej Kozlowski. Following the pope's visit to Poland and the outbreak soon thereafter of major protests at the end of the 1970s, Polish journalists of the dissident persuasion gathered one evening to debate not just if but when the regime would fall. After giving their estimates, the journalists then addressed the question of optimal timing. Typical of their comments in this instance was the following: "I don't want the regime to fall until early 1981, since by that time I will be at the top of the waiting list to get a new apartment (or a new car)."

7 The introduction of reforms was not just a reaction to the pressing need for change; it was also built into the socialist enterprise. Here, a useful analogy has been provided by Vojislav Stanovčić (1989). As he has argued, as with a bicycle, so with socialism constant forward movement was necessary in order to achieve balance (also see Csanádi, 1997). There was, in short, a certain reform mania built into socialism that was a product of both the need to expand and the absence of self-corrective mechanisms.

CHAPTER 3

1 The Romanian case is harder to categorize. On the one hand, Romania was never expelled from the Soviet alliance (as was the case for Yugoslavia and then Albania). On the other hand, Romania was less integrated into the bloc than, say, Hungary, Poland, and others. This was reflected, for example, in the departure of Soviet troops from Romania in 1962; Romanian refusal to participate in the invasion of Czechoslovakia in 1968; subsequent Romanian resistance at times to Warsaw Pact exercises and Comecon negotiations; and the Ceausescu regime's pursuit of a distinctive road to socialism that involved, among other things, the establishment of a patrimonial dictatorship (which, in practice, degenerated into "socialism in one family") and an independent foreign policy stressing Romanian nationalism and close diplomatic and trade relations between Romania and the West and Romania and Third World countries (see especially Linden, 1986).

2 I use the term "national" instead of "ethnic" for three reasons. First, in some of these cases (such as with the Muslims, the constitutive nationality in Bosnia-Herzegovina, the Croatians, the constitutive nationality in Croatia, and the Serbs, the constitutive nationality in Serbia), ethnicity and ethnic distinctiveness are misnomers. Second, in the discourse within these countries during the socialist period (represented, for example, in their constitutions), the emphasis was on the existence of national diversity and nationalities, some of which were alloted political units within the federal structure. Finally, nation connotes the idea of a shared political community, which can be based on ideology, citizenship, language, ethnicity, and/or religion. Indeed, until the final half of the nineteenth century, nation was primarily understood as a category having few implications for language, religion, or ethnicity.

3 For discussions surrounding the purposes behind national federalism in the Soviet Union, see, e.g., Pipes, 1968; Zaslavsky, 1993; Motyl, 1987, 1991; Roeder, 1991; Hodnett, 1967; Suny, 1992, 1993; Slezkine, 1994; Huttenbach, 1990; Gleason, 1990; Dmitrijević, 1995; Stanovčić, 1989; Goati, 1989; Brubaker, 1996; Lapidus, 1992; Lapidus and Walker, 1995; and Goldman, Lapidus and Zaslavskv, 1992.

4 There was a possibility that the formation of Yugoslavia after World War I might have produced a roughly similar structure of federalism with subunits defined in national-territorial terms. This was, for example, the position of the Croats in the deliberations over the formation of the state. However, for a variety of reasons (not the least of which was the absence of much in the way of deliberations involving all affected parties), the "Kingdom of the Serbs, Croats and Slovenes" was formed as a unitary state (see especially Banac, 1984). It should also be noted that the founding of national federalism in Yugoslavia after World War II and the diversification of the republics that followed reflected in part debates within the Yugoslav Communist Party during the interwar period (see Woodward, 1995b: 36–42; also Irvine, 1991).

5 However, only in Yugoslavia was there a "pan-national" category – or "Yugoslav" – that figured not just in the census, but also in official and informal discourse.

6 What also contributed to national identity was the introduction of the internal passport system – as in the Soviet Union, beginning in 1932. This tended to

lock national groups into their homelands, while, in the Soviet case, giving official status to membership in a particular national group.

7 As in domestic socialism in general, so in the federal cases the absence of transparency in pricing, budgets, and the like made it easy to assume discrimination against the republic and, perhaps, favoritism of other republics (see especially Brada, 1994, on this point for the Czechs and Slovaks; and Echols, 1975, on redistribution along republican lines).

8 The sovereignty of the nations that had republics was recognized by the Yugoslav, Soviet, and Czechoslovak constitutions. However, as Robert Hayden (1995a) and Vojislav Stanovčić (1993–1994) have observed, in the Yugoslav case this had less constitutional force, since the right to national self-determination was granted in the preamble to the 1974 (or last) Yugoslav constitution (see *Ustav socijalisticke federativne republike*, 1981: 3). However, at the same time, this was not Serbia's interpretation, since the revised Serbian constitution of 1989 – which predated similar efforts in Slovenia and Croatia – stated Serbian sovereignty quite clearly. My thanks to Tibor Varady for pointing this out to me.

9 Recent work by historians on immediate postwar Yugoslavia indicates, however, that despite draconian purges carried out by the Yugoslav Communists in a manner typical of Leninist regimes, the Yugoslav leadership was nonetheless constrained in what it did from the beginning by the mass public (see, e.g., Bokovoy, 1997; Lilly, 1994).

CHAPTER 4

1 The Albanian case receives less attention in this chapter than the other regimes in the region. This is because decades of isolation has left quite skeletal information on Albania during the socialist period (see Glenny, 1997).

2 It became commonplace, even among specialists, to speak of the sclerosis of Communist systems, especially during the Brezhnev era. However, while it was true that the high rates of elite turnover characteristic of these systems in earlier decades slowed down, it was also true that even Brezhnev introduced a considerable number of policy innovations, including the remarkably risky and, in the socialist context, unorthodox decision to open up the bloc to Western trade and capital. Moreover, in the Brezhnev period, as at other times, policy innovation was cyclical. Virtually all of the major policy initiatives introduced by socialist leaders come at the beginning of their terms in office and become from there onward standard operating procedures (Bunce, 1981; Breslauer, 1982).

3 It is ironic that the phrase "the self-determination of nations" was first mentioned in international documents in response to developments in eastern Europe – most notably, in the Proclamation on the Polish Question endorsed by the London Conference of the First International (Connor, 1972; Esman, 1994). Since that time, the phrase has appeared in the United Nations Charter, Article I, paragraph 2, and, more recently, in the Helsinki Final Act of 1975. It was through the Helsinki process that this idea could be said to have become an influential international norm – in large measure because it had been around so long and because of the procedures for adopting the Final Act.

4 "Glasnost'" was a term that first surfaced during the Alexandrine reforms of the nineteenth century. It was understood then *and* during the Gorbachev era

to be a mechanism by which dictatorships could get the benefit of pluralism (i.e., feedback and criticism) without the costs – the collapse of dictatorial control over the media and public opinion. All this was to occur through the use of publicity in order to expose problems, deficiencies, and the like. See Bunce, 1993, on the many parallels between the Brezhnev-Gorbachev eras and the reigns of Nicholas I and Alexander II.

5 Here, it is interesting to note in passing the parallels between Hungary and Spain. The fear of revolution and counterrevolution had also played a key role in moving Spain to a pacted transition from dictatorship to democracy and, subsequently, to a prominent role within the literature on transitions as "the very model of a modern elite settlement" (see Gunther, 1992; Edles, 1998; Linz and Stepan, 1996: 100–107).

6 This was evident, for example, in the rapid emptying of these Communist parties – as good a measure as any of the decline of ideological commitment and the dominance of opportunists within the party ranks.

7 Albania is included in this list, because, while the events of 1989–1990 were not on the whole violent, they became so, beginning in 1991, in large measure because of the incomplete character of this transition and the breakdown of law and order (see Glenny, 1997).

8 In Chapter 7, we discuss at greater length the role of the military in the Soviet, Yugoslav, and Czechoslovak cases of regime and state transformation. Suffice to note here that other factors must be brought in to account for the peaceful character of the Soviet revolution in particular – that is, the historical role and mission of the Soviet military and its relationship to civilian authority.

CHAPTER 5

1 Beginning in the mid-1970s, with the collapse of the Salazar regime in Portugal, there have been a number of regime transitions from dictatorship to democracy that have been peaceful. However, in most of the Latin American and southern European cases (with Portugal an exception), the processes involved did not include regime collapse. And they certainly did not involve as well a collapse of the state (see especially Fishman, 1990, on Spain).

2 Indeed, even if we add other factors commonly thought to boost the mobilization propensities of large and compact minorities (for instance, level of socioeconomic development relative to other regions and to the overall norm, degree of national consciousness, a prior history of such mobilization, or extent of representation of regions in the central political leadership), we cannot explain the interregional variations in nationalist mobilization in the last years of socialism. On these factors, see, e.g., Gourevitch, 1979; Horowitz, 1981, 1985, 1994; Hechter and Levi, 1979.

3 The literature on the national histories of Yugoslavia and Czechoslovakia is voluminous – for a tasting, see, e.g., Banac, 1984; Burg, 1983; Dubravčić, 1993; Flaherty, 1989; Golubović, 1995; Bičanić, 1973; Bookman, 1990; Krizan, 1993; Lampe, 1996; Stokes, Lampe, and Rusinow with Mostov, 1996; S. Ramet, 1984; P. Ramet, 1985; Vodapivec, 1992; Vujačić, 1996, on Yugoslavia. On Czechoslovakia, see, for instance, Leff, 1988; Wolchik, 1991, 1995; Bartlova, 1995; Musil, 1995b; Pithart, 1995; Rychlik, 1995; Henderson, 1994; Prihoda, 1995).

4 This incorrect rendition of international histories had particular and destructive consequences with respect to Western reactions to the wars of secession in Yugoslavia. In assuming the constancy of inter-national conflict, Western decision makers found it easy to code national conflicts accompanying the collapse of Yugoslavia as typical Balkan politics that were irrational in origin and expression and thereby beyond the control of the (more rational and more civilized) West. On the "Balkan problem," see, e.g., Larrabie, 1990–1991; Kaplan, 1993; Kennan, 1993: 3–11). For insightful critiques of these convenient assumptions, see Todorova, 1994; Lampe, 1996; Donia and Fine, 1994; Gagnon, 1994–1995; Lytle, 1992.

5 Of course, Milošević was aware of Serbian nationalism, given, for example, the Memorandum of the Serbian Academy of Sciences (published in 1986) and a protest signed in January of the same year by two thousand Serbs from Kosovo, which was then published in a Serbian newspaper and followed up by the visit of representatives of the Serbian minority from Kosovo to Belgrade in February and April (see especially Silber and Little 1996: 29–35). However, what the April meeting showed Milošević was the potency *and* utility of Serbian nationalism.

6 What also did not help matters in Yugoslavia was that in the late 1980s, republics (led by Slovenia and Croatia) began to plan for holding competitive elections prior to any plans at the center for scheduling such elections at the federal level. This was in direct contrast to the sequencing of such elections in both the Soviet Union and Czechoslovakia, but in keeping, it must be remembered, with Yugoslav traditions – given, for instance, the holding since the mid-1960s of republican party congresses prior to the federal party congress. By holding competitive elections in the republics first (and, indeed, last), the future of the Yugoslav center, already bleak, became more so; the possibilities for an all-Yugoslav and nonnationalist political movement or party dimmed (though the prime minister, Ante Marković, did throw together such a party, only to see it lose time and again – see Tašić, 1993); and Yugoslav politics and economics were fully captured by the republics and their nationalist leaders and followers (see more generally on the costs of electoral sequencing Linz and Stepan, 1992).

CHAPTER 6

1 This comparison hardly exhausts the variable ways in which ex-Communists and others used nationalism in the post-Communist context in order to further their power and policy goals. One can point, for example, to the case of the ex-Communist Milan Kučan, who, again because of the particular mixture of incentives provided by the context within which he operated, managed to preserve his political future by combining nationalism, liberalism, and secession in Slovenia. One can also point to the case of Vladimír Mečiar, also an ex-Communist, who succeeded in Slovakia by combining nationalism and the threat of secession with a far more tempered vision of economic and especially political liberalization.

2 The final argument was used selectively. When Yel'tsin was building bridges to the liberal intelligentsia, to reformers within the party-state and to republican leaders that linked nationalism with liberalization, the emphasis was placed

on rapid and radical reform. However, when Yel'tsin was reaching out to republican leaders who were less supportive of reform, the emphasis shifted to republican sovereignty and the freedom it would give republican leaders and their followers to define their own economic and political trajectories.

3 These explanations, of course, do not exhaust the possibilities (see Fearon, 1994). One could argue, for example, that the number of units in the federation was important; that the degree of nationalist pluralism was crucial; or that the size of the dominant nation was critical. However, these three arguments are also problematic. From a game theoretic perspective, one could argue that the situation most prone to violence might very well have been the dual structure of Czechoslovakia, or that the number of units involved in both the Soviet and Yugoslav cases was sufficiently large to have produced a wide range of positions on state dismemberment and thus violence in response to these different positions. Second, while Czechoslovakia was the least diverse, featured the most homogeneous republican units, and, thus, would seem to have presented the best case for peaceful division, the similarities between Yugoslavia and the Soviet Union along these dimensions, despite their contrasting processes of state dismemberment, seem to cast doubt on the importance of these variables. Finally, Serbians were a smaller portion of the Yugoslav population than was the case for either Czechs or Russians. However, this would seem to predict that Serbs would be less, not more likely to contest the end of the state and the establishment of new state boundaries along republican lines.

4 On the eve of state collapse, both Czechoslovakia and the Soviet Union had become in fact confederal systems. This had to do with constitutional changes (which were implemented to some degree in Czechoslovakia in 1990–1991, but only proposed in the Soviet Union through the draft of the new Union Treaty) and with more informal dynamics reflecting the weakening of the state along with the regime.

5 It is a telling observation, for example, that both the Czech republic and Russia, on independence, immediately converted those all-union institutions into their own state institutions.

6 What also must be recognized was that the brief war in Slovenia reflected two contradictory influences. On the one hand, the JNA was dispatched to Slovenia to protect Yugoslavia. On the other hand, Milošević and the leader of Slovenia, Milan Kučan, had already made a prior and secret agreement to allow Slovenia to leave (see especially Glenny, 1995, on this point and on the secret agreement between Milošević and Tudjman, the leader of Croatia, to carve up Bosnia; and, for further support, see Kadijević, 1993; Jović, 1995b).

7 There is also some evidence that the JNA prepared for the wars of secession – by, for example, demilitarizing the territorial militias (which proved to be particularly important in Croatia), changing the local command structure, and redrawing the boundaries of military districts, all prior to the breakout of war (see Jović, 1995a; Vasić and Švarm, 1995b).

CHAPTER 7

1 What was also crucial, as discussed in Chapter 6, was the definition of the military's mission in the Soviet Union and in the Warsaw Treaty Organization. Thus, the bloc's military was understood not just to be under the control of the

Soviet Union, but also to be a force focused on external rather than internal threats. This was in contrast to the mission of the military in Yugoslavia in particular – as evidenced by, for example, its repeated interventions in Yugoslav domestic politics, even before the wars in Slovenia and Croatia began in mid-1991.

2 This also explains the contrast between pacted regimes' transitions, as in Poland and Hungary, and mass mobilization, as East Germany, Czechoslovakia, Bulgaria, Romania, and Albania. Thus, pacted transitions occurred where the economy was disastrous and the political environment liberalized. Both pointed to a large contingent of reform Communists that functioned as a bridge between the regime and a fairly large opposition. However, in more hard-line regimes, such a bridge did not exist, and protest led the way out of socialism. What also facilitated protest was the precedents set by Hungary and Poland. Events there weakened the parties elsewhere, while strengthening the opposition – not just because the Communists gave up power in Hungary and Poland, but also because the Soviets acquiesced to this outcome.

3 These preconditions seem to be both necessary and sufficient. Thus, when all four are in place, nationalist mobilization against the state is quite likely, and when one or more is missing, far less likely. This explains, for instance, why all the republics within the Soviet Union, Czechoslovakia, and Yugoslavia (save Montenegro, which had been taken over by Serbia) left the state, and why other political or national units within these three states did not. This also explains one other point that is often overlooked in the recent rush to study nationalism: why national minorities are ubiquitous, but nationalist mobilization against the state exceptional.

These four factors also help us make sense of yet another puzzle: the variations over time in nationalist protests mounted by the Albanian minority in Kosovo, a region within the present, as well as the former Yugoslavia. In the beginning of the 1980s and again in 1998, the Albanian minority living in Kosovo (but not elsewhere in Yugoslavia) mounted protests against Serbian domination. However, in between these two brief outbursts, the Albanians were quiescent – despite the turmoil of state dissolution and the continuity of their status as a large, compact majority within Kosovo, but a small minority within the country as a whole. What seems to explain this variable behavior are changes over time in institutional endowments and opportunities for protest. Thus, just as the early 1980s featured divisions within both the Yugoslav and Serbian political leadership and an increase in the constitutional powers of Kosovo relative to Serbia, so by 1997–1998 the Yugoslav state had weakened considerably, the Serbian leadership was again internally divided, and its Montenegrin allies had begun to go their separate political ways. As a result, Serbian control over Kosovo and the state declined sharply in the first half of the 1980s and, again, from 1997–1998. However, in between these two periods, the Serbian leadership was united, and they exercised dictatorial control over Kosovo. Thus, it was only when geographical compactness and established political boundaries *combined* with expanded institutional resources and opportunities for political change that Albanians in Kosovo mobilized against the state. This was the case, moreover, both during and after socialism, and, for that matter, during and after the Yugoslav state.

4 The discussion that follows excludes one issue: the violent end of Yugoslavia. Here, we would argue that the violent termination of this state, while facilitated by its institutional design, could possibly have been avoided. If Western powers had recognized sooner that Yugoslavia was going to end, instead of pressuring elites to hold the state together, they could have structured the dismemberment process in such a way as to avoid violence. This in turn could have weakened the position of Milošević and Tudjman and, thus, undercut their aggressive designs; allowed for the protection of minority rights; and guaranteed the security of those states, such as Bosnia, that were unusually vulnerable to outside intervention. However, such decisive actions in the context of 1990–1991 seem an unlikely scenario. International involvement in state dismemberment usually takes place, if at all, after states divide, not before or during the process of division. At the same time, such involvement would necessarily have required demilitarization and the stationing of NATO troops throughout Yugoslavia. Moreover, Western elites were still understandably wedded to the importance of stable state boundaries in Europe as a guarantee of peace, and they were, at the same time, absorbed with the turmoil of the Soviet Union and fearful that a division of Yugoslavia would legitimate such behavior in the Soviet Union, thereby producing, it was assumed, a civil war spanning Eurasia.

REFERENCES

Abbott, Andrew (1992). "From Causes to Events: Notes on Narrative." *Sociological Methods and Research* 20 (May): 428–455.

Anderson, Benedict (1991). *Imagined Communities: Reflections on the Origins and Spread of Nationalism.* London: Verso.

Anderson, Perry (1974). *Lineages of the Absolutist State.* London: Verso.

Andrić, Ivo (1945). *The Bridge on the Drina.* Chicago: University of Chicago Press.

Arbatov, Georgii (1991). *Zatianuvsheesia vyzdorovlenie (1953–1985gg): Svidetel'tsvo sovremennika.* Moscow: Mezhdunarodnye otnosheniia.

Arbatov, Georgii, and William Oltmans (1984). *Vystupaia v 80e: Kniga-intervyu ob aktual'nykh sovremennikh mezhdunarodnykh otnoshenni.* Moscow: Novosti.

Armstrong, John (1992). "The Autonomy of Ethnic Identity: Historic Cleavages and Nationality Relations in the USSR." In Alexander Motyl, ed., *Thinking Theoretically about Soviet Nationalities*, 23–43. New York: Columbia University Press.

Arutiunian, Iu. V., and L. M. Drobizheva, (1987). *Mnogoobrazie kul'turnoi zhizn' i narodov SSSR.* Moscow: Mysl'.

Ash, Timothy Garton (1989). "Refolution in Hungary and Poland." *New York Review of Books*, no. 36 (August 17): 9–15.

Azrael, Jeremy (1970). "Varieties of De-Stalinization." In Chalmers Johnson, ed., *Change in Communist Systems*, 135–151. Stanford, Calif.: Stanford University Press.

Bahry, Donna (1987). *Outside Moscow: Power, Politics and Budgetary Policy in the Soviet Republics.* New York: Columbia University Press.

——— (1991). "The Union Republics and Contradictions in Gorbachev's Economic Reform." *Soviet Economy* 7 (July–September): 215–255.

Balcerowicz, Leszek (1995). *Socialism, Capitalism, Transformation.* London: Central European University Press.

Banac, Ivo (1984). *The National Question in Yugoslavia.* Ithaca, N.Y.: Cornell University Press.

Barany, Zoltan (1993). "Civil-Military Relations in Comparative Perspective: East-Central and Southeastern Europe." *Political Studies* 41: 594–610.

(1994). "Living on the Edge: The East European Roma in Postcommunist Politics and Societies." *Slavic Review* 53 (Summer): 321–344.

(1997). "Democratic Consolidation and the Military: The East European Experience." *Comparative Politics* 30 (October): 21–43.

Bartlova, Alena (1995). "Political Power-Sharing in the Interwar Period." In Jiri Musil, ed., *The End of Czechoslovakia*, 159–179. Budapest: Central European Press.

Bates, Robert (1983). "Modernization, Ethnic Competition, and the Rationality of Politics in Contemporary Africa." In Donald Rothchild and Victor A. Olorunsola, eds., *State versus Ethnic Claims: African Policy Dilemmas*, 152–171. Boulder, Colo.: Westview Press.

(1997). "Theory in Comparative Politics?" *APSA – Comparative Politics Newsletter* 8 (Winter): 1–3.

Bates, Robert H., Rui J. P. de Figueiredo Jr., and Barry R. Weingast (1998). "The Politics of Interpretation: Rationality, Culture, and Transition." *Politics and Society* 26 (June): 221–256.

Beissinger, Mark (1993). "Protest Mobilization among Soviet Nationalities." Unpublished manuscript, Department of Political Science, the University of Wisconsin.

(1995a). "The State as Constructor of Nationalism: Nationalist Mobilization before and after the Soviet Union." Paper presented at the Conference on Communism, Post-Communism, and Ethnic Mobilization, Cornell University, Ithaca, N.Y., April 21–22.

(1995b). "The Persisting Ambiguity of Empire." *Post-Soviet Affairs* 11 (April–June): 149–184.

(1996). "How Nationalisms Spread: Eastern Europe Adrift the Tides and Cycles of Nationalist Contention." *Social Research* 63 (Spring): 97–146.

Benderly, Jill, and Evan Kraft, eds. (1994). *Independent Slovenia: Origins, Movements, Prospects*. New York: St. Martin's Press.

Berkowitz, Daniel, and Beth Mitchneck (1992). "Fiscal Decentralization of the Soviet Economy." *Comparative Economic Studies* 34 (Summer): 1–18.

Bernhard, Michael (1993). *The Origins of Democratization in Poland*. New York: Columbia University Press.

Bičanić, Ivo (1995). "The Economic Causes of New State Formation during the Transition." *East European Politics and Societies* 9 (Winter): 2–21.

Bičanić, Rudolf (1973). *Economic Policy in Socialist Yugoslavia*. Cambridge: Cambridge University Press.

Bilandžić, Dusan (1979). *Historija socijalisticke federativne republike Jugoslavije: glavni procesi*. 2d ed. Zagreb: Skolska Knjiga.

Blejer, Mario I., and Fabrizio Coricelli (1995). *The Making of Economic Reform in Eastern Europe: Conversations with the Leading Reformers in Poland, Hungary, and the Czech Republic*. Aldershot: Edward Elgar.

Bogomolov, Oleg, ed. (1989). *Perestroika: Glasnost', demokratiia, sotsializm*. Moscow: Progress Publishers.

Bokovoy, Melissa (1997). "Peasants and Partisans: Politics of the Yugoslav Countryside, 1945–1953." In Melissa Bokovoy, Jill Irvine, and Carol Lilly, eds., *State-Society Relations in Yugoslavia, 1945–1992*, 115–138. New York: St. Martin's Press.

Bolčić, Silvano (1983). *Razvoj i kriza Jugoslavenskog društva u sociološkoj perspektivi*. Belgrade: Radionica SIC.

——— (1989). "O odgovornosti saveza komunista za krizu i osnovnom smeru njegovog preobražaja." In Vladimir Goati, ed., *Smisao jugoslavenskog pluralistickog šoka*, 127–138. Belgrade: Književne novine.

Bookman, Milica Zarković (1990). "The Economic Basis of Regional Autarchy in Yugoslavia." *Soviet Studies* 42 (January): 93–109.

Bossuyt, Marc J. (1995). "Belgium: Bipolar and Centrifugal Federalism." Paper presented at the Conference on Conflict Resolution: The Search for Common Ground, UN Office Vienna, International Centre, July 24–25.

Bozoki, Andras, and Miklos Sukosd (1993). "Civil Society and Populism in the Eastern European Democratic Transitions." *Praxis International* 13 (October): 224–241.

Brada, Josef C. (1994). "The Slovak Economy during the First Year of Independence." In John Hardt and Richard Kaufman, eds., *East-Central European Economies in Transition*, 518–530. Washington, D.C.: U.S. Congress, Joint Economic Committee Government Printing Office.

Brass, Paul (1985). *Ethnic Groups and the State*. Totowa, N.J.: Barnes and Noble.

Bresaluer, George W. (1982). *Khrushchev and Brezhnev as Leaders: Building Authority in Soviet Politics*. London: Allen and Unwin.

——— (1989). "Evaluation of Gorbachev as a Leader." *Soviet Economy* 5 (October–December): 299–319.

Brown, David (1989). "Ethnic Revival: Perspectives on State and Society." *Third World Quarterly* 13: 1–17.

Brown, J. F. (1991) *Surge to Freedom: The End of Communist Rule in Eastern Europe*. Durham, N.C.: Duke University Press.

Brown, Michael E. (1993). "Causes and Implications of Ethnic Conflict." In Michael E. Brown, ed., *Ethnic Conflict and International Security*, 3–26. Princeton, N.C.: Princeton University Press.

Brubaker, Rogers (1995). "National Minorities, Nationalizing States and External Homelands in the New Europe." *Daedalus* 124 (Spring): 107–132.

——— (1996). *Nationalism Reframed*. Cambridge: Cambridge University Press.

Brus, Wlodzimierz (1977). "Stalinism and the People's Democracies." In Robert Tucker, ed., *Stalinism: Essays in Historical Interpretation*, 77–110. New York: Norton.

Bruszt, Laszlo, and David Stark (1992). "Remaking the Political Field in Hungary: From the Politics of Confrontation to the Politics of Competition." In Ivo Banac, ed., *Eastern Europe in Revolution*, 13–35. Ithaca, N.Y.: Cornell University Press.

Buchanan, Allen (1991). *Secession: The Morality of Political Divorce from Fort Sumter to Lithuania and Quebec*. Boulder, Colo.: Westview Press.

Bunce, Valerie (1981). *Do New Leaders Make a Difference? Executive Succession and Public Policy Under Capitalism and Socialism*. Princeton, N.J.: Princeton University Press.

——— (1983a). "Neither Equality Nor Efficiency: International and Domestic Inequalities in the Soviet Bloc." In Daniel Nelson, ed., *Communism and the Politics of Inequality*, 5–34. Lexington, Mass.: Lexington Press.

(1983b). "The Political Economy of the Brezhnev Era: The Rise and Fall of Corporatism." *British Journal of Political Science* 13 (January): 129–158.

(1985). "The Empire Strikes Back: The Transformation of the Eastern Bloc from a Soviet Asset to a Soviet Liability." *International Organization* 39 (Winter): 1–46.

(1989). "Decline of a Regional Hegemon." *East European Politics and Societies* 3 (Spring): 235–267.

(1991a). "Stalinism and the Management of Uncertainty." In Gyorgy Szoboszlai, ed., *The Transition to Democracy in Hungary*, 136–164. Budapest: Hungarian Institute of Political Science.

(1991b). "Two-Tiered Stalinism: A Self-Destructive Order." In Kazimierz Poznaski, ed., *Constructing Capitalism*, 29–46. Boulder, Colo.: Westview Press.

(1993). "Domestic Reform and International Change: The Gorbachev Reforms in Historical Perspective." *International Organization* 47 (Winter): 107–138.

(1994). "Sequencing Political and Economic Reforms." In John Hardt and Richard Kaufman, eds., *East-Central European Economies in Transition*, 49–63. Washington, D.C.: U.S. Congress, Joint Economic Committee: Government Printing Office.

(1995a). "Can We Compare Democratization in the East versus the South?" *Journal of Democracy* 6 (July): 87–100.

(1995b). "Should Transitologists Be Grounded?" *Slavic Review* 54 (Spring): 111–127.

(1998a). "The Historical Origins of the East-West Divide: Civil Society, Political Society and Democracy in Europe." Unpublished manuscript, Cornell University.

(1998b). "The Visegrad Group: Regional Cooperation and European Integration in Postcommunist Europe." In Peter Katzenstein, ed., *Mitteleuropa: Between Europe and Germany*, 240–284. Providence, R. I.: Berghahn Books.

(1998c). "Regional Differences in Democratization." *Post-Soviet Affairs* 17 (July): 3–29.

(1998d). "The Return of the Left and the Future of Democracy in Eastern and Central Europe." In Birol Yesilada, ed., *Comparative Political Parties and Party Elites: Essays in Honor of Samuel J. Eldersveld*. Ann Arbor: University of Michigan Press.

Bunce, Valerie, and Dennis Chong (1990). "The Party's Over: Mass Protest and the End of Communist Rule in Eastern Europe." Paper presented at the annual meeting of the American Political Science Association, San Francisco, August 30–September 2.

Bunce, Valerie, and Maria Csanádi (1993). "Uncertainty in the Transition: Postcommunism in Hungary." *East European Politics and Societies* 7 (Spring): 240–275.

Burawoy, Michael, and Pavel Kratov (1993). "The Economic Basis of Russia's Political Crisis." *New Left Review* 198 (March–April): 49–70.

Burg, Stephen (1983). *Conflict and Cohesion in Socialist Yugoslavia: Political Decision Making since 1966*. Princeton, N.J.: Princeton University Press.

(1995). *War or Peace: Nationalism, Democracy, and American Foreign Policy in Eastern Europe*. Unpublished manuscript, Brandeis University.

Busza, Eva (1994). "Transition and Civil-Military Relations in Poland and Russia: A Theoretical Framework." Paper presented at the annual meeting of the American Association for the Advancement of Slavic Studies, Philadelphia, November 17–20.

Butora, Martin, and Butorova, Zora (1993). "Slovakia after the Split." *Journal of Democracy* 4 (April): 71–83.

Cable, Vincent (1995). "The Diminished Nation-State: A Study of the Loss of Economic Power." *Deadalus* 124 (Spring): 23–54.

Čirković, Sima (1996). "Da li je Jugoslavenska katastrofa bila neminovna?" *Dijalog: umesto monologa*, 1–2 (Spring–Summer): 3–10.

Cohen, Lenard (1993). *Broken Bonds: The Disintegration of Yugoslavia*. Boulder, Colo.: Westview Press.

(1997). "Serpent in the Bosom: Slobodan Milosevic and Serbian Nationalism." In Melissa Bokovoy, Jill Irvine, and Carol Lilly, eds., *State-Society Relations in Yugoslavia, 1945–1992*, 315–344. New York: St. Martin's Press.

Cohen, Stephen F. (1985). *Rethinking the Soviet Experience: Politics and History since 1917*. Oxford: Oxford University Press.

Collier, David (1989). "Letter from the President: Comparative Methodology in the 1990s." *APSA – Comparative Politics Newsletter* 9 (Winter): 1–5.

Collier, David, and James Mahoney (1996). "Insights and Pitfalls: Selection Bias in Qualitative Research." *World Politics* 49 (October): 56–91.

Colton, Timothy (1979). *Commissars, Commanders and Civilian Authority*. Cambridge, Mass.: Harvard University Press.

(1986). *The Dilemma of Reform in the Soviet Union*. New York: Council on Foreign Relations.

Comisso, Ellen (1979). *Workers' Control under Plan and Market: Implications of Yugoslav Self-Management*. New Haven, Conn.: Yale University Press.

(1991). "Political Coalitions, Economic Choices." In Gyorgy Szoboszlai, ed., *Democracy and Poltical Transformation: Theories and East-Central European Realities*, 122–137. Budapest: Hungarian Political Science Association.

(1993). "Federalism and Nationalism in Post-Socialist Eastern Europe." *New Europe Law Review* 1 (Spring): 489–503.

Connor, Walker (1972). "Nation-Building or Nation-Destroying." *World Politics* 24 (April): 319–355.

(1984). *The National Question in Marxist-Leninist Theory*. Princeton, N.J.: Princeton University Press.

Conversï, Daniele (1993). "Domino Effect or Internal Developments? The Influences of International Events and Political Ideologies on Catalan and Basque Nationalism." *Western European Politics* 16 (July): 245–270.

(1994a). "Reassessing Current Theories of Nationalism. Nationalism as Boundary Maintenance and Creation." Unpublished manuscript.

(1994b). "Violence as an Ethnic Border: The Consequences of a Lack of Distinctive Elements in Croatian, Kurdish and Basque Nationalism." Unpublished manuscript.

Cox, Robert, and Erich Frankland (1995). "The Federal State and the Breakup of Czechoslovakia: An Institutional Analysis." *Publius* 25 (Winter): 71–88.

Crawford, Beverly (1996). "Explaining Defections from Cooperation: Germany's Unilateral Recognition of Croatia." *World Politics* 48 (July) : 482–521.

Crowley, Stephen (1994). "Barriers to Collective Action: Steelworkers and Mutual Dependence in the Former Soviet Union." *World Politics* 46 (July) : 589–616.

Csanádi, Maria (1990). "Beyond the Image: The Case of Hungary." *Social Research* 57 (Summer) : 321–346.

——— (1997). *Party-States and Their Legacies in Post-Communist Transformation.* Cheltenham: Edward Elgar.

Curtin, Philip D. (1966). "Nationalism in Africa, 1945–1965." *Review of Politics* 28 (April): 143–153.

Daalder, Hans (1973). "Building Consociational Nations." In S. N. Eisenstadt and Stein Rokkan, eds., *Building States and Nations: Analyses by Region*, 2: 14–31. Beverly Hills, Calif.: Sage.

Dallin, Alexander, and George Breslauer (1970). *Political Terror in Communist Systems.* Stanford, Calif.: Stanford University Press.

Danforth, Loring (1995). *The Macedonian Conflict: Ethnic Nationalism in a Transnational World.* Princeton, N.J.: Princeton University Press.

Daniels, R. V. (1979). "Soviet Politics since Khrushchev." In John Strong, ed., *The Soviet Union under Brezhnev and Kosygin*, 16–25. New York: Van Nostrand Reinhold.

Dawisha, Karen (1980). "Soviet Security and the Role of the Military: The 1968 Czechoslovak Crisis." *British Journal of Political Science* 10 (July): 341–363.

——— (1997). "Post-Communism's Troubled Steps towards Democracy: An Aggregate Analysis of Progress in the 27 New States." Center for the Study of Post-Communist Societies, University of Maryland, College Park.

Dawisha, Karen, and Bruce Parrott, eds. (1997). *The End of Empire: The Transformation of the USSR in Comparative Perspective.* Armonk, N.Y.: M. E. Sharpe.

deNevers, Renee (1993). "Democratization and Ethnic Conflict." In Michael E. Brown, ed., *Ethnic Conflict and International Security*, 61–78. Princeton, N.J.: Princeton University Press.

Denich, Bette (1994). "Dismembering Yugoslavia: Nationalist Ideologies and the Symbolic Revival of Genocide." *American Ethnologist* 21 (May): 367–390.

Derlugian, Georgii (1995). "Historical Sociological Interpretation of Nationalist Separatism in the Four Former Soviet Autonomous Republics: Tataria, Chechnya, Abkhazia and Ajaria." Ph.D. dissertation, State University of New York at Binghamton.

Deudney, Daniel, and G. John Ikenberry (1991–1992). "The International Sources of Soviet Change." *International Security* 16: 74–118.

Dion, Douglas (1998). "Evidence and Inference in the Comparative Case Study." *Comparative Politics* 30 (January): 127–146.

Djilas, Milovan (1988). "Djilas on Gorbachev." *Encounter* 23 (Fall): 33–42.

——— (1990). "Eine Revolutionare Demokratische Vision von Europa." *Europa-Archiv* 45 (1990): 28–41.

Dmitrijević, Vojin (1995). "The Post-Communist Apotheosis of the Nation-State and the Old and New Minorities." Paper presented at the Interdisciplinary Workshop on Multicultural Existence in the European Context. Sponsored by the Soros Foundation, the Institute of Social Sciences, Belgrade, and the University of Essex, September 24–26.

Donia, Robert J., and John V. A. Fine Jr. (1994). *Bosnia Herzegovina: A Tradition Betrayed*. New York: Columbia University Press.

Draft Union Treaty (1991). *FBIS-SOV* – 91 – 158. August 15, pp. 22–27.

Drobizheva, Leokadia (1992). "Perestroika and the Ethnic Consciousness of Russians." In Gail Lapidus, Victor Zaslavsky, and Philip Goldman, eds., *From Union to Commonwealth: Nationalism and Separatism in the Soviet Republics*, 98–113. Cambridge: Cambridge University Press.

Dubravčić, Dinko (1993). "Economic Causes and Political Context of the Dissolution of Multinational Federal States: The Case of Yugoslavia." *Communist Economies and Economic Transformation* 5, no. 3: 259–272.

Dunlop, John (1993a). *The Rise of Russia and the Fall of the Soviet Empire*. Princeton, N.J.: Princeton University Press.

(1993b). "Russia: Confronting a Loss of Empire." In Ian Bremmer and Ray Taras, eds., *Nation and Politics in the Soviet Successor States*, 43–72. Cambridge: Cambridge University Press.

Easter, Gerald (1997). "Preference for Presidentialism: Postcommunism Regime Change in Russia and the NIS." *World Politics* 49 (January): 184–211.

Echols, John M. (1975). "Politics, Budgets, and Regional Equality in Communist and Capitalist Systems." *Comparative Political Studies* 8 (October): 259–292.

Edles, Laura (1998). *Symbol and Ritual in the New Spain*. Cambridge: Cambridge University Press.

Eggertsson, Thrain (1990). *Economic Behavior and Institutions*. Cambridge: Cambridge University Press.

Ekiert, Grzegorz (1991). "Democratization Processes in East Central Europe: A Theoretical Reconsideration." *British Journal of Political Science* 21, no. 3: 285–313.

(1996). *The State against Society: Political Crises and Their Aftermath in East Central Europe*. Princeton, N.J.: Princeton University Press.

(1998). "Patterns of Postcommunist Transition in Eastern Europe." Paper presented at the Conference of the Council for European Studies, Baltimore, February 26–28.

Ekiert, Grzegorz, and Jan Kubik (1996). "Cycles of Protest and Popular Mobilization under State-Socialism, 1945–1989." *Working Paper Series*, no. 5, International Studies Center, University of Michigan.

(1997). *Rebellious Civil Society: Popular Protest and Democratic Consolidation in Poland, 1989–1993*. Unpublished manuscript.

Elazar, Daniel J. (1982). *Governing Peoples and Territories*. Philadelphia: Institute for the Study of Human Issues.

(1993). "International and Comparative Federalism." *Political Science* (June): 190–195.

Eley, Geoff (1996). Introduction. In Geoff Eley and Ronald G. Suny, eds., *Becoming National: A Reader*, 3–38. Oxford: Oxford University Press.

Elster, Jon (1995). "Explaining the Break-up of the Czechoslovak Federation: Consenting Adults or the Sorcerer's Apprentice." *East European Constitutional Review* 4 (Winter): 36–41.

(1996). *The Roundtable Talks and the Breakdown of Communism*. Chicago: University of Chicago Press.

Ermakoff, Ivan (1997). "Crisis and Abdication: A Comparative Inquiry into Processes of Democratic Breakdowns." Ph.D. dissertation, University of Chicago.

Esman, Milton (1994). *Ethnic Politics*. Ithaca, N.Y.: Cornell University Press.

Esman, Milton, and Shibley Telhami, eds. (1995). *International Organizations and Ethnic Conflict*. Ithaca, N.Y.: Cornell University Press.

Evangelista, Matthew (1995). "The Paradoxes of State Strength: Transnational Relations, Dominant Structures and Social Policy of Russia and the Soviet Union." *International Organization* 49 (Winter): 1–38.

(1998). *Taming the Bear: Transnational Relations and the Demise of the Soviet Threat*. Ithaca, N.Y.: Cornell University Press.

Fearon, James (1994). "Ethnic War as a Commitment Problem." Paper presented at the annual meeting of the American Political Science Association, New York, September 2–5.

Fearon, David, and David Laitin, (1996). "Explaining Inter-Ethnic Cooperation." *American Political Science Review* 90 (December): 715–735.

Finer, Samuel (1983). "State-Building, State Boundaries and Border Control." *Social Science Information* 13, no. 415: 79–126.

Fish, M. Steven (1995). *Democracy from Scratch: Opposition and Regime in the New Russian Revolution*. Princeton, N.J.: Princeton University Press.

(1996). "The Travails of Liberalism." *Journal of Democracy* 7 (April): 105–117.

(1997). "The Predicament of Russian Liberalism: Evidence from the December 1995 Parliamentary Elections." *Europe-Asia Studies* 49 (March): 191–220.

(1998). "The Determinents of Economic Reform in the Postcommunist World." *East European Politics and Societies* 12 (Winter): 31–78.

Fisher, Sharon (1994). "Czech-Slovak Relations Two Years after the Elections." *RFE/RL Research Report* 3 (July): 9–17.

Fishman, Robert (1990). "Rethinking State and Regime: Southern Europe's Transition to Democracy." *World Politics* 42 (April): 422–440.

Flaherty, Diane (1989). "Plan, Market and Unequal Regional Development in Yugoslavia." *Soviet Studies* 11 (January): 100–124.

Foran, John, and Jeff Goodwin (1993). "Revolutionary Outcomes in Iran and Nicaragua: Coalition Fragmentation, War and the Limits of Social Transformation." *Theory and Society* 22 (April): 209–247.

Friedland, Roger, and Robert R. Alford (1991). "Bringing Society Back In: Symbols, Practices and Institutional Contradictions." In Walter Powell and Paul DiMaggio, eds., *The New Institutionalism in Organizational Analysis*, 232–263. Chicago: University of Chicago Press.

Friedman, Francine (1997). "The Bosnian Muslims: The Making of a Yugoslav Nation." In Melissa Bokovoy, Jill Irvine, and Carol Lilly, eds., *State-Society Relations in Yugoslavia, 1945–1992*, 267–290. New York: St. Martin's.

Friedrich, Carl J. (1966). "Federalism and Opposition." *Government and Opposition* 1 (April): 286–296.

Furtado, Charles F., Jr., and Michael Hechter (1992). "The Emergence of Nationalities Politics in the USSR: A Comparison of Estonia and Ukraine." In Alexander Motyl, ed., *Thinking Theoretically about Soviet Nationalities*, 169–204. New York: Columbia University Press.

Gaddis, John Lewis (1986). "The Long Peace: Elements of Stability in the Postwar International System." *International Security* 10 (Spring): 99–142.

Gagnon, V. P., (1994). "Serbia's Road to War." In Larry Diamond and Marc F. Plattner, eds., *Nationalism, Ethnic Conflict and Democracy*, 117–131. Baltimore: Johns Hopkins University Press.

(1994–95). "Ethnic Nationalism and International Conflict." *International Security* 19 (Winter): 130–166.

(1995). "Ethnic Conflict as an Intra-Group Phenomenon: A Preliminary Framework." *Revija za Sociologiju* nos. 1–2: 81–90.

Gaidar, Egor (1995). *Gosudarstvo i evoliutsiia*. Moscow: Evratsiia.

Gaidar, Egor, and Victor Yaroshenko (1988). "Nulevoi tsikl." *Kommunist* 8: 74–86.

Garthoff, Raymond (1985). *Detente and Confrontation: American-Soviet Relations from Nixon to Reagan*. Washington, D.C.: Brookings Institution.

Gellner, Ernest (1983). *Nations and Nationalism*. Oxford: Basil Blackwell.

(1994). *Conditions of Liberty: Civil Society and Its Rivals*. London: Penguin.

(1995). Introduction. In Peruwal Sukumar, ed., *Notions of Nationalism*, 1–7. Budapest: Central European University Press.

Gitelman, Zvi (1970). "Power and Authority in Eastern Europe." In Chalmers Johnson, ed., *Change in Communist Systems*, 235–263. Stanford, Calif.: Stanford University Press.

(1992). "The Politics of Socialist Restoration in Hungary and Czechoslovakia." In Jack Goldstone, ed., *Revolutions: Theoretical, Comparative and Historical Studies*, 268–279. New York: Harcourt Brace Jovanovich.

Gleason, Gregory, ed. (1990). *Federalism and Nationalism: The Struggle for Republican Rights in the USSR*. Boulder, Colo.: Westview Press.

Glenny, Misha (1992). *The Fall of Yugoslavia: The Third Balkan War*. London: Penguin.

(1995). "Yugoslavia: The Great Fall." *New York Review of Books*, no. 42 (March 23): 56–61.

(1997). "Albania: Heart of Darkness." *New York Review of Books*, no. 44 (August 14): 32–36.

Gligorov, Vladimir (1992). "Balkanization: A Theory of Constitution Failure." *East European Politics and Societies* 6 (Fall): 283–301.

Goati, Vladimir, (1989). "Reforma SKJ i političkog sistema." In Vladimir Goati, ed., *Smisao jugoslavenskog pluralističkog šoka*, 169–184. Belgrade: Knjizevne novine.

(1990). *Jugoslavija na prekretneci: od monizma do gradjanskog rata*. Belgrade: Institut za novinarstvo.

(1995). "Temptations of Democracy in the Third Yugoslavia." Paper presented at the Interdisciplinary Workshop on Multicultural Existence in the European Context. Sponsored by the Soros Foundation, the Institute of Social Science, Belgrade and the University of Essex, September 24–26).

Golan, Galia (1973). *Reform Rule in Czechoslovakia: The Dubcek Era, 1968–1969.* Cambridge: Cambridge University Press.

Goldman, Philip, Gail Lapidus, and Victor Zaslavsky (1992). "Introduction: Soviet Federalism – Its Origins, Evolution and Demise." In Gail Lapidus and Victor Zaslavsky with Philip Goldman, eds., *From Union to Commonwealth: Nationalism and Separatism in the Soviet Republics*, 1–21. Cambridge: Cambridge University Press.

Goldstone, Jack (1991). *Revolution and Rebellion in the Early Modern World.* Berkeley: University of California Press.

Golubović, Zagorka (1988). *Kriza identita savremenog jugoslavenskog društva: jugoslavenski put u socijalizam viden iz različitih uglova.* Belgrade: Filip Visnjić.

(1995). "Nacionalism kao dominantan društveni odnos i kao dispozicija karaktera." In Zagorka Golubović, Bora Kuzmanović, Mirjana Vasović, eds., *Društveni karakter i društvene promene u svetlu nacionalnih sukoba*, 133–167. Belgrade: Filip Višnjić.

Golubović, Zagorka, Bora Kuzmanović, and Mirjana Vasović, eds. (1995). *Društveni karakter i društvene promene u svetiu nacionalnih sukoba.* Belgrade: Filip Višnjić.

Goodwin, Jeffrey (1988). "States and Revolutions in Third World Countries: A Comparative Analysis." Ph.D. dissertation, Harvard University.

Gorbachev, Mikhail (1993). *Gody trudnykh reshenii: izbrannoe, 1985–1992gg.* Moscow: Tortura.

Gordon, Ellen, and Luann Troxel (1995). "Ethnic Mobilization without War: Comparing Cases from Bulgaria and Lithuania." Paper presented at the Conference on Post-Communism and Ethnic Mobilization, Cornell University, Ithaca, N.Y., April 20–21.

Gorlin, Alice (1983). "Plan Fulfillment and Growth in Soviet Ministries: Industrial Nondefense Ministries, 1966–79." *Journal of Comparative Economics* 7 (December): 415–431.

Gourevitch, Peter Alexis (1979). "The Reemergence of 'Peripheral Nationalisms': Some Comparative Speculations on the Spatial Distribution of Political Leadership and Economic Growth." *Comparative Studies in Society and History* 21 (July): 303–322.

Gow, James (1992). *Legitimacy and the Military: The Yugoslav Crisis.* New York: St. Martin's Press.

Grabher, Gernot, and David Stark, ed. (1997). *Restructuring Networks in Post-Socialism: Legacies, Linkages and Localities.* Cambridge: Cambridge University Press.

Graham, Loren (1993). *The Ghost of the Executed Engineer: Technology and the Fall of the Soviet Union.* Cambridge, Mass.: Harvard University Press.

Grdešić, Ivan (1992). "1990 Elections in Croatia." *Political Science Review* 1: 91–99.

Grdešić, Ivan, Mirjana Kasapović, and Ivan Šiber, eds. (1989). *Interesi i ideje u SKJ: Struktora idejnih stavova i političkih poruka I. konferencije SKJ.* Zagreb: Ivan Prpić.

Grdešić, Ivan, Mirjana Kasapović, Ivan Šiber, and Nenad Zakošek (1991). *Hrvatska u izborima '90*. Zagreb: Naprijed.

Greenfeld, Liah (1992). *Nationalism: Five Roads to Modernity*. Cambridge: Cambridge University Press.

Greskovits, Bela (1998). *The Political Economy of Protest and Patience*. Budapest: Central European University Press.

Gunther, Richard (1992). "Spain: The Very Model of a Modern Elite Settlement." In John Higley and Richard Gunther, eds., *Elites and Democratic Consolidation in Latin America and Southern Europe*, 36–80. Baltimore: Johns Hopkins University Press.

Gurr, Ted Robert (1974). "Persistence and Change in Political Systems, 1800–1971." *American Political Science Review* 68: 1482–1504.

Hadžić, Miroslav (1994). "Ratni udeo JNA." In *Filozofija i društvo VI: Teorijske pretpostavke razumevanja raspada Jugoslavije*, 189–208. University of Belgrade: Institute for Philosophy and Social Theory.

Haggard, Stephen, and Robert Kaufman (1995). *The Political Economy of Democratic Transitions*. Princeton, N.J.: Princeton University Press.

Hall, John (1995). "Nationalism, Classified and Explained." In Peruwal Sukumar, ed., *Notions of Nationalism*, 8–33. Budapest: Central European University Press.

Hall, Peter A. (1997). "The Role of Interests, Institutions, and Ideas in the Comparative Political Economy of the Industrialized Nations." In Mark Irving Lichbach and Alan S. Zuckerman, eds., *Comparative Politics: Rationality, Culture, and Structure*, 174–207. Cambridge: Cambridge University Press.

Hall, Peter A., and Sidney Tarrow (1998). "Globalization and Area Studies: When Is Too Broad Too Narrow?" *Chronicle of Higher Education* 44 (January 23): B4–B5.

Hann, Chris (1995). "Subverting Strong States: The Dialectics of Social Engineering in Hungary and Turkey." *Daedalus* 124 (Spring): 133–154.

Haraszti, Miklós (1987). *The Velvet Prison: Artists under State Socialism*. Translated by Katalin Landesman and Stephen Landesmann with the help of Steve Wasserman. New York: Basic Books.

Harding, Neil (1984). "Socialism, Society and the Organic Labour State." In Neil Harding, ed., *The State in Socialist Society*, 1–50. Albany: State University of New York Press.

Harris, Chauncy D. (1993). "The New Russian Minorities: A Statistical Overview." *Post-Soviet Geography* 34: 1–27.

Harris, James (1998). *The Great Urals: Regional Interests and the Evolution of the Soviet System*. Ithaca, N.Y.: Cornell University Press.

Harsanyi, Nicolae, and Michael D. Kennedy (1994). "Between Utopia and Dystopia: The Liabilities of Nationalism in Eastern Europe." In Michael D. Kennedy, ed., *Envisioning Eastern Europe*, 149–179. Ann Arbor: University of Michigan Press.

Harun-or-Rashid (1990). "Bangladesh: The First Successful Secessionist Movements in the Third World." In Ralph R. Premdas, S. W. R. de A. Samarasingha, and Alan B. Anderson, eds., *Secessionist Movements in Comparative Perspective*, 83–94. New York: St. Martin's Press.

Hauslohner, Peter (1987). "Gorbachev's Social Contract." *Soviet Economy* 31: 54–89.

Havel, Václav (1998). "The State of the Republic." *New York Review of Books*, no. 45 (March 5): 42–46.

Hayden, Robert (1992). "Constitutional Nationalism in the Formerly Yugoslav Republics." *Slavic Review* 51: 654–673.

——— (1995a). "Constitutional Nationalism and the Wars in Yugoslavia." Paper presented at the Conference on Post-Communism and Ethnic Mobilization, Cornell University, Ithaca, N.Y., April 21–23.

——— (1995b). "The 1995 Agreements on Bosnia and Herzegovina and the Dayton Constitution: The Political Utility of Constitutional Illusion." *East European Constitutional Review* 4: 12–15.

Hechter, Michael (1977). *Internal Colonialism: The Celtic Fringe in British National Development, 1536–1966*. Berkeley: University of California Press.

——— (1987). *Principles of Group Solidarity*. Berkeley: University of California Press.

——— (1992). "The Dynamics of Secession." *Acta Sociologica* 35: 267–283.

Hechter, Michael, and Malka Appelbaum (1982). "A Theory of Ethnic Collective Action." *International Migration Review* 16: 412–434.

Hechter, Michael, and Margaret Levi (1979). "The Comparative Analysis of Ethnoregional Movements." *Ethnic and Racial Studies* 2 (July): 260–274.

Held, David (1996). "The Decline of the Nation State." In Geoff Eley and Ronald G. Suny, eds., *Becoming National: A Reader*, 407–417. Oxford: Oxford University Press.

Helf, Gavin (1994). "All the Russias: Center, Core and Periphery in Soviet and Post-Soviet Russia." Ph.D. dissertation, University of California at Berkeley.

Henderson, Karen (1994). *Czechoslovakia: Cutting the Gordian Knot*. Dordrecht, Netherlands: Kluwer.

Hirszowicz, Maria (1986). *Coercion and Control in a Communist Society: The Visible Hand in a Command Economy*. New York: St. Martin's Press.

Hobsbawn, Eric (1968). *Industry and Empire*. London: Penguin.

——— (1992). *Nations and Nationalism since 1780: Programme, Myth, Reality*. 2d ed. Cambridge: Cambridge University Press.

Hodnett, Grey (1967). "The Debate over Soviet Federalism." *Soviet Studies* 18 (April): 458–481.

——— (1975). "Succession Contingencies in the Soviet Union." *Problems of Communism* 24 (March–April): 1–21.

Hodnett, Gary, and Peter Potichnyj, (1970). *The Ukraine and the Czechoslovak Crisis*. Canberra: Department of Political Science, Research School of Social Sciences, Australian National University.

Hodson, Randy, Dusko Sekulic, and Garth Massey (1994). "National Tolerance in the Former Yugoslavia." *American Journal of Sociology* 99 (May): 1534–1558.

Höhmann, Hans-Hermann (1979). "The State and the Economy in Eastern Europe." In Jack Hayward and R. N. Berki, eds., *State and Society in Contemporary Europe*, 141–157. New York: St. Martin's Press.

Holloway, David (1989–1990). "State, Society and the Military under Gorbachev." *International Security* 14 (Winter): 5–24.

Horowitz, Donald (1981). "Patterns of Ethnic Separatism." *Comparative Studies in Society and History* 23 (April): 165–195.

(1985). *Ethnic Groups in Conflict.* Berkeley: University of California Press.

(1992). "How to Begin Thinking Comparatively about Soviet Ethnic Problems." In Alexander Motyl, ed., *Thinking Theoretically about Soviet Nationalities*, 9–22. New York: Columbia University Press.

(1994). "Democracy in Divided Societies." In Larry Diamond and Marc F. Plattner, eds., *Nationalism, Ethnic Conflict and Democracy*, 35–55. Baltimore: Johns Hopkins University Press.

Horvat, Branko (1982). *The Political Economy of Socialism.* Armonk, N.Y.: M. E. Sharpe.

Hough, Jerry F. (1969). *The Soviet Prefects: The Local Party Organs in Industrial Decision-Making.* Cambridge, Mass.: Harvard University Press.

(1990). "Gorbachev's Endgame." *World Policy Journal* 7 (Fall): 639–672.

Hroch, Miroslav (1995). "National Self-Determination from a Historical Perspective." In Sukumar Periwal, ed., *Notions of Nationalism*, 65–82. Budapest: Central European University Press.

(1996). "From National State to the Fully Formed Nation: The Nation-Building Process in Europe." In Geoff Eley and Ronald G. Suny, eds., *Becoming National: A Reader*, 60–78. Oxford: Oxford University Press.

Hughes, J. (1994). "Regionalism in Russia: The Rise and Fall of Siberian Agreement." *Europe-Asia Studies* 46: 1133–1161.

Huttenbach, Henry R., ed. (1990). "Introduction: Towards a Unitary State: Managing a Multinational Society, 1917–1985." In Henry Huttenbach, ed., *Soviet Nationality Policies: Ruling Ethnic Groups in the USSR*, 1–8. London: Mansell Publishing.

Iankova, Elena Atanassova (1997). "Social Partnership after the Cold War: The Transformative Corporatism of Post-Communist Europe." Ph.D. dissertation, Cornell University.

Innes, Abby (1997). "The Break-up of Czechoslovakia: The Impact of Party Development on the Separation of the State." *East European Politics and Societies* 11 (Fall): 393–435.

Irvine, Jill (1991). "Tito, Hebrang and the Croat Question, 1943–1944." *East European Politics and Societies* 5 (Spring): 306–340.

(1997a). "Introduction: State-Society Relations in Yugoslavia, 1945–1992." In Melissa Bokovoy, Jill Irvine, and Carol Lilly, ed., *State-Society Relations in Yugoslavia, 1945–1992*, 1–26. New York: St. Martin's.

(1997b). "Ultranationalist Ideology in Croatia." *Problems of Postcommunism* 44 (July – August): 30–43.

Jackson, Robert H., and Carl G. Rosenberg (1982). "Why Africa's Weak States Persist: The Empirical and the Juridical in Statehood." *World Politics* 35 (October): 1–24.

Jedanaesti kongres SKJ: dokumenti (1978). Belgrade: Komunist.

Jones, Chris (1981). *Soviet Influence in Eastern Europe: Political Autonomy and the Warsaw Pact.* New York: Praeger.

Jović, Borisav (1995a). "Dnevnik srditog predsednika." *Vreme International*, November 13, pp. 40–44.

(1995b). "Presecanje Hrvatske." *Vreme International*, November 27, pp. 40–43.

Kadijević, Veljko (1993). *Moje vidjenje raspada-vojska bez države*. Belgrade: Politička izdavačka delatnost.

Kaiser, Philip J. (1994). "The Czech Republic: An Assessment of the Transition." In John Hardt and Richard Kaufman, eds., *East-Central European Economies in Transition*, 506–517. Washington, D.C.: U.S. Congress, Joint Economic Committee, Government Printing Office.

Kaminski, Antoni (1992). *An Institutional Theory of Communist Regimes: Design, Function and Breakdown*. San Francisco: ICS Press.

Kaplan, Robert (1993). *Balkan Ghosts: A Journey through History*. New York: St. Martin's Press.

Karklins, Rasma (1993). *Ethnopolitics and Transition to Democracy: The USSR and Latvia*. Baltimore: Johns Hopkins University Press.

Kautsky, John (1962). "An Essay in the Politics of Development." In John Kautsky, ed., *Political Change in Underdeveloped Countries: Nationalism and Communism*, 3–119. New York: John Wiley & Sons.

Keeler, John (1993). "Opening the Window for Reform: Mandates, Crises and Extraordinary Policy-Making." *Comparative Political Studies* 25 (January): 435–486.

Kennan, George (1993). *The Other Balkan Wars: A 1913 Carnegie Endowment Inquiry in Retrospect*. Washington, D.C.: Carnegie Endowment for International Peace, distributed by the Brookings Institution.

Kerr, C., and A. Siegel (1954). "The Inter-Industry Propensity to Strike: An International Comparison." In William Kornhauser, ed., *Industrial Conflict*, 189–212. New York: McGraw-Hill.

King, Gary (1996). "Why Context Should Not Count." *Political Geography* 15: 159–164.

King, Gary, Robert Keohane, and Sidney Verba, eds. (1994). *Designing Social Inquiry: Scientific Inference in Qualitative Research*. Princeton, N.J.: Princeton University Press.

Kirkh, A. V., P. E. Iarve, and K. P. Khaav, (1988). "Etnosotsial'naia differentsiia gorodskogo naseleniia Estonii." *Sotsiologicheskie issledovaniia* 3 (1988): 30–35.

Kirow, Peter (1995). "Regional Warlordism in Russia: The Case of Primorskii krai." *Europe-Asia Studies* 47, no. 6 (September): 923–949.

Kolarska-Bobinska, Lena (1994). *Aspirations, Values and Interests: Poland, 1989–1994*. Warsaw: IFiS Publishers.

Kolkowicz, Roman (1967). *The Soviet Military and the Party*. Princeton, N.J.: Princeton University Press.

Kornai, Janos (1979). *The Economics of Shortage*. Stockholm: Institute for International Economic Studies.

"Korrenoi vopros perestroiki: Beseda s akademikom T. Zaslavskoi" (1988). *Izvestiia*, June 4, p. 3.

Kramer, Mark (1998). "The Czechoslovak Crisis and the Brezhnev Doctrine." In Carole Fink, Philip Gassert, and Detlef Junker, eds., *1968: The World Transformed*. Oxford: Oxford University Press.

Križan, Mojmir (1993). "Nationalismen in Jugoslawien. Von postkommunistischer nationaler Emanzipation zum Krieg." *Osteuropa* 42 (February): 121–140.

Krygier, Martin (1997). "Virtuous Circles: Antipodean Reflections on Power, Institutions, and Civil Society." *Eastern European Politics and Societies* 11 (Winter): 36–88.

Kubik, Jan (1994). *The Power of Symbols against the Symbols of Power: The Rise of Solidarity and the Fall of State Socialism in Poland.* University Park: Pennsylvania State University Press.

Kuran, Timur (1992). "Now Out of Never: The Element of Surprise in the Eastern European Revolutions of 1989." In Nancy Bermeo, ed., *Liberalization and Democratization*, 7–45. Baltimore: Johns Hopkins University Press.

Kuzmanović, Bora (1995). "Etatism kao specifican oblik authoritarne svesti." In Zagorka Golubović, Bora Kuzmanović, and Mirjana Vasović, eds., *Društveni karakter i društvene promene u svetlu nacionalnih sukoba*, 95–110. Belgrade: Filip Višnjić.

Laba, Roman (1991). *The Roots of Solidarity: A Political Sociology of Poland's Working Class Democratization.* Princeton, N.J.: Princeton University Press.

     (1996). "How Yeltsin's Explanation of Ethnic Nationalism Brought Down an Empire." *Transition*, no. 2 (January 12): 5–13.

Laïtin, David (1992). "The Four Nationality Games and Soviet Politics." *Journal of Soviet Nationalities* 2 (Spring): 1–37.

Lampe, John (1996). *Yugoslavia as History: Twice There Was a Country.* Cambridge: Cambridge University Press.

Lane, David (1997). "Ruling Elites in Transition: Nomenklatura or Political Class?" Paper presented at the Conference on Institution-Building in the Transformation of Central and Eastern European Societies, European Science Foundation, Budapest, December 5–7.

Lane, David, and Cameron Ross (1995). "The CPSU Ruling Elite: Commonalities and Divisions." *Communist and Post-Communist Studies* 28 (September): 339–360.

Lapidus, Gail (1992). "From Democracy to Disintegration: The Impact of Perestroika on the National Question." In Gail Lapidus and Victor Zaslavsky with Philip Goldman, eds., *From Union to Commonwealth: Nationalism and Separatism in the Soviet Republics*, 45–70. Cambridge: Cambridge University Press.

Lapidus, Gail, and Edward W. Walker, (1995). "Nationalism, Regionalism and Federalism: Center-Periphery Relations in Post-Communist Russia." In Gail Lapidus, ed., *The New Russia: Troubled Transformation*, 79–113. Boulder, Colo.: Westview Press.

Lapidus, Gail, and Victor Zaslavsky with Philip Goldman, eds. (1992). "Introduction: Soviet Federalism – Its Origins, Evolution and Demise." In Gail Lapidus and Victor Zaslavsky with Philip Goldman, eds., *From Union to Commonwealth: Nationalism and Separatism in the Soviet Republics*, 1–21. Cambridge: Cambridge University Press.

Larrabie, F. Stephen (1990–1991). "Long Memories and Short Fuses: Change and Institutionalization on the Balkans." *International Security* 15 (Winter): 58–91.

Lebow, Richard Ned, ed. (1995). *International Relations Theory and the End of the Cold War*. New York: Columbia University Press.

Leff, Carol (1988). *National Conflict in Czechoslovakia: The Making and Remaking of a State, 1918–1987*. Princeton, N.J.: Princeton University Press.

———— (1997). *The Czech and Slovak Republics: Nation versus State*. Boulder, Colo.: Westview Press.

Lepingwell, John (1994). "The Russian Military in the 1990s: Disintegration or Renewal?" In Douglas Blum, ed., *Russia's Future: Consolidation or Disintegration*. 109–126. Boulder, Colo.: Westview Press.

Levesque, Jacques (1997). *The Enigma of 1989: The USSR and the Liberation of Eastern Europe*. Berkeley: University of California Press.

Levi, Margaret (1997). "A Model, a Method, and a Map: Rational Choice in Comparative and Historical Analysis." In Mark Irving Lichbach and Alan S. Zuckerman, eds., *Comparative Politics: Rationality, Culture, and Structure*, 19–41. Cambridge: Cambridge University Press.

Lewin, Moshe (1988). *The Gorbachev Phenomenon: A Historical Interpretation*. Berkeley: University of California Press.

Lieven, Anatol (1993). *The Baltic Revolution*. New Haven, Conn.: Yale University Press.

Lijphart, Arend (1971). "Comparative Politics and the Comparative Method." *American Political Science Review* 65: 682–693.

———— (1996). "The Puzzle of Indian Democracy: A Consociational Interpretation." *American Political Science Review* 90 (June): 258–268.

Lilly, Carol S. (1994). "Agitprop in Postwar Yugoslavia." *Slavic Review* 53 (Summer): 395–413.

Lind, Michael (1994). "In Defense of Liberal Nationalism." *Foreign Affairs* 75 (June): 87–99.

Lindblom, Charles (1977). *Politics and Markets*. New York: Basic Books.

Linden, Ronald (1986). "Socialist Patrimonialism and the Global Economy: The Case of Romania." *International Organization* 40 (Spring): 347–380.

Linz, Juan (1973). "Early State-Building and Late Peripheral Nationalisms against the State: The Case of Spain." In S. N. Eisenstadt and Stein Rokkan, eds., *Building States and Nations: Analyses by Region*, 2: 32–116. Beverly Hills, Calif.: Sage.

Linz, Juan, and Alfred Stepan (1992). "Political Identities and Electoral Sequences: Spain, the Soviet Union, and Yugoslavia." *Daedalus* 121 (Spring): 123–139.

———— (1996). *Problems of Democratic Transition and Consolidation: Southern Europe, South America, and Post-Communist Europe*. Baltimore: Johns Hopkins University Press.

Locke, Richard, and Kathleen Thelen (1998). "Problems of Equivalence in Comparative Politics: Apples and Oranges, Again." *APSA – Comparative Politics Newsletter* 9 (Winter): 9–12.

Lohmann, Suzanne (1994). "Dynamics of Informational Cascades: The Monday Demonstrations in Leipzig, East Germany, 1989–1991." *World Politics* 47 (October): 42–101.

Loveman, Brian (1994). "Protected Democracies and Military Guardianship: Political Transitions in Latin America, 1978–1993." *Journal of Interamerican Studies and World Affairs* 36 (Spring): 105–189.

Luebke, David Martin (1997). *His Majesty's Rebels: Communities, Factions and Rural Revolt in the Black Forest, 1725–1745*. Ithaca, N.Y.: Cornell University Press.

Lukić, Reneo, and Allen Lynch (1996). *Europe from the Balkans to the Urals: The Disintegration of Yugoslavia and the Soviet Union*. New York: Oxford University Press.

Luong, Pauline Jones (1996). "Ethnopolitics, Strategic Bargaining and Institutional Design: Setting the Rules of Electoral Competition in Post-Soviet Eurasia." *International Negotiation* 1: 1–26.

Lustick, Ian (1987). "Israeli State-Building in the West Bank and the Gaza Strip: Theory and Practice." *International Organization* 41 (Winter): 151–171.

(1990). "Becoming Problematic: Breakdown of a Hegemonic Conception of Ireland in Nineteenth Century Britain." *Politics and Society*, 18: 39–73.

Lynch, Allen (1992). *The Cold War Is Over – Again*. Boulder, Colo.: Westview Press.

Lynch, Allen, and Reneo Lukić (1996). "The Russian Federalism Will Remain United." *Transition*, no. 2 (January 12): 18–21.

Lytle, Paula Franklin (1992). "U.S. Policy toward the Demise of Yugoslavia: The 'Virus of Nationalism.'" *Eastern European Politics and Societies* 6 (Fall): 303–318.

Magaš, Branka (1993). *The Destruction of Yugoslavia: Tracking the Break-up, 1980–1992*. London: Verso.

Mann, Michael (1987). *The Sources of Social Power*. Cambridge: Cambridge University Press.

(1995). "A Political Theory of Nationalism and Its Excesses." In Peruwal Sukumar, ed., *Notions of Nationalism*, 44–64. Budapest: Central European University Press.

Maravall, Jose Maria (1993). "Economic Reform in Southern Europe." In Luiz Carlos Bresser Pereira, Jose Maria Maravall, and Adam Przeworski, eds., *Economic Reforms in New Democracies: A Social-Democratic Approach*, 77–131. Cambridge: Cambridge University Press.

March, James, and Johan Olsen (1984). "The New Institutionalism: Organizational Factors in Political Life." *American Poltical Science Review* 78 (September): 734–749.

Martin, Pierre (1995). "When Nationalism Meets Continentalism: The Politics of Free Trade in Quebec." *Regional and Federal Studies* 5 (Spring): 1–27.

Martiniello, Marco (1995). "The National Question and the Political Construction of Ethnic Communities in Belgium." In Alec G. Hargreaves and Heremy Leaman, eds., *Racism, Ethnicity and Politics in Contemporary Europe*, 131–144. London: Edward Elgar.

(1998). "The Uses of Images of Cultural Differences in Belgian Political Life." Paper presented at the Conference on Federalism, Nationalism, and Secession, Cornell University, Ithaca, N.Y., May 1–2.

Massell, Gregory J. (1974). *The Surrogate Proletariat*. Princeton N.J.: Princeton University Press.

McAdams, Doug, Sidney, Tarrow, and Charles Tilly (1997). "Towards an Integrated Perspective on Social Movements and Revolution." In Mark Irving Lichbach and Alan S. Zuckerman, eds., *Comparative Politics: Rationality, Culture and Structure*, 142–173. Cambridge: Cambridge University Press.

McAdams, James (1997). "Germany after Unification: Normal at Last?" *World Politics* 49 (January): 282–308.

MccGwire, Michael (1987). *Military Objectives in Soviet Foreign Policy*. Washington, D.C.: Brookings Institution.

McCarthy, John D., and Mayer N. Zald (1987). "Resource Mobilization and Social Movements: A Partial Theory." In John D. McCarthy and Mayer N. Zald, eds., *Social Movements in an Organizational Society: Collected Essays*, 15–48. New Brunswick, N.J.: Transaction Books.

McCauley, Martin, and Peter Waldron (1988). *The Emergence of the Modern Russian State, 1855–1881*. Totowa, N.J.: Barnes and Noble.

McFaul, Michael (1995). "State Power, Institutional Change and the Politics of Privatization in Russia." *World Politics* 47 (January): 210–243.

———— (1997). "When Capitalism and Democracy Collide in Transition: Russia 'Weak' State as an Impediment to Democratic Consolidation." Working Paper no. 1, Davis Center for Russia Studies, Harvard University.

Meadwell, Hudson (1989). "Ethnic Nationalism and Collective Choice Theory." *Comparative Political Studies* 22 (July): 139–154.

———— (1994). "Transitions to Independence and Ethnic Nationalist Mobilization." In William James Booth, Patrick James, and Hudson Meadwell, eds., *Politics and Rationality*, pp. 191–213. Cambridge: Cambridge University Press.

Meadwell, Hudson, and Pierre Martin (1996). "Economic Integration and the Politics of Independence." *Nations and Nationalism* 2 (1): 67–87.

Mearsheimer, John (1990). "Back to the Future: Instability in Europe after the Cold War." *International Security* 15 (Summer): 5–56.

Medrano, Juan Díez (1995). *Divided Nations: Class, Politics, and Nationalism in the Basque Country and Catalonia*. Ithaca, N.J.: Cornell University Press.

Menon, Rajan (1994). "Post-Mortem: The Causes and Consequences of the Soviet Collapse." *Harriman Review* 7 (November): 1–10.

Meyer, Stephen M. (1991–1992). "How the Threat (and the Coup) Collapsed: The Politicization of the Soviet Military." *International Security* 16 (Winter): 5–38.

Migdal, Joel (1988). *Strong Societies and Weak States: State-Society Relations and State Capabilities in the Third World*. Princeton, N.J.: Princeton University Press.

Mikheyev, Dmitri (1996). *Russia Transformed*. Indianapolis, Ind.: Hudson Institute.

Milenkovitch, Deborah (1971). *Plan and Market in Yugoslav Economic Thought*. New Haven, Conn.: Yale University Press.

Miller, Nicholas J. (1997). "Reconstructing Serbia, 1945–1991." In Melissa Bokovoy, Jill Irvine, and Carol Lilly, eds., *State-Society Relations in Yugoslavia, 1945–1992*, 291–314. New York: St. Martin's Press.

Mlynar, Zdenek (1980). *Night Frost in Prague: The End of Humane Socialism*. Translated by Paul Wilson. New York: Kay Publishers.

Modrić, Šanja, and Nino Djula (1994). "Delozacije – Meko etnicko čišćenje." *Novi List*, November 4, pp. 6–7.

Moe, Terry (1984). "The New Economics of Organization." *American Journal of Political Science* 28 (November): 739–777.

Moore, Barrington (1978). *Injustice: The Social Bases of Obedience and Revolt.* White Plains, N.Y.: M. E. Sharpe.

Morrony, James D. (1994). *Game Theory for Political Scientists.* Princeton, N.J.: Princeton University Press.

Motyl, Alexander, ed. (1992). *Thinking Theoretically about Soviet Nationalities.* New York: Columbia University press.

    (1987). *Will the Non-Russians Rebel?: State, Ethnicity and Stability in the USSR.* Ithaca, N.Y.: Cornell University Press.

    (1991). "Empire or Stability: The Case for Soviet Dissolution." *World Policy Journal* 8 (Summer): 499–524.

    (1993). *Dilemmas of Independence: Ukraine after Totalitarianism.* New York: Council on Foreign Relations.

Muiznieks, Nils R. (1995). "The Influence of the Baltic Popular Movements on the Process of Soviet Disintegration." *Europe-Asia Studies* 47, no. 1: 3–25.

Musil, Jiri, ed. (1995a). *The End of Czechoslovakia.* Budapest: Central European Press.

    (1995b). "Czech and Slovak Society." In Jiri Musil, ed., *The End of Czechoslovakia,* 77–96. Budapest: Central European Press.

Nahaylo, Bohdan, and Victor Swoboda (1989). *Soviet Disunion: A History of the Nationalities Problem of the USSR.* London: Free Press/Macmillan.

"Natsional'naia politika partii v sovremennykh usloviiakh (platforma KPSS)" (1989). *Pravda,* August 17, pp. 1–2.

Nichols, Thomas (1993). *The Sacred Cause: Civil-Military Conflict over Soviet National Security, 1917–1992.* Ithaca, N.Y.: Cornell University Press.

Nodia, Ghia (1994). "Nationalism and Democracy." In Larry Diamond and Marc F. Plattner, eds., *Nationalism, Ethnic Conflict and Democracy,* 3–22. Baltimore: Johns Hopkins University Press.

North, Douglass (1981). *Structure and Change in Economic History.* New York: Norton.

Nove stranke Srbije: Dokumenti novih političkih stranaka i grupa u Srbiji. (1990). Belgrade: Institut za politicke studije.

Nove, Alec (1979). "Socialism, Centralised Planning and the One-Party State." In T. H. Rigby, Archie Brown, and Peter Reddaway, eds., *Authority, Power and Policy in the USSR: Essays Dedicated to Leonard Schapiro,* 77–97. New York: St. Martin's Press.

    (1980). "The Soviet Economy: Problems and Prospects." *New Left Review* 119 (January – February): 3–19.

Oberschall, A. (1994). "Rational Choice in Collective Protests." *Rationality and Society* 6 (January): 79–100.

O'Donnell, Guillermo (1979). "Tensions in the Bureaucratic-Authoritarian State and the Question of Democracy." In David Collier, ed., *The New Authoritarianism in Latin America,* 285–318. Princeton, N.J.: Princeton University Press.

    (1997). "Polyarchies and the (Un)Rule of Law in Latin America." Paper presented at the annual meeting of the American Political Science Association, Washington, D.C., August 28–31.

O'Donnell, Guillermo, Phillipe Schmitter, and Laurence Whitehead, eds. (1987).

Transitions from Authoritarian Rule. Vols. 1–4. Baltimore: Johns Hopkins University Press.

Olson, Mancur (1982). *The Rise and Decline of Nations: Economic Growth, Stagflation, and Social Rigidities.* New Haven, Conn.: Yale University Press.

O'Neil, Patrick (1996). "Revolution from Within: Institutional Analysis, Transitions from Authoritarianism, and the Case of Hungary." *World Politics* 48 (July): 579–603.

Ost, David (1990). *Solidarity and the Politics of Anti-Politics: Opposition and Reform in Poland since 1968.* Philadelphia: Temple University Press.

Parrott, Bruce (1997). "Analyzing the Transformation of the Soviet Union in Comparative Perspective." In Karen Dawisha and Bruce Parrott, eds., *The End of Empire: The Transformation of the USSR in Comparative Perspective*, 3–29. Armonk, N.Y.: M. E. Sharpe.

Peled, Yoav (1992). "Ethnic Democracy and the Legal Construction of Citizenship: Arab Citizens of the Jewish State." *American Political Science Review* 86 (June): 432–443.

Perlmutter, Amos, and William Leogrande (1982). "The Party in Uniform: Toward a Theory of Civil-Military Relations in Communist Political Systems." *American Political Science Review* 76 (December): 778–789.

Pesić, Vesna (1996). "Serbian Nationalism and the Origins of the Yugoslavian Crisis." Washington, D.C.: U.S. Institute for Peace, April.

Pipes, Richard (1968). *The Formation of the Soviet Union.* New York: Atheneum.

Pi-Sunyer, Oriol (1984). "The Political Economy of the Catalan Nationalist Movement." In Hans Vermeulen and Jeremy Boissevain, eds., *Ethnic Challenge: The Politics of Ethnicity in Europe*, 152–168. Goettingen: Heredot.

Pithart, Petr (1995). "Towards Shared Freedom, 1968–1989." In Jiri Musil, ed., *The End of Czechoslovakia*, 201–222. Budapest: Central European Press.

Powell, Walter, and Paul Di Maggio, (1991). "Introduction." In Walter Powell and Paul Di Maggio, eds., *The New Institutionalism in Organizational Analysis*, 1–38. Chicago: University of Chicago Press.

Pravda, Alex (1981). "East-West Interdependence and the Social Compact in Eastern Europe." In Morris Bornstein, Zvi Gitelman, and William Zimmerman, eds., *East-West Relations and the Future of Eastern Europe*, 162–190. London: Allen and Unwin.

Premdas, Ralph R. (1990). "Secessionist Movements in Comparative Perspective." In Ralph R. Premdas, S. W. R. de A. Samarasingha, and Alan B. Anderson, eds., *Secessionist Movements in Comparative Perspective*, 12–31. New York: St. Martin's Press.

Premdas, Ralph R., S. W. R. de A. Samarasingha, and Alan B. Anderson, eds. (1990). *Secessionist Movements in Comparative Perspective.* New York: St. Martin's Press.

Prihoda, Peter (1995). "Mutual Perceptions in Czech-Slovak Relations." In Jiri Musil, ed., *The End of Czechoslovakia*, 128–138. Budapest: Central European Press.

Prucha, Vaclav (1995). "Economic Development and Relations, 1918–1989." In Jiri Musil, ed., *The End of Czechoslovakia*, 40–76. Budapest: Central European Press.

Przeworski, Adam (1982). "The Man of Iron and Men of Power in Poland." *Political Science*, 15 (Winter): 18–31.

(1986). "Some Problems in the Study of the Transition to Democracy." In Guillermo O'Donnell, Philippe Schmitter, and Laurence Whitehead, eds., *Transitions from Authoritarian Rule: Prospects for Democracy*, 47–63. Baltimore: Johns Hopkins University Press.

(1991). *Democracy and the Market*. Cambridge: Cambridge University Press.

Przeworski, Adam, and Henry Teune (1970). *The Logic of Comparative Social Inquiry*. New York: Wiley-Interscience.

Pusić, Vesna (1992). "A Country by any Other Name: Transition and Stability in Croatia and Yugoslavia." *East European Politics and Societies* 6 (Fall): 242–259.

(1996). "The Origin of Croatian Political Identity." *Erasmus* 15 (February): 3–8.

(1997). "Mediteranski model na zalasku autoritarnih država." *Erasmus* 20 (January): 2–18.

Ragin, Charles (1987). *The Comparative Method: Moving beyond Qualitative and Quantitative Strategies*. Berkeley: University of California Press.

(1998). "Comparative Methodology, Fuzzy Sets, and the Study of Sufficient Causes." *APSA – Comparative Politics Newsletter* 9 (Winter): 18–22.

Rakove, Milton (1975). *Don't Make No Waves – Don't Back No Losers: An Insider's Analysis of the Daley Machine*. Bloomington: Indiana University Press.

Ramet, Pedro, ed. (1985). *Yugoslavia in the 1980s*. Boulder, Colo.: Westview Press.

Ramet, Sabrina P. (1984). *Nationalism and Federalism in Yugoslavia, 1963–1983*. Bloomington: Indiana University Press.

(1996). *Balkan Babel: The Disintegration of Yugoslavia from the Death of Tito to Ethnic War*. 2d ed. Boulder, Colo.: Westview Press.

Remington, Robin (1969). *Winter in Prague: Documents on Czechoslovak Communism in Crisis*. Translated by Michael Berman. Cambridge, Mass.: MIT Press.

(1985). "Political-Military Relations in Post-Tito Yugoslavia." In Pedro Ramet, ed., *Yugoslavia in the 1980s*, 56–75. Boulder, Colo.: Westview Press.

(1996). "State Cohesion and the Military." In Melissa Bokovoy, Jill Irvine, and Carol Lilly, eds., *Partisans to Patriots: State and Society Relations in Yugoslavia, 1945–1992*. Boulder, Colo.: Westview Press.

Rice, Condoleezza (1987). "The Party, the Military and Decision Authority in the Soviet Union." *World Politics* 40 (October): 55–81.

Rigby, T. H. (1977). "Stalinism and the Mono-Organizational Society." In Robert Tucker, ed., *Stalinism: Essays in Historical Interpretation*, 53–76. New York: Norton.

(1990). *The Changing Soviet System: Mono-Organizational Socialism from Its Origins to Gorbachev's Restructuring*. Aldershot: Edward Elgar.

Riker, William (1964). *Federalism: Origin, Operation, Significance*. Boston: Little Brown.

Risse-Kappen, Thomas (1996). "Exploring the Nature of the Beast." *Journal of Common Market Studies* 34 (March): 53–80.

Rizman Rudolf (1995). "Slovenia's Non-Violent Road to Independence." Paper presented at the Conference on Nationalism and Secession in Europe, Cornell University, Ithaca, N.Y., April 12–14.

Roeder, Philip (1991). "Soviet Federalism and Ethnic Mobilization." *World Politics* 43 (January): 196–232.

(1994). "Varieties of Post-Soviet Authoritarian Regimes." *Post-Soviet Affairs* 10, no. 1 (January–March): 61–101.

Roksandić, Drago (1991). *Srbi i Hrvatskoj od 15 stoljeca do naših dana.* Zagreb: Vjesnić.

"The Role of Theory in Comparative Politics: A Symposium" (1995). Atul Kohli, Peter Evans, Peter J. Katzenstein, Adam Przeworksi, Susanne Hoeber Rudolph, James C. Scott, and Theda Skocpol contributors. *World Politics* 48 (October): 1–49.

Rose, Richard (1996). "Ex-Communists in Post-Communist Societies." *Political Quarterly* 67 (January – March): 14–26.

Rush, Myron (1982–1983). "Guns over Growth in Soviet Policy." *International Security* 7 (Winter): 167–79.

Rusinow, Dennison, ed. (1988). *Yugoslavia: A Fractured Federalism.* Washington, D.C.: Wilson Center Press.

Rutland, Peter (1992). *The Politics of Economic Stagnation in the Soviet Union.* Cambridge: Cambridge University Press.

Rybovski, L. I., and I. V. Tarasova (1990). "Migratsionnye protsessy v SSSR: Novaya iavleniya." *Sotsiologicheskie issledovaniia* 7: 3–14.

Rychard, Andrzej (1991). "Stare i nowe instytucje zycia publicznego." In *Polacy 90,* 28–39. Warsaw: Polish Academy of Sciences.

Rychlik, Jan (1995). "From Autonomy to Federation, 1938–1968." In Jiri Musil, ed., *The End of Czechoslovakia,* 180–200. Budapest: Central European Press.

Sadikov, V. (1986). "Plan i interes." *Izvestiia,* March 13, p. 3.

Safran, William (1994). "Non-Separatist Policies Regarding Ethnic Minorities: Positive Approaches and Ambiguous Consequences." *International Political Science Review* 15 (January): 61–80.

Schamis, Hector (1994). "Re-Forming the State: The Politics of Privatization in Chile and Britain." Ph.D. dissertation, Columbia University.

Schmitter, Philippe C., and Terry Lynn Karl (1994). "The Conceptual Travels of Transitologists and Consolidologists: How Far to the East Should They Attempt to Go?" *Slavic Review* 53 (Spring): 173–185.

Scobell, Andrew (1992). "Why the People's Army Fired on the People: The Chinese Military and Tiananmen." *Armed Forces and Society* 18 (Winter): 193–213.

Scott, James (1985). *Weapons of the Weak: Everyday Forms of Peasant Resistance.* New Haven, Conn.: Yale University Press.

Searing, Donald (1991). "Roles, Rules, and Rationality in the New Institutionalism." *American Political Science Review* 85 (December): 1239–1260.

Senn, Alfred Erich (1990). *Lithuania Awakening.* Berkley: University of California Press.

Share, Donald (1982). *The Making of Spanish Democracy.* New York: Praeger.

Shea, Christopher (1997). "Political Scientists Clash over the Value of Area Studies." *Chronicle of Higher Education* 58 (January 10): A13–A14.

Sheehy, Ann (1991). "The All-Union and RSFSR Referendums of March 17." *RFE/RL Report on the USSR* 13, no. 13 (March 29): 19–23.

Shoup, Paul (1968). *Communism and the Yugoslav National Question.* New York: Columbia University Press.

Silber, Laura, and Allen Little (1996). *Yugoslavia: Death of a Nation*. New York: Penguin USA (TV Books).

Simić, Pedrag (1995). "Dynamics of Yugoslavian Crisis." *Security Dialogue* 26, no. 2 : 153–172.

Singer, Daniel (1985). "Bitter Hope in a Cold Climate." *Nation*, no. 240, June 22: 760–764.

Sinha, Aseema (1998). "The Politics of Inter-governmental Relations: Federalism and Regulation in India." Paper presented at the Conference on Federalism, Nationalism, and Secession, Cornell University, Ithaca, N.Y., May 1–2.

Skocpol, Theda (1979). *States and Social Revolutions*. Cambridge: Cambridge University Press.

Slezkine, Yuri (1994). "The USSR as a Communal Apartment, or How a Socialist State Promoted Ethnic Particularism." *Slavic Review* 53 (Summer): 414–452.

Slocum, John (1995). "Disintegration and Consolidation, National Separatism and the Evolution of Center-Periphery Relations in the Russian Federation." Occasional paper, Peace Studies Program, Cornell University, Ithaca, N.Y.

Smith, Anthony (1986). *The Ethnic Origins of Nations*. Oxford: Basil Blackwell.

   (1989). "The Origins of Nations." *Ethnic and Racial Studies* 12 (July): 340–367.

   (1992). "Ethnic Identity and Territorial Nationalism in Comparative Perspective." In Alexander Motyl, ed., *Thinking Theoretically about Soviet Nationalites*, 45–65. New York: Columbia University Press.

Smooha, Sammy, and Theodore Manf (1992). "The Diverse Modes of Conflict Resolution in Deeply Divided Societies." *International Journal of Sociology* 33, nos. 1–2: 26–47.

Snyder, Jack (1990). "Averting Anarchy in the New Europe." *International Security* 14 (Spring): 5–41.

   (1994). "Russian Backwardness and the Future of Europe." *Daedalus* 123 (Spring): 179–202.

Snyder, Tim, and Milada Vachudova (1997). "Are Transitions Transitory? Two Types of Political Change in Eastern Europe since 1989." *East European Politics and Societies* 11 (Winter): 1–35.

Solnick, Steven (1996). "The Political Economy of Russian Federalism: A Framework for Analysis." *Problems of Post-Communism* 43 (November–December): 13–25.

   (1998a). *Stealing the State: Control and Collapse in Soviet Institutions*. Cambridge, Mass.: Harvard University Press.

   (1998b). "Territorial Coalitions in Transitional States: Russia in Comparative Perspective." Paper presented at the annual meeting of the Midwest Political Science Association, Chicago, April 24.

Šorčulija, Zivko (1995). "Nationalism and the Position of National Minorities in the Post-Communist Countries." In Vojin Dmitrijević, ed., "The Post-Communist Apotheosis of the Nation-State and the Old and New Minorities." Paper presented at the Interdisciplinary Workshop on Multicultural Existence in the European Context. Sponsored by the Soros

Foundation, the Institute of Social Science, Belgrade and the University of Essex, September 24–26.

Staniszkis, Jadwiga (1984). *Poland's Self-Limiting Revolution*. Edited by Jan T. Gross. Princeton, N.J.: Princeton University Press.

——— (1991). *The Dynamics of the Breakthrough in Eastern Europe: The Polish Experience*. Translated by Chester Kisiel. Berkeley: University of California Press.

Stanovčić, Vojislav (1989). "Reforma političkog sistema." In Vladimir Goati, ed., *Smisao jugoslavenskog pluralističkog šoka*, 141–168. Belgrade: Knjizevne novine.

——— (1993). "National Self-Determination and Secession: Ideas and Problems." *Arhiv za pravnici društvene nauke* 4 (October–December): 747–762.

Stargardt, Nicholas (1995). "Origins of the Constructivist Theory of Nation." In Periwal Sukumar, ed., *Notions of Nationalism*, 83–105. Budapest: Central European University Press.

Stark, David (1992). "Can Designer Capitalism Work in Central and Eastern Europe?" *Transition: The Newsletter about Reforming Economies* 3 (May): 1–4.

——— (1996). "Recombinant Property in East European Capitalism." *American Journal of Sociology* 101 (January): 993–1027.

Steinmo, Sven, Kathleen Thelen, and Frank Longstreth (1992). *Structuring Politics: Historical Institutionalism in Comparative Analysis*. Cambridge: Cambridge University Press.

Stern, Jessica Eve (1994). "Moscow Meltdown: Can Russia Survive?" *International Security* 18 (Spring): 40–65.

Stokes, Gale (1993). *The Walls Came Tumbling Down: The Collapse of Communism in Eastern Europe*. Oxford: Oxford University Press.

Stokes, Gale, John Lampe, and Dennison Rusinow, with Julie Mostov (1996). "Instant History: Understanding the Wars of Yugoslav Succession." *Slavic Review* 55 (Spring): 136–160.

Strange, Susan (1995). "The Defective State." *Daedalus* 124 (Spring): 55–74.

Suda, Zdenek (1995). "Slovakia in Czech National Consciousness." In Jiri Musil, ed., *The End of Czechoslovakia*, 106–127. Budapest: Central European Press.

Sukumar, Peruwal, ed. (1995). *Notions of Nationalism*. Budapest: Central European University Press.

Suny, Ronald (1992). "State, Civil Society and Ethnic Cultural Consolidation in the USSR: Roots of the National Question." In Gail Lapidus and Victor Zaslavsky with Philip Goldman, eds., *From Union to Commonwealth: Nationalism and Separatism in the Soviet Republics*, 22–44. Cambridge: Cambridge University Press.

——— (1993). *The Revenge of the Past: Nationalism, Revolution, and the Collapse of the Soviet Union*. Stanford, Calif.: Stanford University Press.

——— (1995). "Ambiguous Categories: States, Empires and Nations." *Post-Soviet Affairs* 11 (April–June): 185–196.

Szczepanski, Jan (1970). *Polish Society*. New York: Random House.

Szporluk, Roman (1989). "Dilemmas of Russian Nationalism." *Problems of Communism* 38 (July–August): 15–35.

Szucs, Jeno (1983). "The Three Historical Regions of Europe: An Outline."

Acta Historica: Revue de L'academie des Sciences de Hongrie 29 (2–4): 131–184.

Taagepera, Rein (1993). *Estonia: Return to Independence.* Boulder, Colo.: Westview Press.

Taras, Ray (1993a). *Polish Communists and the Polish Road to Socialism.* Stanford, Calif.: Stanford University Press.

——— (1993b). "Making Sense of Matrioshka Nationalism." In Ian Bremmer and Ray Taras, eds., *Nation and Politics in the Soviet Successor States,* 513–538. Cambridge: Cambridge University Press.

Tarkowski, Jacek (1990). "Endowment of Nomenklatura, or Apparatchiks Turned into Entrepreneurchiks, or from Communist Ranks to Capitalist Riches." *Innovation* (Vienna) 3: 89–105.

Tarrow, Sidney (1994). *Power in Movement: Social Movements, Collective Action, and Politics.* Cambridge: Cambridge University Press.

——— (1995). "Mass Mobilization and Elite Exchange: Democratization Episodes in Italy and Spain." *Democratization* 2 (August): 221–245.

Tašić, Predrag (1993). *Kako sam branio Antu Markovića.* Skopje: NIP.

——— (1994). *Kako je ubijena druga Jugoslavia.* Skopje: AI Press.

Thomas, Daniel (1997). "Norms, Politics and Human Rights: The Helsinki Process and Decline of Communism in Eastern Europe." Ph.D. dissertation, Cornell University.

Thomson, Janice (1995). "State Sovereignty in International Relations: Bridging the Gap between Theory and Empirical Research." *International Studies Quarterly* 39 (June): 213–234.

Tilly, Charles (1975). "Western State-Making and Theories of Political Transition Form." In Charles Tilly, ed., *The Formation of National States in Western Europe,* 601–638. Princeton, N.J.: Princeton University Press.

——— (1992a). *Coercion, Capital, and European States, AD 990–1992.* London: Basil Blackwell.

——— (1992b). "Prisoners of State." *International Social Science Journal* 133 (August): 329–342.

——— (1993). *European Revolutions, 1492–1992.* Oxford: Oxford University Press.

Tito, Josip Broz (1971/1980). "Šovinizam i nacionalizam zu baza klasnog neprijatelja." In *Jugoslavenska revolucija i socijalizam,* 2: 204–210. Zagreb: Globus.

Todorova, Maria (1994). "The Balkans: From Discovery to Invention." *Slavic Review* 53 (Summer): 453–482.

Tökes, Rudolf (1996). *Hungary's Negotiated Revolution: Economic Reform, Social Change and Political Succession.* Cambridge: Cambridge University Press.

Treisman, Daniel (1996). "The Politics of Intergovnernmental Transfers in Post-Soviet Russia." *British Journal of Political Science* 26 (July): 299–335.

——— (1997). "Russia's Ethnic Revival: The Separatist Activism of Regional Leaders in a Postcommunist Order." *World Politics* 49 (January): 212–249.

Trimberger, Ellen (1978). *Revolution from Above: Military Bureaucrats and Development in Japan, Turkey, Egypt, and Peru.* New Brunswick, N.J.: Transaction Books.

Urban, Laszlo (1991). "Why Was the Hungarian Transition Exceptionally Peaceful?" In Gyorgy Szoboszlai, ed., *Democracy and Political Transformation:*

Theories and East-Central European Realities, 303–309. Budapest: Hungarian Political Science Association.

Urban, Michael (1990). *More Power to the Soviets: The Democratic Revolution in the USSR*. Aldershot: Edward Elgar.

Ustav socijalisticke federativne republike jugoslavije/Ustav socijalisticke republike Hrvatske (1981). Zagreb: Narodne novine.

Vajda, Mihaly (1981). *The State and Socialism: Political Essays*. New York: St. Martin's Press.

Van Evera, Stephen (1990–1991). "Primed for Peace: Europe after the Cold War." *International Security* 15 (Winter): 7–57.

——— (1994). "Hypotheses on Nationalism and War." *International Security* 18 (Spring): 5–39.

Vanous, Jan (1982). "East European Economic Slowdown." *Problems of Communism* 31 (July–August): 1–19.

Vanous, Jan, and Michael Marrese (1983). *Soviet Subsidization of Trade with Eastern Europe: A Soviet Perspective*. Berkeley: Institute of International Studies, University of California.

Varady, Tibor (1997). "Minorities, Majorities, Law, and Ethnicity: Reflections of the Yugoslav Case." *Human Rights Quarterly* 19 (February): 9–54.

Vardys, Stanley (1983). "Polish Echoes in the Baltics." *Problems of Communism* 32 (July–August): 21–34.

Varshney, Ashutosh (1997). "Postmodernism, Civic Engagement, and Ethnic Conflict." *Comparative Politics* 30 (October): 1–20.

Vasić, Miloš, and Filip Švarm, (1995a). "Generalski crni petak." *Vreme International*, December 25: 26–29.

——— (1995b). "Povrtac v stanje." *Vreme International*, December 25: 12–16.

Verdery, Katherine (1991). *National Ideology under Socialism: Identity and Cultural Politics in Ceausescu's Romania*. Berkeley: University of California Press.

——— (1993a). "Nationalism in Romania." *Slavic Review* 52 (Summer): 179–203.

——— (1993b). "Whither 'Nation' or 'Nationalism'?" *Daedalus* 122 (Summer): 37–46.

——— (1996). *What Is Socialism and What Comes Next?* Princeton, N.J.: Princeton University Press.

Vermeulen, Hans, and Jeremy Boissevain, eds. (1984). *Ethnic Challenge: The Politics of Ethnicity in Europe*. Goettingen: Heredot.

Vinogradov, Boris (1996). "Ikh nazyvaiut izgoriami sodruzhestva." *Izvestiia* 50 (March 16): 1.

Vodapivec, Peter (1992). "Slovenes and Yugoslavia, 1918–1991." *East European Politics and Societies* 6 (Fall): 220–241.

Volten, Peter (1982). *Brezhnev's Peace Program: A Study of Soviet Domestic Political Process and Power*. Boulder, Colo.: Westview Press.

Von Hagen, Mark (1995). "Does Ukraine Have a History?" *Slavic Review* 54 (Fall): 658–673.

Vujacic, Veljko (1996). "Historical Legacies, Nationalist Mobilization and Political Outcomes in Russia and Serbia: A Weberian View." *Theory and Society* 25 (December): 763–801.

Vujacic, Veljko, and Victor Zaslavsky (1991). "The Causes of Disintegration in the USSR and Yugoslavia." *Telos* 85 (Summer): 120–140.

Vukomanović, Dijana (1995). "The Serbian Nationalism and the Vicious Circle of Ethnonationalism." Paper presented at the Interdisciplinary Workshop on Multicultural Existence in the European Context. Sponsored by the Soros Foundation, the Institute of Social Science, Belgrade and the University of Essex, September 24–26.

Walton, John (1984). *Reluctant Rebels: Comparative Studies of Revolution and Underdevelopment*. New York: Columbia University Press.

Walton, John, and David Seddon (1994). *Free Markets and Food Riots: The Politics of Global Adjustment*. Oxford: Basil Blackwell.

Wasilewski, Jacek, and Edmund Wnuk-Lipinski (1995). "Poland: Winding Road from the Communist to the Post-Solidarity Elite." *Theory and Society* 25 (October): 669–696.

Weingaast, Barry (1994). "Institutionalizing Trust: The Political and Economic Roots of Ethnic and Regional Conflict." Paper presented at the Conference on The New Institutionalism, University of Maryland at College Park, October 14–15.

White, Stephen (1990). "Democratization of the USSR." *Soviet Studies* 42 (January): 3–25.

Williams, Brackette (1989). "A CLASS ACT: Anthropology and the Race to Nation across Ethnic Terrain." *Annual Review of Anthropology* 18: 401–444.

Wippman, David (1995). "Ethnic Conflict, International Powersharing, and International Law." Paper presented at the Conference on Powersharing, Cornell University Law School, Ithaca, N.Y., November 10–11.

Wnuk-Lipinski, Edmund (1992). "Economic Deprivations and Social Transformation." In Wladyslaw W. Adamski, ed., *Societal Conflict and Systematic Change: The Case of Poland, 1980–1992*, 71–92. Warsaw: IFiS Publishers.

Wolchik, Sharon (1991). *Czechoslovakia in Transition: Politics, Economics and Society*. London: Pinter.

(1994). "The Politics of Ethnicity in Post-Communist Czechoslovakia." *East European Politics and Societies* 8 (Winter): 153–188.

(1995). "The Politics of Ethnicity and the Breakup of Czechoslovakia." Paper presented at the Conference on Communism, Post-Communism, and Ethnic Mobilization, Cornell University, Ithaca, N.Y., April 21–22.

(1997). "The Czech Republic: Havel and the Evolution of the Presidency since 1989." In Ray Taras, ed., *Postcommunist Presidents*, 168–194. Cambridge: Cambridge University Press.

Wolfe, Eric (1982). *Europe and the People without a History*. Berkeley: University of California Press.

Wood, John R. (1981). "Secession: A Comparative Analytical Framework." *Canadian Journal of Political Science* 14: 107–134.

Woodward, Susan (1995a). *Balkan Tragedy: Chaos and Dissolution after the Cold War*. Washington, D.C.: Brookings Institution.

(1995b). *Socialist Unemployment*. Princeton, N.J.: Princeton University Press.

Yel'tsin, Boris (1994). *The Struggle for Russia*. New York: Random House.

Young, Crawford (1976). *The Politics of Cultural Pluralism*. Madison: University of Wisconsin Press.

(1993). "The Dialectics of Cultural Pluralism: Concept and Reality." In Crawford Young, ed., *The Rising Tide of Cultural Pluralism: The Nation-State at Bay?*, 245–278. Madison: University of Wisconsin Press.

Zak, Vaclāv (1995). "The Velvet Divorce of Institutional Foundations." In Jiri Musil, ed., *The End of Czechoslovakia*, 245–278. Budapest: Central European Press.

Zaslavskaya, Tatyana (1984). "The Novosibirsk Report." Translated by Teresa Cherfas. *Survey* 28 (Spring): 88–108.

——— (1986). "Taktika peremen." *Izvestiia*, April 18: 4.

Zaslavsky, Victor (1982). *The Neo-Stalinist State: Class, Ethnicity and Consensus in Soviet Society.* Armonk, N.Y.: M. E. Sharpe.

——— (1993). "Success and Collapse: Traditional Soviet Nationality Policy." In Ian Bremmer and Ray Taras, eds., *Nations and Politics in the Soviet Successor States*, 29–42. Cambridge: Cambridge University Press.

"Završne analize." (1995). In Zagorka Golubović, Bora Kuzmanović, and Mirjana Vasović, eds., *Društveni karakter i društvene promene u svetlu nacionalnih sukoba*, 325–334. Belgrade: Filip Višnjić.

"Završna razmetranja" (1995). In Zagorka Golubović, Bora Kuzmanović, and Mirjana Vasović, eds., *Društveni karakter i društvene promene u svetlu nacionalnih sukoba*, 335–352. Belgrade: Filip Višnjić.

Zic, Zoran (1994). "Democratic Transition and Self-Determination in Multiethnic Societies: The Different Cases of Spain and the Former Yugoslavia." Paper presented at the 18th European Studies Conference, University of Nebraska at Omaha, October 5–7.

Zimmerman, Warren (1995). "The Last Ambassador: A Memoir of the Collapse of Yugoslavia." *Foreign Affairs* 74 (March–April): 2–20.

Zimmerman, William (1987). *Open Borders, Nonalignment, and the Political Evolution of Yugoslavia.* Princeton, N.J.: Princeton University Press.

——— (1994). "Markets, Democracy and Russian Foreign Policy." *Post-Soviet Affairs* 10 (April–June): 103–126.

Županov, Josip (1983). *Marginalije o društvenoj krisi.* Zagreb: Globus.

INDEX